# FAMILY ROOTS OF
# SCHOOL LEARNING
# AND BEHAVIOR DISORDERS

# FAMILY ROOTS OF SCHOOL LEARNING AND BEHAVIOR DISORDERS

*Edited by*

## ROBERT FRIEDMAN, Ph.D.

*Assistant Clinical Professor of Psychiatry (Psychology)*
*School of Medicine, University of Southern California*
*Children's Hospital, Los Angeles, California*

Consultant
*Kaiser Foundation Parent-Child Guidance Center*
*Los Angeles, California*

CHARLES C THOMAS • PUBLISHER
*Springfield • Illinois • U.S.A.*

301.56
F 911

Published and Distributed Throughout the World by
CHARLES C THOMAS · PUBLISHER
BANNERSTONE HOUSE
301-327 East Lawrence Avenue, Springfield, Illinois, U.S.A.

© 1973, by CHARLES C THOMAS · PUBLISHER
ISBN 0-398-02469-3 (cloth)
ISBN 0-398-02472-3 (paper)
Library of Congress Catalog Card Number: 76-190322

With THOMAS BOOKS *careful attention is given to all details of
manufacturing and design. It is the Publisher's desire to present books
that are satisfactory as to their physical qualities and artistic possibilities
and appropriate for their particular use.* THOMAS BOOKS *will be true
to those laws of quality that assure a good name and good will.*

*Printed in the United States of America*
*Y-2*

# CONTRIBUTORS

## ROSE M. BROMWICH, Ed.D.

*Professor, Department of Psychological Foundations of Education*
*San Fernando Valley State College*
*Northridge, California*

## SAUL L. BROWN, M.D.

*Chief, Department of Child Psychiatry*
*Cedars-Sinai Medical Center*
*Associate Clinical Professor of Psychiatry*
*School of Medicine*
*University of Southern California*
*Los Angeles, California*
*Faculty member, Pacific Oaks College*
*Pasadena, California*
*Instructor, Southern California Psychoanalytic Institute*
*Los Angeles, California*

## EVIS J. CODA, M.D.

*Medical Director, Kennedy Child Study Center*
*Santa Monica, California*
*Child Psychiatrist*
*Formerly Medical Director, Louisiana Center for Exceptional Children*
*New Orleans, Louisiana*

## WILLIAM W. CULP, M.A.

*Coordinator of Psychological Services, Administrative Area A*
*Los Angeles City Unified School District*
*Los Angeles, California*

## ALFRED H. FOSTER, M.A.

*Coordinator, Counseling and Psychological Services, Administrative Area E*
*Los Angeles City Unified School District*
*Los Angeles, California*
*School Psychologist, Licensed Psychologist, State of California*

## ROBERT FRIEDMAN, Ph.D.

*Assistant Clinical Professor of Psychiatry (Psychology)*
*School of Medicine*
*University of Southern California*
*Children's Hospital*
*Consultant, Kaiser Foundation Parent-Child Guidance Center and*
*Department of Psychiatry*
*Southern California Permanente Medical Group*
*Los Angeles, California*
*Diplomate in School Psychology, ABPP*
*Private Practice*

## EDWARD L. GREEN, M.D.

*Chief, Department of Psychiatry*
*Southern California Permanente Medical Group*
*Los Angeles, California*
*Administrative Consultant, Kaiser Foundation Parent-Child Guidance Clinic*
*Hollywood, California*
*Medical Director, Kaiser Foundation Parent-Child Center*
*Watts, California*

## GERALD I. LUBIN, M.D.

*Assistant Professor of Psychiatry and Pediatrics*
*School of Medicine*
*University of Southern California*
*Children's Hospital*
*Director of Training in Child Psychiatry and Assistant Program Director*
*University Affiliated Training Program*
*Children's Hospital*
*Los Angeles, California*

## DAVID MELTZER, M.D.

*Member, Los Angeles Psychoanalytic Institute*
*Supervisor of Child Psychotherapy, Reiss-Davis Child Study Center and*
*Cedars-Sinai Medical Center*
*Los Angeles, California*
*Private Practice in Adult and Child Psychoanalysis*

## MORTIMER M. MEYER, Ph.D.

*Director of Psychological Services and Director of Training*
*Reiss-Davis Child Study Center*
*Instructor, California School of Professional Psychology*
*Formerly Chief Psychologist, Veterans Administration*
*Mental Hygiene Clinic*
*Los Angeles, California*

## HARRY PANNOR, M.S.W.

*Casework Director for the Parent-Child Guidance Service, Volunteer*
*Big Brother Program, and Camp Max Straus of*
*Jewish Big Brother Association of Los Angeles County*
*Private Practice*

## FRANK S. WILLIAMS, M.D.

*Medical Director, Julia Ann Singer Preschool Psychiatric Center*
*Assistant Chief, Department of Child Psychiatry*
*Cedars-Sinai Medical Center*
*Assistant Clinical Professor of Psychiatry*
*University of Southern California School of Medicine*
*Instructor, Southern California Psychoanalytic Institute*
*Los Angeles, California*

# PREFACE

THE importance of the link between the family and the school has been well established. We know that it is in the family that the child has his first learning experience, his initial contact with authority, and the beginning of his socialization as a person. Parental attitudes, values, and goals concerning education have a strong impact on the child. Parent-child relationships and family interactional systems can promote or hinder school adjustment. In a sense, the child takes his family to school with him. Reciprocally, school comes home to the family. The success or failure of the child in school can affect the child's standing in the family and may also serve as a kind of test of the family. Success in school can enhance the child's status in his family and validate the family's worth. A school learning or behavior problem, on the other hand, can have the opposite effect and may also disrupt family harmony and generate serious conflict between family members.

This book focuses on one aspect of the family-school link—the familial roots of school-related problems. Learning and behavior disorders are separated for purposes of discussion; it is recognized, however, that these categories overlap and are often found in combination. *School*, as the term is used in this text, encompasses the range of preschool through high school, *family* refers not only to the two-parent intact family unit but also to the one-parent, extended, and other family groupings. It should be noted that although school is referred to as a unitary entity, there are a wide spectrum of types and much variation in quality among schools. While families in the United States have many similarities in structure and function, there are also differences, both along and across racial, ethnic, and class lines.

School learning and behavior disorders often have a complex etiology. Physiological, psychological, and cultural determinants may all be involved. The premise of this text is that while the family aspect

ix

is not a critical factor in all school difficulties, it is the decisive element in many. The purpose of this volume, therefore, is to provide a broad framework for understanding the interconnection between the family and school disorders, and to suggest effective diagnostic procedures and intervention approaches. The first part of the book explores the familial factors in school maladjustment. In part two, evaluation of the family component is discussed. Parts three and four, respectively, illustrate specific methods of working with parents and families in clinical treatment and school guidance.

Those of us who are engaged in dealing with school difficulties know that the needs are many and the resources limited. The family has the potential of being an important ally in the process of changing unproductive school behavior. It is our hope that this book will encourage a fuller utilization of that potential.

# ACKNOWLEDGMENTS

The editor would like to thank the following people for their assistance with the manuscript: Jan Fintcher and Barbara King, typists; Sandy Friedman, copy reader; Ethelyn Rafish, librarian at the Reiss-Davis Child Study Center; Betty S. Woodward and Karen Hittson, associate editors, and Payne E. L. Thomas of Charles C Thomas, Publisher. Appreciation is expressed to Gloria Martin for cover design consultation.

The encouragement of my wife, Blanche, and my son, Keith, has been especially helpful in the course of the book's development.

R. F.

# TABLE OF CONTENTS

# FAMILY ROOTS OF
# SCHOOL LEARNING
# AND BEHAVIOR DISORDERS

# PART ONE

# THE FAMILY AND SCHOOL DIFFICULTIES

*Chapter I*

# FAMILY EXPERIENCE AND CHANGE

SAUL L. BROWN

Mᴏꜱᴛ of us have lived in families. Our memories of childhood form in the flow of family experiences lived out over the years of time now past. Early we learned that those adults around us who are now old used to be young, that some who are at times spoken of are no longer alive, that those now young would in time change and become older, would marry, would move away, and would have children of their own. From time to time new members of the family were born and others died.

Out of these experiences came a deeply engrained awareness of the inexorability of change in family life.

Our wisdom about life incorporates the notion of a progressive and yet recurring cycle of change. The phrase "family life cycle" is reflective of that wisdom and feels right to us even though it does not stand up easily before semantic criticism. A "life cycle" ordinarily refers to *organisms* that pass through a series of stages in their biological development from birth to death. Through all the stages, the organism remains discrete, well defined, and in some degree physically autonomous.

Families, while they have many characteristics of organisms, are not the physically discrete entities of scientific biology. Social psychology uses more exact phrasing by referring to families as "biosocial systems." What this means is that a family group functions like a general system with many interlocking and interacting subcomponents or subsystems. Within the family, the subsystems include the husband-wife dyad, father-child dyads, mother-child dyads, sibling groups, and others. Other subsystems within the larger family system are those of the parents with their own siblings, the parents to their

5

respective parents and each other's parents (in-laws), the children and their uncles and aunts and grandparents, etc. In some instances father's or mother's relationships with their employers or with close friends can become subsystems of the family system. Also there are "interactional subsystems" which I shall describe in a later section. Thus the subsystems are both biologic *and* social. Families are simultaneously a social invention and a result of biological evolution and need. The biosocial units which we call families function at any given moment in accordance with social and biological dynamisms. They progress through a cycle of change which has certain characteristics. I will use the phrase "family life cycle" in speaking of this phenomenon while acknowledging its semantic limitations. But before pursuing this theme, a few additional comments about individual development may be helpful.

## DEVELOPMENTAL PHASES OF THE INDIVIDUAL
### The Property of Many Disciplines

Charting the process of change in an individual human life is an engrossing project. The number of variables that affect such a process are infinite and range from the biologic to the psychologic to the sociologic and cultural. The large number of disciplines devoted to the study of individual human development attests to the complexity of the subject; included are behavorial psychology, neurophysiology, pediatric physiology, psychoanalysis, social psychology, educational psychology, cultural anthropology, and others. Each has its vocabulary, its theories, its tools for observation, its own hypotheses and biases. The territory is large and there seems to be enough room for any explorers who care to enter! Common to all is the view that discrete phases can be discerned in the continuing flow of development in each individual.

### The Psychoanalytic Perspective

A most influential contributor to understanding individual human development has been the psychoanalyst Erik Erikson. The model he developed in the 1940's for describing characteristics of the psychosocial development of infants has been of enduring value[7]. He clarified how the almost infinite variety of factors involved in each infant's development coalesce into a series of "developmental crises" reflecting the dominant forces in each phase. These relatively discrete moments in the life history of each person become the nodal points around which the ego (personality) evolves or fails to evolve. Extending the traditional psychoanalytic instinctual drives, Erikson emphasizes understanding each major developmental phase in terms of polarities of ego function arising in an interpersonal context.

Thus the developmental crisis of the earliest phase of infancy involves the establishment of a deep psychic and physical mutuality between mother and infant. Success or relative failure of ego development is characterized as "trust versus basic mistrust." In the next developmental stage of the child, that of "the toddler," the psychologic forces at work produce a crisis whose resolution is characterized by Erikson as the polarity of "autonomy versus shame and doubt." Failure to evolve a vibrant sense of autonomy at this age leads to an ego with life-long feelings of self-doubt and a readiness to feel ashamed of one's self. Subsequent crises of ego development are characterized by the polarities: "initiative versus guilt" (ages three to five); "industry versus inferiority" (ages five to ten); "identity versus role diffusion" (adolescence); and "intimacy versus isolation" (early adulthood).

Most important is Erikson's notion that failure or imperfect resolution significantly colors the ways in which the crisis of the next phase is met and resolved; for example, where there has been a failure of mutual trust between mother and infant, the child lacks the ability to relax in relation to others. This hampers his ability later to establish ego functions that lead to deep personal relationships. In his subsequent search for autonomy he is unable to draw upon warm relationships from others for the periodic support that he will need. Because he is left mistrustful of intimate ties to others, he becomes manipulative of people while remaining incurably (usually secretly and often unconsciously) self-doubting. In short, a compounding of failures of personality development may occur, eventually becoming evident in various aspects of a person's behavior and psychological functioning. I must emphasize that this summary of Erikson's model is extremely simplified and barely does justice to his extensive and searching formulations.

## DEVELOPMENTAL PHASES IN THE FAMILY LIFE CYCLE

Drawing upon Erikson's frame of reference, I have tried to conceive of the developmental progression of a family group in somewhat analogous terms; just as the ego functions of an individual evolve through a series of developmental tasks and crises, so do the interactional patterns of an entire family group. And just as failures in individual development contaminate later phases in definite ways, so do familial failures to master the major phases of the family cycle affect the psychological functioning of the family members in each successive period of development.

When does a family group begin? It begins with each newly married couple even though such a couple continues to be a part of two prior family groups; that is, the husband's family and the wife's. As children are born to the couple, the numbers in the new family group multiply. The fact that a new family cycle begins with each marriage does not negate the fact that the family cycles of the prior families of origin still exist. The young couple continues the family life cycles of each original family group at the same time that it begins its own family cycle. The breaking away of the newly married couple from each one's nuclear family may create subtle crises for everyone— the two sets of in-laws as well as each of the newlyweds. There is no scarcity of jokes and folk humor about this situation. But it is a very serious problem indeed and it may be that the large number of in-law jokes are only a reflection of the feelings of helplessness it evokes in both generations.

### Phase A: Primary Commitment

The developmental task of this phase is a successful disconnection from the two prior families and a crystallization of a single new family group. Primary commitment begins, in the most discrete sense, on the day of the wedding. It becomes worked out over some period of time thereafter. The ways in which the small day-to-day crises of this phase are worked out are very much a function of the social and cultural expectations that play upon a couple, the respective ties and involvements that each partner has with his or her parents, the inner psychodynamics of the young husband and the young wife, the surrounding life's circumstances, and many other factors so numerous I shall not attempt to list them.

A summarizing polarity that characterizes the ultimate failure or success of this phase is "primary commitment versus fractional dispersion."

Where a primary commitment is established in the early phase of the marriage, husband and wife relegate prior emotional involvements with parents, siblings, and friends to a secondary level of investment. The marriage is now the dominant structure in the life of each partner. When there is a failure of primary commitment, the emotions of each partner become fractionated and dispersed among others. When this occurs in a major way, it sets the stage for disruption of the next important developmental phase. Each spouse is constantly looking away, in effect, to other relationships and to a variety of involvements and distractions outside the marriage.

A continuing overloaded tie to parents or relatives inevitably affects the children in later stages of family development. I recall a diagnostic family interview with a bright three-year-old boy and his parents. There were two play telephones in the interview room. He picked both up and simulated a talk with both of his grandmothers simultaneously! The fact was that his parents were in the midst of a titanic struggle with both grandmothers and he had become the vehicle for the struggle.

The "ground rules" for primary commitment are not the same in all ethnic or cultural groups. The romantic tradition of our western society is very demanding of a marital relationship. It calls for a commitment of profound and encompassing love between two people in a marriage. This has not always been the case. "Arranged marriages" are a well-known exception. In the European upper classes it has been traditional that romantic involvements may continue outside the marriage. Some believe this is becoming prevalent in the United States. A primary commitment may exist short of total romantic love if both husband and wife are fully concerned with establishing a family and raising children. The commitment may therefore be to the marriage but not so fully to each other. This can occur only if the culture sanctions it. Problems arise when one of the two partners has a very different agenda for commitment than the other one has, regardless of the society in which they live.

## Phase B: The Nurturing System

A fundamental accommodation that must be made by *all* participants in a family group is one that insures everyone's survival. For the very young this includes not only feeding, but holding, calming, stroking, and stimulating. John Bowlby[2], a psychoanalytically trained observer of infant development, has outlined the elements of "attachment behavior" necessary for an infant's physical *and* psychological survival. Attachment behavior as he describes it is reciprocal between infant and mother. It includes various modalities such as smiling, visual following, clinging, and sucking. These reflexes are released in the infant by a nurturing person, usually the mother. Each bit of behavior in turn sets off reciprocal responses in the mothering person and becomes the basis for the later feelings of mutuality and basic trust that Erikson speaks of. As the first year of life progresses the infant's behavior grows more complex. The more initiative it shows, the more response it evokes from the adults in the immediate environment. Other psychoanalysts have carefully studied this early phase and have produced interesting formulations. Among them are Sylvia Brody[3], Margaret Mahler[14], L. W. Sander[18], Rene Spitz[20], D. W. Winnicott[21], Ernst Kris[12], Samuel Ritvo[17], and Albert Solnit[19]. The focus of their reports is upon the subtleties of interaction between mothers and infants. Taken in totality, these interactions can be characterized as "basic nurturing" of infants.

My own focus in this chapter will be upon family interaction. In this frame of reference, basic nurturing becomes an item of total family experience. Nothing in this view contradicts the fact that, in general, mothers are the most direct and effective providers of basic nurturing in early infancy. Other important factors are at work, however, and need to be recognized; for example, in the United States, welfare workers have often observed that much of an infant's nurturing in poor homes where mother has many children may be carried out by older siblings.

In many families there is an overall nurturing attitude that can be discerned. When the generalized *nurturing attitude* is positive, effective, direct physical nurturing of the youngest member is an inevitable result. A crucial outcome of the phase of primary commitment is the fact that husband and wife are genuinely committed to working together and finding pleasure in this. Equally important, they become open to and responsive to dependency needs in each other. Later, these elements of the marriage become generalized into a positive nurturing attitude toward their children. It is important to note that the children themselves reinforce nurturing impulses in the parents and add vitality to the process. A child's pleasure cheers the parents! I cannot emphasize enough that this is a reciprocal interactional system with feedback going on all the time. What results is the growth of a storehouse of good will and warmth that family members need to draw upon in their responses to each other. Successful progress through later developmental phases is dependent upon at least a minimum of such good will and warmth.

For theoretical purposes I find it useful to think in terms of interactional subsystems. This is a little different from the structural subsystems that I referred to earlier. Within the major familial interactional system, the subsystem of basic nurturing develops its own momentum. It produces feedback to each of the participants, children and parents alike. Other interactional subsystems of family life, to be described in following sections, relate to the nurturing subsystem and are enhanced *or* depleted in accord with how well they function. If we follow out the notion of an interactional subsystem affecting individual family members, we can see that if the subsytem of basic intrafamilial nurturing falters, a generalized feeling of coldness and distance between family members results. A nurturing subsystem with negative coloration produces negative effects.

A new infant introduces change into a family system. For any number of reasons the family may falter in responding effectively to this change and may fail to meet the minimum requirement for nurturing the infant. A postpartum depression in the mother or a psychotic-dissociative reaction in the father following birth of an infant are extreme but well-known clinical situations which interfere with the smooth evolution of the nurturing phase. Episodes in the life of the family that are psychologically traumatic leave aftereffects for everyone. The episodes themselves may become obscured or almost forgotten as time moves on. In recent years the phenomenon of the "battered child syndrome" has focused our attention on the fact that certain parents are simply incapable of meeting the early nurturing phase. There are instances in which babies are left to themselves for hours at a time or situations in which infants are exposed to hazards without careful protection. These situations do not always become openly recognized because of the shame and guilt they evoke. Yet they may linger as family secrets.

Extreme failures in familial response to the nurturing phase may be reflected through symptoms in the infant. Symptoms may range from obvious physical problems such as malnutrition, to more subtle phenomena such as infantile depressive states, or serious developmental lags in the first year. These phenomena have been observed in their most extreme form in institutionalized infants. The symptoms of severe failures of familial nurturing may appear as psychophysiological imbalances in the infant. Examples are hyperactivity, overexcitability, severe sleep disturbance, frequent vomiting, or even proneness to infection. Children who are viewed to be suffering minimal brain damage may in some instances be manifesting the result of early failures in the family nurturing subsystem. The same seems to be true of many autistic children.

When both parents are unable to meet the direct nurturing needs of an infant, others in the family may take over. One of the older siblings or a competent grandmother or an in-law or aunt or uncle may provide what amounts to a compensatory nurturing subsystem. Sometimes the compensatory subsystem can become a problem later. An example is that of a grandmother who moves in to care for the family because mother is unable to do so. She may stay on like "the man who came to dinner," becoming a force in the family life thenceforth. What begins as a necessary and effective compensatory nurturing mechanism in a family may evolve into a self-perpetuating pathological subsystem.

What meaning do these concepts have for educators? When there is generalized mutuality and warmth in the family, children and adults feel safe. They are comfortable about exploring their environment, asking questions of each other, sharing findings and thoughts, and showing enthusiasm for each other's achievements. A positive attitude about learning and experiencing arises out of such a family milieu.

When, on the other hand, the nurturing subsystem is characterized by coolness and detachment between family members, a closing down of learning and exploration is likely to occur. Sharing of thoughts and ideas is felt to be threatening. New experience is resisted. It is quite true that some children from such families do develop good learning skill. It has been my observation, however, that they are usually children who happen to have been born with unusual capacity. Moreover, they use learning as an overcompensation for what is missing in the emotional sphere of their lives. They throw themselves into learning, but at the expense of warm, interpersonal experience with others. Their intellects tend to be mechanized (like "Dr. Strangelove") rather than humanistic. Educators who value "pure achievement" and who are unconcerned with the "feeling side" of learning may not view these results so negatively as I do!

When there is a severe absence of a nurturing attitude in the current life of a family, both educators and therapists need to assess what modifications may be possible for that family. Not infrequently the problem is so complex that the helping professional has to settle for very small gains. The most that may be possible in some instances is an accepting, nonjudgmental attitude on the part of the professional person. Exhortation or censure rarely leads to change. But often acknowledgement of the limitations in a situation helps professionals to remain objective enough so that they can offer help but not become overwhelmed by the problem.

The difficulties related to deficient nurturing in families are not just the phenomena of economic poverty. Often the failure of a nurturing attitude is dramatically evident in very wealthy families. Also, in my estimation, it is frequently a by-product of those families that are most deeply committed to extreme rationalism or to the "gods of technology," or to "making it big" in the profit system.

When the problem in a child is a result of a more-or-less episodic and not overwhelming failure of nurturing in the family, brief interventions by therapists or educators can often help a great deal. A case illustration of brief intervention follows:

> Lisa's mother had been hospitalized three different times between Lisa's third and sixth birthdays. The mother suffered from a recurring kidney problem. Each time she came home from the hospital she was weak for extended periods and could not be up and around very much.
>
> It was in the periods of her mother's convalescence that Lisa suffered most. While mother was at the hospital both of her grandmothers helped care for her. But once mother returned home, Lisa felt deep longings for attention from her. Even when mother was not physically weak, however, she was occasionally depressed because of her insistent physical problem. Many times she would turn Lisa away from her. Lisa's father was not a particularly tender person. He was steady and kept things going but he did not respond much to his little girl's need for cuddling and affection.
>
> Lisa developed some strong undercurrents of "meanness." She was usually "good," but when other children seemed to be getting special

favors from adults she could be seen to build up tension and become provocative to the point of sadism with some of the children in her class.

Evaluation of her family and of her by a school psychologist shed light on her behavior. Her teacher became more sensitive to what set Lisa's "meanness" off and, also, she became less judgmental of her than she had been before the evaluation. The teacher was counseled by the psychologist to be firm with Lisa but also to talk with her about her feelings at times when it was evident that she felt competitive with other children.

Fortunately, the psychologist in this instance had developed skill in meeting with families. He had three such meetings with Lisa's parents and Lisa. The teacher attended one of these. In the meeting, some of Lisa's "problems" were talked about, but also Lisa was helped to express her feelings of "being gypped" when her mother was not feeling well. Some effort was made to get father to see that Lisa would benefit from an occasional sign of affection from him.

The joint effort led to marked reduction in Lisa's provocativeness in school and the children showed her much more acceptance in the weeks that followed this professional help.

## Phase C: Familial Encouragement of Individuation and Autonomy

In the individual development of each child we observe how bits of autonomous behavior oscillate with momentary or sometimes more prolonged returns to dependency refuge. This phenomenon occurs countless times during a day. Margaret Mahler,[14] a psychoanalytic student of the early phase of infant development, has brought the issue of separation and individuation in the first four years of life into particularly sharp focus. In her work she has emphasized that space exploration through crawling and early walking, and the manipulation of objects, all occurring in the first year-and-a-half, are the precursors of a psychic sense of independence and autonomy. In the toddler phase a child moves away from mother in ever-widening circles, and this repetitive daily activity provides an ever-elaborating proliferation of mechanisms for later autonomy. By the age of two a child walks into other rooms out of sight of mother and others, and sustains independent play for extended periods of time. With passing weeks new explorations are undertaken.

Each venture away from mother has implications for the growing sense of independent identity in a child. Conversely, each venture toward independence evokes reciprocal reactions in mother. How she responds is a function of her own personal history. Separation and independent action can be threatening to some mothers and exciting to others. Most mothers greet their children's independent explorations and initiative with enthusiasm and pleasure, some with gloom and anxiety or even with punishment, while others may show neutrality or a kind of indifference. Each style of maternal reaction affects the child (and the other family members).

Once again I wish to redirect our attention to the total family experience. Family nurturance of emerging autonomy in the infant and toddler is part and parcel of a total familial attitude toward self-expression and autonomous development. Not only each mother but each family has its own style. Beginning with the ways in which husband and wife relate to each other, values evolve for the children. The subsystem that I defined as "primary commitment," evolving in the earliest phase of the marriage, interlocks with the subsystem of basic nurturing and these, in turn, with the subsystems of autonomy and individuation. If during the phase of primary commitment a married couple defines some workable balance of togetherness and separateness, a model for the family behavior grows out of this and penetrates the nurturing phase that follows it.

Interpersonal warmth in the nurturing phase and genuine working together derived from the phase of primary commitment affect the subsequent evolution of autonomy and individuation for husband and wife, as well as children, in a positive fashion. Each family member receives recognition for being a person in his own right. The small crises of independent assertion that occur each day are met constructively. In any human group each person's bid for autonomy inevitably produces stress upon others. It upsets comfortable group equilibrium. There is always some resistance to the changes that increasing individuation evokes. In a successfully functioning family, positive accommodations and supportive reactions are the rule. The result is that children and adults have a clear sense of identity and value. They enjoy their feelings of initiative and freedom. Later, school and learning are experienced as places of pleasurable challenge.

In families where individuation is poorly supported or where it is felt as threatening, conflicts occur both between the parents and between them and the children. Between the parents this shows up in the form of struggles for power, excessive pressure to control each other, and in a variety of maneuvers in which each manipulates the other either through clinging dependence or through authoritarian dominance. Indeed, the resistance to accepting another person's individuality is very deep in almost all of us. Working out a vibrant respect for each person's individuality within a family is a lifelong demanding project.

Children in families where there is a great resistance to personal autonomy become either very timid and submissive or compulsively rebellious. A common "battle ground" for autonomy occurs around bowel training. The excretory function lends itself to struggle around autonomy because it is one that the child can control (or refuse to control). Success or failure in this training has powerful effects upon parents. Also, the anal phase coincides with the phase of increasing motility. Those children who become caught up in a battle with parents to establish their feelings of individuality develop extreme reactions to bowel training.

Somewhat later the matter of autonomy becomes dramatized around major events of separation, such as being left at nursery school or in nonfamiliar environments. Children with poorly integrated experiences in the phase of autonomy and individuation greet nursery school or kindergarten with separation anxiety and sometimes with phobic avoidance. In families where clinging and excessive mutual dependency are characteristic, the children may fear moving out into the world of school and peers. They are infected by their parents' anxiety.

Another kind of clinically observed reaction in children occurs in certain families where dependency is rejected and early independence is applauded. This is the reaction of "pseudomaturity." Often pseudomaturity arises in the nurturing phase and becomes accentuated all over again in response to the phase when autonomy is normally in the ascendency. Such children appear to handle separation and independence with aplomb when they are toddlers. It becomes evident as we observe them closely, however, that they overreject dependent gratifications that are appropriate for their age. They turn their backs on hugs and affection. They often resist close engagement with other children. Although competent and independent, they are on the way to being "loners." In school they do not lend themselves to guidance from teachers and they resist shared activities and pleasures. Their maturity and autonomy are at the expense of gratifying basic needs. Teachers are familiar with children who, because of poorly balanced autonomy, fail to be productive participants in classrooms. They may be the timid and inhibited ones on the one hand, or the compulsively rebellious ones or the nervously clinging ones or the "loners," on the other. Understanding a child's behavior in the light of his family experience introduces objectivity. A teacher with such understanding avoids reactions that are too subjective. Insight into a child's problems placed in the context of his family patterns helps define realistic approaches to him.

Conferences with families can be useful for evaluating developmental deficits as well as for discerning family styles and disruptive forces. Psychotherapists experienced with family interviews can offer help in uncovering factors that are responsive to educational or therapeutic intervention. Following are two brief samples of such conferences. They illustrate how the process works, given certain kinds of problems. In the first, "Carl" is in the third grade and is present at the interview. His family's style in dealing with autonomy is to create authoritarian controls:

TEACHER (*to parents*). I'm puzzled about why Carl always seems to go against rules—yet I know he's not mean. He's really a nice person. Do you have any ideas?

MOTHER. It has always been so with Carl—practically since he could crawl.

FATHER. We certainly give him rules at home—I don't believe in permissiveness—I wasn't raised that way—and my wife wasn't either—Carl certainly knows what we want!

TEACHER. But somehow things aren't working right—Carl is giving me a hard time—practically every time I give an assignment . . ..

FATHER. Don't teachers have to figure out punishment and rewards?

TEACHER. Mr. Martin, we do have to do that, it's true. But for some children ordinary punishments and rewards don't seem to work. That's why with Carl I'm in a quandary.

FATHER. Well, I didn't mean to be critical but . . ..

MOTHER. No, we really don't—but . . ..

TEACHER. Maybe the point is that we have to work this out together—Carl has to help too. From what you say, you folks are used to strong rules in your family—but it seems that's not working for Carl at school. So maybe you have to reconsider some things.

FATHER. For example?

TEACHER. Well, I'd like you to consider whether Carl's rebelling at school because he's afraid to at home. Could it be that you hold the reins too tight? I don't really know—but something isn't going well and Carl's getting a reputation for being a rebel. It seems you do have to reevaluate whether there are too many rules at home.

MOTHER. It's true we don't always explain *why* we want something done. I know my husband has that attitude—he expects things to happen right now. When we were young I couldn't learn to drive a car from him—I got nervous, and inside I got mad—he was so cut and dried—almost military. *(Mother and Father laugh uneasily).*

TEACHER. Carl—could you help? What do you think could get you off the habit of always going against rules?

CARL. I don't know.

TEACHER. Maybe Carl is too shy to say. It's hard, Carl, to talk about this. Anyway I do believe that everyone needs to rethink things a little. Carl is off on the wrong foot at school. You folks like rules and I can understand that—I do too. But sometimes they need to be modified. Maybe you do need to think more about how to take Carl in on your thinking so he doesn't feel things are just being pushed onto him. I've noticed that in class when I take time to explain a "why" to Carl, he often goes along with what I ask and doesn't seem to need to rebel.

Comment: In this example, teacher stayed very close to her own conviction and experience, which was that Carl would cooperate if he weren't coerced. The father's attitude was clear. The teacher couldn't undertake to change the father or the family. She could only try to help them reflect and reevaluate. Such a discussion in front of Carl might serve to start him on the road to some reflection about his impulsive behavior and to trying to make some changes.

A second illustration is one in which there are family problems at many levels. Whatever may have been the initial marital commitment, it is no longer present. Quite the opposite. The nurturing in the family is sporadic. Mother is insensitive to separation fears in her daughter, is overwhelmed by life's pressures, and is barely able to provide the basic needs of a family cycle. Teacher meets with Mrs. Rogg and Sheila, who is six:

TEACHER. I guess it was hard for you and Sheila to get here—all the work you have and the other kids on top of it.

MRS. ROGG. You know it—I feel I can't make it sometimes—it's just too much.

TEACHER. I hate to push more problems on you, but let's talk a little. Sheila's a handful when she gets nervous.

MRS. ROGG. They all are—so was their father—thank God at least he's not around anymore.

TEACHER. I can understand, although you know Sheila still loves her father—she draws pictures of him.

MRS. ROGG. No kidding? She never mentions him to me—but maybe I don't take time to listen.

TEACHER. Do you want to know how I see Sheila's problem?

MOTHER. Sure—that's why I'm here.

TEACHER. Well, I think she's so clinging and jumpy in school because she is afraid sometimes that you won't come home.

MOTHER. That's ridiculous—I always come home—sometimes I stay out late, but everybody needs some fun.

TEACHER. Of course. But maybe if you could just spell out very clearly to Sheila when you will be around and when you won't— maybe just take time to explain, or call her at a certain time in the evening if you'll be very late—just so she knows she's in your mind.

MOTHER. You think she needs that?

TEACHER. Sheila, what do you think?

SHEILA. Sometimes she don't wanna come home—sometimes she wants to run off.

MOTHER. Oh, come on—I say that when I'm blue, but I never have run off—come on Sheila, you know that.

TEACHER. Well, try anyway to spell things out to Sheila—it could help.

Comment: No single family conference produces miracles. A family conference can, however, set new wheels in motion. The child's presence at the meeting is important. Even if the parents do not change, the child takes from the experience a new perspective about himself and the teacher and the parents. Self-perception is the beginning of a process of maturing. The family conference may bear fruit months or years later. A teacher must keep optimal distance in order not to crowd the parents and also to avoid arousing unrealistic expectations in the child. Too much personal involvement by a teacher with a family can arouse complex emotions between parents and the school. Teachers should learn how to tailor family meetings to the issue at hand. Understanding the family cycle helps.

The main issue at hand in the case of Sheila and Mrs. Rogg is separation. Mother's spontaneous attitude toward Sheila suggests that while basic nurturing has been adequate, her own problems in achieving individuation and autonomy are still adolescent-like, and blind her to Sheila's needs as a separate person.

In the case of the Martins, father's personal solution to the problems of individuality and autonomy has been to be authoritarian and a setter of rules. His wife has complied with this approach. When Carl reached the phase of independent activity in his personal development, the familial reaction was to force him into an authoritarian mold. But it has not worked well, and Carl has displaced his struggle with parental authority onto the school.

## Phase D: Family Organization of Ego Mastery

The concept of "the ego" in individual psychology is complex. It has evolved through three generations of psychoanalytic research, beginning with Freud. I will begin this section with a short review of individual development and then return to the family development theme.

### Basic Ego Functions

In the toddler phase of development a remarkably rapid proliferation of behaviors and of inner psychic processes occurs. Certain basic *ego functions* become well crystallized in the first year-and-a-half and form the base upon which even more complex psychic mechanisms develop later. These ego functions are the capacity to *perceive*, to *think logically*, to *remember*, to *imagine and fantasy*, to *communicate through speech*, to *move about and explore surroundings*, to *integrate bodily sensation with thought processes*, and to *express a wide range of emotions*. In totality, these functions constitute the matrix for mastering interpersonal and objective experiences, but they are only the beginning of psychic experience in human beings (much in contrast to lower levels of animal life).

### Defense Mechanisms

Within each person, the ego functions I have just listed interweave with complex psychological processes that psychoanalysts call "defense mechanisms." In the first three to five years of life, defense mechanisms and a variety of "coping behaviors" take form at a bewildering rate of speed. This occurs so subtly that unless adults take time to observe children of this age very closely, the whole phenomenon of ego formation may not register in their minds. They view young children as "cute little objects" rather than as complex young people.

Because our sense of ourselves in the world is forever shifting, we strive for equilibrium in our lives. In order to achieve this kind of mastery, defense mechanisms and coping behaviors become elaborated and become the basis of our psychic survival. Of the defense mechanisms, the most common are rationalization, dissociation, repression, denial, displacement, intellectualization, and projection.

Every educator is familiar with *rationalization*—hearing it daily from students who find innumerable "logical" reasons why they failed to do what was expected. *Dissociation* is something teachers see often but may not define in this way; that is, behavior which a person carries without realizing he is doing it. A child who impulsively pushes others and then reacts with tears when others attack him is often only vaguely aware of his own provocative behavior. His side of the act has become dissociated from his consciousness. *Repression* is most common of all. Everyone—children, teachers, principals, and custodians—seems to be expert at forgetting what he said to others or what may have been said in return. The more emotionally distressful, the more likely is an event to be repressed. *Displacement* is an unfortunate but very frequent behavior in classrooms—children displacing anger from unhappy events at home or with siblings onto classmates; even teachers displacing irritations from their own personal lives onto their students! *Projection* is an ego mechanism that is very complex. It involves unwittingly attributing motives and intentions to others that really reside in one's self. Children frequently accuse others of what they themselves might wish to have done. They often assume that teachers or principals harbor critical or angry feelings toward them which may in fact be only projections of their own hostile-aggressive feelings toward authorities. They react against what they consider to be criticism before it is even there.

The various mechanisms I have reviewed are the ways in which humans master the anxieties of life. They become sources of interpersonal confusion when they function in an overly rigid way. When they operate with a degree of conscious understanding and control, they become buffers between the individual and the disruptive events of daily life. Intellectualization, for example, produces a one-sided person if it is overused. In moderation, intellectualization becomes an excellent balance to overwhelming emotion or impulse. Some repression is necessary for survival, since acute and gross memory of every painful experience would make life unbearable. Similarly, displacement of anger into constructive channels such as a competitive sport or a sharp debate helps master anger that cannot be properly acted out toward intimates.

### Coping Behavior

Side-by-side with the defense mechanisms of the ego, and always interwoven with them, are "coping" behaviors. These are the endless varieties of observable human behaviors through which individuals master life's circumstance. They include constructive bodily skills, social skills, intellectual competence, occupational activities, and creative endeavors of various kinds.

### The "Total Mix" of the Personality

The psychic processes I have described are an awesomely intricate tangle of phenomena. They constitute the "total mix" of personality functions that are generally categorized under the term "ego functions." Much has been written about each of the processes to which I referred. There are innumerable studies of each of the basic ego functions, of the defense mechanisms, and of various coping behaviors. Many studies concentrate on the developmental aspect of these processes. Others attend to the difficult question of how integration of the ego occurs and what constitutes ego strength and weakness. Others concentrate on clinical and educational applications.

In recent years the emergence of the field of "family therapy" has opened new vehicles for understanding the formation of ego processes. Coincidentally, educators concerned with the life experiences of children in ghettoes or in environments deficient in formal learning opportunities have become interested in how family experience affects the development of those aspects of the ego that relate to cognition. Understanding has surged forward as a result of these new fields of effort.

### Family Process and Ego Mastery

The work of family therapists particularly emphasizes the reciprocal interactions within a family. It is out of that experience that I have become sensitized to the themes of this chapter and particularly to the concepts that follow in this section on family organization of ego mastery.

Returning to my original thesis, I reiterate that parallel to the developmental process of each child, a developmental process goes on in each parent and in the family as a whole. Mechanisms for mastering life's experiences become much more intricate and subtle as the years of family life go on. There is a long path from the recently married young couple living alone with each other in a one bedroom apartment to the same couple five or ten years later with two or three children, managing household and finances, making plans and decisions about each child, reacting to each other's needs, interacting with relatives and neighbors, participating in the world of work, keeping in touch with the social and intellectual progress of each child, and sustaining a minimum of personal equilibrium.

We have reviewed the first phases of family development as prelude to this much more complex one of organizing ego mastery. How does this mastery occur? I shall try to explore this by discussing several major familial mechanisms which may be viewed as essential interactional subsystems in the phase of family organization of ego mastery. Those I shall discuss are *closeness and separation, communication of emotion, communication of ideas and perceptions, response to body experience, clarification of reality from fantasy, resolution of conflicts, fulfillment of goals, use of memory,* and *definition of roles.* Much more might be said of any of these than I can attempt to elaborate upon in this chapter.

CLOSENESS AND SEPARATION. Throughout the life of a family the contradictory forces of being close to others and at the same time accepting separation from them are forever in need of integration. Earlier experiences of individuation and autonomy in the family affect this process as it unfolds.

In a successfully functioning family the coping mechanisms for separation are delicately interwoven into the *daily* experience of the younger children. Mothers and fathers take time to clarify the reasons for their departures even when it is only for a few minutes or a few hours. They attend sympathetically to the feelings evoked in the very young members when they are left behind. Just as important perhaps, they attend to each other's feelings in relation to separation and loneliness. Through this model and through day-by-day practice, everyone develops appropriate mechanisms for mastering the distressful feelings that are a part of separation from each other. When it is time for attending school, both mother *and* child greet the event with emphasis upon pleasurable anticipation rather than upon separation distress. The interest parents show a child in what he experiences at school during a day becomes an encouragement to him for mastering the ambivalence he feels over leaving the comfort of his home. A consequence of this mastery is pleasure in the activities of the school.

When separation is poorly managed, exaggerated ego defenses evolve which make it difficult for the child to function autonomously and to learn in the absence of parents. Open expression of feelings about arrivals and departures of parents and siblings is not allowed in families where stoicism is prized. In such families children learn to feel ashamed of sentiment and they become "cool." There are certain families, on the other hand, that resist separation (and autonomy) altogether. In these the children are often clinging and demanding. Everyone is stuck to each other. This becomes something more than a feeling of warm connection.

In some children hyperactivity and restlessness are symptoms of an underlying fear of closeness and its necessary counterpart, separation. Their very hyperactivity serves to avoid intimacy and, therefore, the anxiety of separation which has to accompany all intimacy. Listen to popular love songs for evidence of how preoccupied young people are with these twin phenomena of intimacy and separation anxiety!

Observers of children in certain ghetto environments have demonstrated how the harshness of early life causes such children to avoid investing themselves in close interpersonal relations. When they are pressed to relate to another person (teacher) they resist. Only under persistent and skillfully guided interpersonal contacts with professionals do such children open up to warm relationships. When they do, they begin to experience painful separation anxieties which heretofore they had avoided through restless, aimless hyperactivity and shallow relationships with others. The educational problems with children whose difficulties emanate from a family experience that lacked sensitivity to separation are formidable. When they are built upon an absence of a nurturing attitude in a family, such problems may make it impossible for the child to function in the regular classroom because they are so deep. The combination of inadequate basic nurturing plus an absence of interpersonal connection produces a child devoid of deep pleasure in any undertaking.

COMMUNICATION OF EMOTIONS. Communication of emotions occurs all the time whether consciously intended or not. Frustration and anger are inevitable in interpersonal experience. The ways in which these are responded to and talked about among family members define ways in which the children will meet the same emotions in peer groups and at school. The same is true for anxiety and for tenderness. When emotions are attended to with genuine interest and supportively responded to, inner disruptions become fewer. Constancy of inner emotions allows children to maintain focused attention on learning. Acceptance of and ease with emotions arise out of sensitive sharing of feelings between family members. What I am referring to here constitutes an enormously complex communication process. Much of it is nonverbal. Many families react to an open show of emotion by inducing shame or self-doubt in those who were transgressors! Anger or tenderness is suppressed or scoffed at or disregarded. Usually this kind of suppression is at work between the parents themselves when the children are very young. Not only does it have far-reaching consequences for the interpersonal life within the family but it affects the independent lives of each member outside the family. People who cannot communicate feelings become isolated or slip into computer-like existence. They do sometimes become brilliant in a narrow range of academic achievement. When this happens they may not present problems to educators.

Achieving an inner integration of conflicting or ambivalent feelings and learning to meet and express both hostility and tenderness are lifelong challenges. The early years of family life define the later course for expressing feelings and receiving feelings from others.

PERCEPTUAL COMPETENCE. Almost everyone sees and hears and touches. Yet, in some families communication of perceptual experiences is encouraged and reinforced, while in others it seems to create tension and irritability. Some families seem to require that everyone avoids looking or hearing or smelling or touching. The reasons vary. But where avoidance of accurate sensory perception is the style of life, the children become narrow and avoid new experiences. Children from such families need to be actively taught how to use and find pleasure in their perceptual abilities and also how to communicate experience to others. Perceptual clarity enhances one's ability to cope with life's stresses. Educators have long understood how effective sharing of perceptions underlies good learning ability. New ways need to be found to reach children whose families fail to reward communication of perceptions.

COMMUNICATION OF IDEAS. Shortly after learning their first few words, toddlers begin to communicate increasingly complex ideas. Much of the time they do this through questions or through play with objects. Soon they do so in play with their contemporaries. Adults often seem oblivious of the colorful and direct ways that children of this age use to communicate ideas. Nursery school teachers or others who are sensitized to communication in young children often surprise parents when they point out the richness of children's communications. In my own experiences with families in therapy I have often observed startled reactions in parents when I succeed in drawing out their three-year-old about what he thinks of his father or mother or a sibling! Parents are often not only startled but often dismayed when they are required to listen to what their own teenagers have to say in family interviews.

Unfortunately, the "ideas" of children frequently meet resistance in adults. Just as unfortunately, adults greet the ideas of other adults with at least equal resistance. In fact, most people do poorly in "taking in" the ideas of others. Most of us tend to love our own ideas the most. The family style and standards about how one person listens to another have long-lasting and powerful effects on the children. Their openness to ideas at school and elsewhere grows out of a "listening attitude" at home. How a conversation flows around the dinner table is indicative of the way in which family members deal with each other's ideas.

LANGUAGE IN FAMILIES. A core element in communication of ideas is *effective use of language*. Many families use language in a primitive fashion—just enough to get across basic feelings but not enough to refine them. Language that is so limited may be sufficient for living in the very stark circumstances of life or death, but in order for humans to become "human," refinement of language communication is essential. Human feeling has so many subtle components that sensitive and reasonably accurate exchange becomes impossible without clear verbalization. The possibilities for misunderstanding between people are infinite. When misunderstanding occurs, anxiety and hostility result. Cumulative misunderstandings lead to mutual fear between people and to gross and insensitive manipulation of one by another. Pain and personal disaster often result from the long-term mistrust that arises out of inability to communicate through language. Salvador Minuchin and coauthors[15] have described this vividly in their book, *Families of the Slums.* Development in middle- and upper-class families also suffers when ideas are incompletely formulated and communicated. The everchanging language of adolescents and the gradual incorporation of these changes into adult vocabularies illustrate how language reverberates in a family. In earlier years parents often pick up and use the language of their toddlers.

Bodily Freedom and Pleasure in Families. Some religions of the past, out of zealous preoccupation with spirituality and virtue, have unfortunately created feelings of shame and rejection toward the human body. This has led to peculiar attitudes about sexual function and even the sexual anatomy. When feelings of pleasure and gratification in the body are made shameful and driven underground, perverse sexuality results. Guilt and shame lead sex and the body to be dealt with secretly, "out in the barn" or in a variety of pornographic outlets. Accepting bodily pleasure in appropriate degree and balance leads to the capacity for a feeling of freedom and an absence of self-consciousness. Underground sexuality, by contrast, exerts a magnetic pull upon thinking and fantasy and blocks effective learning and genuine interpersonal experience. Rigidity and punitive attitudes are frequent in people who are ashamed of their bodies and who are very guilty about sexual pleasure.

Family attitudes about the body are of powerful significance. The ease with which family members give or accept embraces, touching, occasional (nonexcitatory) nudity, and open talk about sexual and other bodily functions (appropriate to age) determine the ways in which the child will feel about his own bodily experience. This is a large subject and mere discussion of it meets great uneasiness and resistance in many segments of the population. Its significance for education lies in the area of how free and comfortable young people can be about themselves. Also, children who are preoccupied with thoughts about sex, resulting from too much suppression at home or too much excited secrecy, are not likely to keep their minds on formal learning. They are excitable and provocative and introduce constant distractions in classrooms.

Overcompensatory behavior is most common in the areas of body function. Under the surface of many daredevils and muscular bullies lie major anxieties about body intactness. Many "sexy" girls are profoundly fearful about their feminine selves. Other youngsters who walk or move rigidly or with exaggerated motions frequently reflect longstanding family tensions in their bodily movements. Once again emphasizing the reciprocity of attitudes in a family, it is of interest to note how, in the current scene, the attitudes toward body and sex that adolescents show are reducing "old-fashioned" rigidities in the older generation. Much earlier in the family cycle, a toddler's exploration of his own body and his candid questions have a strong impact on the adults. Unfortunately, the natural curiosity of the toddler or the later bumptiousness of the adolescent may provoke rigid and constricted reactions in adults. Most parents need guidance and a chance to talk over their subjective reactions to all of this.

CLARIFYING REALITY AND FANTASY. The boundaries of reality are never fully fixed for any of us. Interpretations of reality vary according to generation, social group, economic needs, ethnic background, educational level, and many other factors. Each of us tends to hold tenaciously to our own brand of "reality."

Children perceive the world in ways that are characteristic for them. Indeed, they do have their own reality. In the broad view, reality is an intricate admixture of the child's world and the adult environment. Hopefully, the child's fanciful verbalizations reawaken the imaginations and the mental imagery of the older family members.

In the toddler phase it is age-appropriate to feel omnipotent. Along with this feeling, a toddler believes in magical forces and causes. Unfortunately there are many adults who have never modified magical ways of thinking. When their children expect the impossible (or fear the impossible), these adults have difficulty in helping them differentiate what is likely to happen and what is unlikely to happen. Instead of providing the child a sensitive mutual explanation of what is probable and what is improbable, the superstitions or hysteria or even grandiosity of such parents may prevail. On the other hand and just as unfortunately, many parents deal harshly with children's fantasies. The family style becomes one of dogged and colorless "realism" and the children are incapable of using their imaginations creatively.

Parents must understand and temper their own magical fantasies because in their leadership of a growing family group adults cannot rely on magic to work out their problems. As family members watch television stories together and talk about them, or discuss newspaper events, or talk about Halloween or Santa Claus or spacemen or whatever, they forge a sense of reality for each other. Each family has its own mechanisms. Those educators who are able to achieve insight into the familial experiences of a particular child may avoid frustration and may be able to help clarify that child's misconceptions. Too often, educators have "flown blind" in the face of deeply entrenched cultural and familial beliefs.

Ethnic and cultural differences add to the complexity of a teacher's task. Certain cultural environments tend to be very matter-of-fact (rural environments and communities where families are mainly technicians or engineers are examples). Children from such families become embarrassed with open sharing of imagination in school and they need continuous encouragement.

The fantasy and imaginative production of children in "black ghetto" neighborhoods are likely to express very different emotional conflicts and intellectual preoccupation than are those of children from the "all white suburbs." Even within each of these there are wide variations. No two "engineers' families" are actually alike, any more than are two "black families" alike. Each has its individual history and structure. This uniqueness is what makes the concept of family life cycles such an intriguing one.

RESOLUTION OF INTERPERSONAL CONFLICTS. Interpersonal conflicts are the constant preoccupation of all humans living together in groups. The unceasing presence of war and the seeming increase of violence in the world suggests how gigantic is the task ahead. Long before the arrival of children, a married couple evolves intricate mechanisms for dealing with conflict. These mechanisms are at work not only between husband and wife but between the couple as a unit in relation to in-laws, friends, neighbors, and others. The mechanisms for dealing with or avoiding anger or conflict are one group of "coping behaviors." They are sometimes referred to as "the games people play."

Each partner in the marriage carries a long and complex personal history derived from identifications in each one's prior family. Much of what constitutes the developmental task of the phase of primary commitment in marriage has to do with finding ways of resolving conflicts. The question of conflict in marriage has far-reaching implications for our society. Too often the process of defining mechanisms for conflict resolution is poorly worked out. Instead, a variety of devices become relied upon for obscuring or masking or repressing conflicts. Alcohol is one device; intimidation by threats to leave one another or to turn to other relationships are common. In some marriage relationships guilt provocation or shaming become means for distracting from meaningful resolution of conflict. In others, withdrawal into long silences or carrying grudges or retreating to tears or lashing out with irritability or depreciation are substitutes for working out of conflicts. It is clear that when one person always needs to win or have his or her way, the model that is set for children in the family will be a skewed one.

When children enter the oppositional phase (anal-motile phase) with the great pressure for autonomy that occurs at this time, they put their parents to a new test of flexibility in resolving differences. Many parents become wildly exasperated when they run into a succession of willful "no's" from their toddlers. The child's growing verbalization and thinking ability add to the difficulties for parents, hopefully stimulating them to greater maturity and self-restraint. Unfortunately, those parents who have failed to work out a rich variety of mechanisms for conflict resolution earlier, now resort to rigid or punitive or even childish confrontations with their children. The child's pressure upon them reopens conflicts between the parents.

Currently the term "negotiation" has become popular. Ideally it reflects a greater degree of maturity between groups and nations. Within a family the ability to slow down the interaction at times of conflict and try to hear one another out and *empathize* with the other creates a high potential for constructive resolution of conflict. This produces a hopefulness in the children that their needs and views will be responded to with seriousness. A listening attitude and an emphatic tendency become extended into behavior with peers at school. Empathy is a direct derivative of a warm, nurturing attitude in the early phase of the family. In this chapter I have not defined *empathy* as a specific familial developmental task, but it may well merit separate attention.

The familial pattern in regard to conflict is frequently quite obvious in a child's behavior at school.

> One teacher said to a consultant, "Patricia clams up when others resist her suggestions. . . . I have seen her mother's lips tighten at a PTA meeting when others disagree with her. . . . Patricia once told me, 'My Mommy and Daddy didn't talk to each other for two whole days. . . .' " The consultant and the teacher went on to discuss ways in which Patricia could be induced to talk her feelings out at times when she was in conflict with other children.

In the phase of organizing ego mastery, all members of the family add to their personal range of skills and flexibility in resolving conflict. Not only do the children learn from their parents, but parents grow in response to the pressures placed on them by their children. Successful resolution of conflict occurs when each person feels listened to. The result is a reinforcement of a feeling of mutuality in all family members.

FULFILLING GOALS AND COMPLETING PROJECTS. Organizing and carrying through are virtues familiar to those with the Puritan heritage about responsibility and work. They are the virtues that have civilized wild frontiers and have carried the industrial revolution forward to its remarkable results. They are the virtues shared by the great engineers and captains of industry, as well as by scientists, teachers, skilled craftsmen, and occasionally politicians!

Children in the age range of three to five years lend themselves with great enthusiasm to games and activities of a kind that lead to a clear result. They love to build cities and structures with blocks and to survey their completed work. With encouragement, they love to create artistic work as well, unless the expectations placed upon them become rigid or overly exacting.

Some families are so "project oriented" they appear to be in a blaze of productive activity all the time. Those children in such families who get into rhythm with this become "winners." Those who do not, tend to become compulsive rebels. Currently we see many middle-class youngsters from such families going to radical extremes in "dropping out." The dropping away from high-powered family goals reaches self-destructive proportions for that minority of young adults who compulsively reject goals and organization to the point of blanking out on drugs. They regress to a state of monotonous nonproductivity in their flight from the achievement expectations of their parents.

There are great variations in the kinds of goals and projects families value. For some, athletics or sports become the core of organized family activities; for others, intellectual or cultural activities predominate. The family whose members work together in a business or on the farm provides a daily structure for project organization and completion. That kind of family tends to be something of the past in the United States. In its day it exerted a powerful effect on the whole family life. Many who seek to create communes are hoping to revive some of the feeling of a "caring group" in which common work goals are defined and where all the participants share in the group effort.

Families in middle-class apartment-house settings may need to invent and carefully structure activities that involve all the members in common effort. Drawing the children into the daily domestic activities may be a major vehicle, although there are dangers of becoming involved in power struggles around such intrafamilial projects. Planning outings and trips together can be a way of pulling everyone into projects that involve a cycle of thinking and imagining together, organizing action, and bringing action to a gratifying result.

The teacher who works with children from families who have no tradition of working on projects or moving toward goals will have a long road to travel in order to involve such children in organized activities. Children need repeated encouragement and reward to develop pleasure in this area of ego activity.

Teachers of the very rich and of the very poor find a common problem in that many children from such families are not able to find pleasure in working toward relatively distant goals. The tragedy is greater for the latter—those locked into ghettos that offer minimal or no rewards for achievement. Teachers may find it impossible to educate children whose families are too poor or are too fragmented to establish realistic life goals.

MEMORY. Like gravity or the sun or the air around us, memory is ever-present and always affecting us. In family life it may be a constructive factor in interpersonal communication, but it may, under more negative circumstances be used as a cudgel. Shared well, memory becomes the basis for mutuality in family experience. Children at age three or four make frequent references to past events. Their comments often surprise and delight their parents who then become involved in sharing memories with their children out of the sheer pleasure of doing so.

Positively recalled family events of the past and references to past achievements of various members—parents or children—build individual identity and positive attitudes toward mastering experience. Memory used to remind one another of past failures or sins, on the other hand, becomes a vehicle for evoking guilt and anxiety. How memory is used in a family is of major importance in the early years of childhood, since it is then that children learn whether to trust it in communication or to take flight from it because it only reopens hurts or guilt. When memory is felt to be alien and a burden, the attitude toward learning in school and elsewhere becomes crippled. Between husband and wife, memory may be used as a means of attack.

In our work in the therapeutic nursery school at the Cedars-Sinai Medical Center's Child and Family Study Center, we have learned that many families with disturbed preschool children have failed to create a positively toned memory system for their children. Our teachers regularly put together a biographic photo album of each child and his family which he receives on graduation. Through this medium the family and school experiences become recorded in permanent visual memories. A sense of the past and a recognition of the reality of change evolve from seeing one's self and one's family in various scenes of the recent and remote past.

Some families become so treasuring of the past that they "live with their memories." We have all met or read about members of the dispossessed aristocrary such as those from Tsarist Russia or pre-Castro Cuba or Indo-China, or even the "old South" in the United States. In situations of that kind memory becomes a retrogressive force. For some families, nostalgia and tradition and "the past" are clung to as the model of life. While a feeling of security can derive from "living in the past," it stultifies growth and development.

DEFINING OF ROLES. Roles are defined and redefined throughout the cycle of a family, although certain basic structural roles crystallize and change very little; namely, "Pop," "Mom," "Grandpa," "Grandma," "big brother," "kid sister," and so on. But even so, behavorial expectation within those role designations changes as the aging process proceeds.

Throughout the phase of *familial organization of ego mastery*, intense and constant experimentation with many roles is a central experience for the children. The parents are simultaneously taking on new roles in relation to friends, in-laws, and the community. A young couple in their midtwenties experience a rapid change in social role from being a pair of "young married kids" to being "Mr. and Mrs. Jones." It is in these years that father is clarifying his career role, his role as a member of community groups, as a person in his neighborhood and in his family of origin. Something similar goes on for mother. With the "Women's Lib" movement, shifting of mother's roles becomes an even more powerful factor in family life. Parental roles become complex and variegated at the very time that their children's role experimentations are most active.

In fantasy role play, children become Daddy, Mommy, policemen, doctors, bus drivers, kings, queens, bosses, baseball players, robbers, spacemen, batmen, supermen, jungle queens, etc. These roles are played out in relationship to peers, and in the process many subtleties of two-person (dyadic) interaction are tried out and become part of coping behavior. The models for various role behaviors are to a great degree the ways the parents act with each other and with others. There are many other models. Grandparents are important, as well as uncles and aunts, family friends, nursery school teachers, characters in stories, television personalities (real and fictional), and of no small importance, children in the neighborhood. The place of a family in the economic and social scene is of crucial importance. The recent "black revolution" has convincingly shown how a whole ethnic group can suffer tragically from having been overtrained into rigidly defined roles and role behavior. The "Uncle Tom" role that so many black people find offensive is one such rigidification. Other rigidly defined black roles were the "Stepin Fetchet" character of the movies and Jack Benny's houseman, "Rochester." Even successful black athletes and entertainers have been forced into rigidly stereotyped roles in the popular mind.

There are many ways of fulfilling the roles of big sister, little sister, older brother, first cousin, or grandchild. Every role has a reciprocal partner—a "big brother" implies the presence of a "little" brother or sister. Similarly, innumerable reciprocal roles exist between parents and children. Some of these become overloaded; e.g.,

"Daddy's little princess," or "Grandpa's favorite," or "Mom's little helper." Difficult personality problems may arise because of exaggerated behaviors and self-images that accompany rigid role designations.

In a family certain roles fulfill psychological needs for everyone. Some children play out the role of scapegoat or "the loser"; others become overly idealized because of intellectual or athletic skill or unusual beauty. If these roles are rigidly set, serious problems may occur. Teachers frequently are able to spot such children in their classrooms because their personalities are so obvious. "The loser" is often shy, or silly, or provocative in a way that leads him to be ostracized or rejected. "The intellectual" demands constant acknowledgment beyond what is appropriate. "The athlete" feels he has no other responsibilities to fulfill. I have mentioned only a few of the stereotyped role behaviors that are familiar to teachers.

Each child needs to balance his role in relation to each parent. This is an extremely complex process referred to by psychoanalysts as the "Oedipal phase." By the time children are five or six they imagine adult roles for themselves in relation to their parents of the opposite sex. A little girl pretends the role of attentive and charming and even "sexy" wife to her father. Exaggerated behavior of this kind evokes feelings in father, and in mother, too. There are innumerable variations. A relatively firm crystallization of the parental roles in relation to sex, authority, decision making, and impulse control needs to occur during the phase of ego mastery in the family cycle. Parental failure at this point leads to confusion for everyone. If the marriage was poorly knit in the first place, the stress arising in this new phase may be enough to bring about a breakdown of the family unit. Some children emerge from the phase of early ego mastery in roles excessively advanced for their age and actual competence. One not uncommon example is when a father retreats into alcoholism or too much passivity during this phase of the family cycle and his little son inherits the role of "mother's husband." This is much too heavy a responsibility.

As I have noted, teachers recognize easily those children whose roles are overly defined in their families; for example, the family genius, the family clod, or the family clown. Often it is difficult to reverse such roles in the family. If the origin of such roles can be discerned, the teacher's objectivity is enhanced and there is less tendency to respond to the behavior of these children in a subjective way. Indeed, with understanding, a teacher can carefully avoid playing into the child's role behavior and can open opportunities for the child to change it.

In an ideal family cycle, everyone learns a broad spectrum of role behaviors that are appropriate to time and circumstance. While flexible, they must not be undermining of the central identity of each person. It is possible to understand and play out many roles while remaining a genuine person, but the process for achieving this is a slow and complex one. The school and the family environment interrelate in relation to role behaviors in even more intricate ways as the years go on. Children who fail to develop good one-to-one role exchanges with parents or siblings become "loners" in school, or sometimes manipulators of others. They do not experience substantial give-and-take relationships. Those who become caught-up in a poorly balanced three-way relationship with mother and father may become forever jealous and envious, disrupting friendships of others. They may be so preoccupied with achieving primary acceptance and notice that they are unable to invest themselves in the learning process at school. Examples are "Daddy's favorite girl" or "Mom's perfect son" types of children.

Distorted role expectations at home become projected onto teachers or comrades in school. For such children those who are authorities become equated with parents at home. Peers are perceived in the roles of siblings. Behavior in a classroom is often a carry-over of home experience. The reactions a child expects from adults will be based upon what he sees adults do in his family. If the role behavior of adults at home is unpredictable or shifting or poorly defined or "immature" or ungratifying for them, children will carry over great ambivalence of feeling about adults in general, as well as about those in their school environment. Ideally, teachers should be able to help a child define appropriate adult behaviors. This definition occurs more easily when teachers understand what familial values are at work for a particular child. Of course the defining of behavior reflects the teacher's own family experience as well. Teachers do not grow up in a vacuum. Each of us has at some time been a part of an influential family experience. We all know that we often function more objectively in our professional roles than in our own families.

Following is a example of a boy who is struggling with his role in relation to a female authority figure, his teacher.

> TEACHER. I guess, Jerry, you think fathers are supposed to know a lot more than mothers—like ladies can't know as much as men.
>
> JERRY. Well—my Dad says women don't think clear—they just babble but they don't know much. . . .
>
> TEACHER. So maybe it bothers you if a lady teacher like me corrects you. . . .
>
> JERRY. I guess teachers are different . . . but I don't think you know as much as Mr. Carter.
>
> TEACHER. Maybe, but try to listen to me anyway—sometimes ladies know things too.

*Comment*: In this case, the teacher has to be aware of her own feelings about being "put down" by men.

## Phase E: The Middle Years of the Family

This is the period in the life of the family when children and parents move out into the world. Characterizing this very extended phase as "centrifugal" may be an overdramatization, but what happens is a bit like centrifugal force where everything spins away from the center. The household remains very much the center of the family interaction. But with most of the children in full attendance at school, dispersion of the family members into innumerable activities outside the home occurs. The middle phase encompasses many years, including adolescence and the period of early adulthood when children move away. It merits much more detailed discussion than is possible in this chapter.

Each parent's individual development in this developmental period affects not only the marital relationship but the day-to-day familial transactions. Some parents, out of a failure to develop "their own thing," try to hold on to their children and avoid the signs of growing independence. Mothers are perhaps more likely to do this than fathers. Children's growth of interest in peers and activities away from home threatens the inner familial cohesion of earlier years. If each parent has become relatively comfortable as a person in his or her own right, this new development is met optimistically. It is in the middle years of the family cycle that mothers often take on full-time work outside the home. Many women become active in organizations. Mother's outside activities can produce stress and disequilibrium in the family routine and require readaptations between all members. How these adaptations occur are very much a function of how each of the earlier phases has progressed. Issues of individuation and autonomy remain paramount.

Frustrations and angers may arise in the marriage and spill over into the family's interaction. Sibling competitiveness is often more manifest in this period, since areas for success are highly defined and youngsters either "make it" or they don't. Success or failure in social relationships and in school and career all become the focus of attention. If earlier phases have progressed with some degree of success, an enlarging sense of mutual respect and good feeling within the family occurs. Opportunities are present for identifying with each other's experiences, for sharing successes and empathizing with problems, for traveling, for learning together, for defining values and points of view about life, and for developing depth and range of understanding.

Inevitable conflicts between generations arise in these years. Many parents in the process of "maturing" leave the more experimental ideas of their youth behind. For some, a rigidification occurs and sensitivity to young people becomes defensively dulled. Conflicts of values and attitudes toward life take on force between the generations as the children become adolescents. All over again issues of autonomy come to the fore. Adolescents characteristically view themselves as relatively omnipotent. They tend to "put down" the realistic cautions that the older generation raises. In their longing to establish themselves as independent persons, adolescents often depreciate the sensitivities and wisdom of parents and of school authorities. Usually this kind of exaggerated self-assertion is of fairly brief duration and does not lead to major problems if adults do not become entrenched in rigid counterpositions. The need for adolescents to turn inward and share their thoughts or experiences only sporadically and when they feel like it, does threaten certain parents who feel left out.

Many adolescents fail to progress in this period because they cannot disentangle from the family matrix. Tragic results may occur because of the inability of the parents to master the anxieties of separation.

The effect of adolescence upon parents has become the subject of recent films, stories, essays, and magazine articles, and is a chapter in itself. The fact that parents are usually in their late thirties or early forties as their children reach adolescence is of great importance. It is in these years that many adults enter a period of personal insecurity about aging, careers, finances, physical health, etc. Just as their young become most challenging, parents are most personally vulnerable. The imminence of children leaving home or of finding excitement "out there" evokes fear or envy or defensiveness in parents. Lines of conflict and hostility often become drawn in families. Explosions, withdrawals, flight, accusations, and counteraccusations all occur. Marital relationships frequently undergo new stress as each parent has to give up attachments to the child and intensify the relationship with each other. The work of teachers and educators with adolescents becomes even more difficult because society is undergoing such a rapid change. The natural volatility of youth becomes more intensified by the shifting values and uncertain nature of society at large.

It falls upon teachers to help adolescents define goals and directions in life. But teachers are themselves being cast about on uncertain waves and are not sure of what they have to offer young people. They find theselves being criticized by parents who want certainty to occur in the schools and by the adolescents who are resistant to "the establishment." Young people from families who have failed to progress through a relatively well-defined life cycle may find it difficult to trust teachers or cooperate with what schools ask of them. The problem of defining educational goals needs to be met from both sides: families on the one hand and schools on the other.

Educational institutions do need to modify their systems of procedure and organization so as to adapt more realistically to the kinds of family experience their students have known. Otherwise teachers may find themselves at an impasse with many of their students. Sensitivity to the dynamics of family life is a key that may reopen healthy exchange between educators and the young. With new knowledge and skills being developed in the field of "small group dynamics," it becomes possible to envision a day when schools will foster many kinds of intergeneration discussion groups, psychodrama, "rap sessions," and so on. There are many ways that the generations can come into productive exchange with one another. Schools have been slow to explore such avenues, perhaps out of fear of the unknown.

## SUMMARY

I have tried in this chapter to tie a very complex knot. Drawing upon concepts from social psychology, developmental sociology,

individual personality development, psychoanalysis, and family therapy, I have reviewed some of the dynamics and phenomena underlying the developmental cycle of families. In order to structure thinking about the family cycle, I have suggested the following phases of
development: primary commitment, the nurturing system, familial
encouragement of individuation and autonomy, family organization
of ego mastery, and the middle years of family life.

A two-sided thesis underlies everything I have formulated here. It
is that growth and development of individuals always occurs in a
*context,* and *contexts are forever changing.*

Insofar as we view "the family" to be a context in which human
beings develop, we need to look at how the cycle of change occurs
in families.

If one takes seriously the thesis that change is always present in
human experience, then one may learn how to move *with* rather than
*against* children, parents, students, and families. But to accept change
and to move with it does not mean that we must become so fluid that
no expectations nor directions can be charted. What a serious
acceptance of the notion of change demands of us is a willingness to
understand what the process is, what its dynamics are, and how
distortions of the natural process of change occur.

For educators, the process of change in family life holds implications somewhat different from those of economists or real estate sales-
men or psychotherapists. Educators meet the process of family change
at a point where formal learning is the issue. Since formal learning is
not something all human children take to with equal enthusiasm,
educators meet an enormously varied range of receptivity. It has
become clear in recent years that the receptivity to formal learning
in young people is a function of many factors. "Pure intelligence,"
if there is such a thing, is only one factor.

How can comprehension of the developmental cycle of families
aid educators to assess or modify or increase the child's receptivity to
formal learning? Perhaps most directly by helping to understand
not only where certain resistances to learning have come from, but
what is *perpetuating the resistances.*

Through comprehending the stages of development of families,
one becomes more objective than one might formerly have been in
responding to learning resistances in children. It may be helpful to

imagine the case of "Tim." Is his fearfulness and reticence in the classroom a result of deep inner anxiety or is it a reflection of under-developed ego functions? How can this be assessed? A most effective vehicle for such an assessment is through a family meeting. In such a meeting it soon becomes evident whether there is a vibrant sense of mutual respect and warm feeling in the family or whether, on the other hand, there is rigidity or authoritarianism or a "put down" attitude between the family members. If the latter is the case, Tim's problem is most probably one of deep inner anxiety and self-doubt. A healthy sense of self is not encouraged in his family. Tim's needs will be beyond what school can provide. Deep emotional support and a psychotherapeutic approach are needed.

On the other hand, Tim's problems in the classroom may be the result of insufficient family training in ego competence. Warmth and good feeling may prevail, but there is a lack of knowledge in the various areas of ego function. A supportive educational approach together with family guidance may be adequate to reduce the problem.

What if it turns out that Tim's family "just doesn't care," and that no one in the family gives much to anyone else? Then a profound conclusion may need to be drawn. Tim is likely to be obsessively oriented toward what he gets or does not get from others. Formal learning for him is probably going to remain a rather remote concern. About all a teacher can hope to strive for with him if this is the case, is a benign warm relationship.

Lest what I have said seem too pessimistic, I wish to emphasize that the very introduction of constructive concern into the family (for example, from an educator or from an educational institution that cares) sets new intrafamilial forces to work. Early, if the nurturing phase is faltering, warm interest in the family from teachers, such as has occurred in many Project Head Start Centers, can help the family members into a more nurturing attitude toward each other. Later effective and sympathetic interest in a family may help parents become less authoritarian and suppressive, or more organized and supportive, whichever is needed.

The various problems that I have noted may seem to create more challenges for educators than many feel inclined to take on! Increasingly, our understanding tells us that the problems and the challenges of youth can be met only through open-minded and willing cooperation of all professional persons whose careers are committed to human service. Educators need not stand alone in providing education to children. They need day-to-day cooperation from mental health professionals, family counselors, group dynamicists, and whoever else remains sensitive and responsive to the awesome phenomena of human development.

Mental health clinicians, in contrast to educators, tend to focus on what is sometimes called the "intrapsychic" dynamics of the personality. The implication of the term "intrapsychic" is that personality problems and difficulties in living are a function of internal conflicts and failures of ego development. Those of us who do clinical work with families have repeated confirmation, almost within each consultation session, of the fact that personality problems are a function of both what goes on within each person and what goes on in that person's interpersonal relationships. Moreover, we see that a powerful source of difficulty for each individual is the fact that much as he is dependent upon the positive forces of family life for his personal development, he is also hampered at times by the failures or the conflicts within his family.

With each year of my own clinical work, it becomes clearer to me that the beginning of most psychotherapeutic effort should be through an overall evaluation of an individual's family. Whenever feasible this evaluation should include a meeting with the entire family. Family therapists, including myself, have published a great deal about the rich data that emerge through even a single family interview. Central to my view is that the data that emerge in this way are not simply static information to be placed in a clinical chart. Rather, the data become, as they emerge, the very content of the clinical process. Thus, as some of the examples throughout this chapter suggest, learning within a consultation session with an entire family that the father is disparaging and scoffing about "intellectuals" provides the interviewing clinician (or educator) with working material. In the moment that datum emerges from the father, it becomes possible to enter into an exploration with everyone in the family of the meaning of father's attitude for each family member.

I do not intend to imply that one begins a cross-examination; I wish to emphasize that this is an exploration. If in the course of that exploration with the family one keeps in mind the notion of a developmental cycle of families, the opportunity is present to review with the family members how the father's attitude became formed in the life of this family. Everyone is invited to consider what purpose it has served in earlier years, and how it now affects the personalities and the learning capacities of the children. The clinician's part in all of this is not to lecture the father and argue with him about his attitude toward intellectual effort, but rather to investigate and review what goes on in such a way that the father himself may be inclined to modify his negative attitude. Even if he resists, the sheer experience of the exploration itself gives everyone in the family an opportunity to think in a new way. This, then becomes the entrance to a new phase of familial development as well as personal progress for each person.

## REFERENCES

1. Ackerman, Nathan: *Psychodynamics of Family Life.* New York, Basic Books, 1956.
2. Bowlby, John: Attachment, vol. I of *Attachment and Loss.* New York, Basic Books, 1969.
3. Brody, Sylvia: *Patterns of Mothering.* New York, International Universities Press, 1956.
4. Brown, Saul L.: Family therapy viewed in terms of resistance to change. *Psychiatric Research Report 20,* American Psychiatric Association, 1966.
5. Brown, Saul L.: Psychiatric consultation for Project Head Start. *Community Mental Health J, 2,* 1966.
6. Brown, Saul L.: Coordinating professional efforts for children with school problems. *Children, 15,* 1968.
7. Erikson, Erik H.: *Childhood and Society, 2nd ed.* New York, W.E. Norton, 1963.
8. Freud, Anna: *The Ego and the Mechanisms of Defense.* New York, International Universities Press, 1964.
9. Grey, Alan L. (Ed.): *Man, Woman and Marriage.* New York, Atherton Press, 1970.
10. Herndon, James: *The Way It Spozed to Be.* New York, Simon & Schuster, 1968.
11. Kohl, Herbert R.: *Teaching the Unteachable.* New York, New York Review Book, 1967.
12. Kris, Ernst: Decline and recovery in the life of a 3-year-old. In *Psychoanal Study Child.* New York, International Universities Press, 1962, Vol. 17.
13. Lidz, Theodore: *The Person.* New York, Basic Books, 1968.

14. Mahler, Margaret, and LaPerriere, Kitty: Mother-child interaction during separation-individuation. *Psychoanal Q, 34,* 1965.
15. Minuchin, Salvador, Montalvo, B., Guerney, B.G., Rosman, B.L., and Schumer, F.: *Families of the Slums.* New York, Basic Books, 1967.
16. Provence, Sally A., and Lipton, Rose C.: *Infants in Institutions.* New York, International Universities Press, 1963.
17. Ritvo, Samuel, and Solnit, Albert J.: Influences of early mother-child interaction in identification process. In *Psychoanal Study Child.* New York, International Universities Press, 1958, Vol. 13.
18. Sander, Louis W.: Issues in early mother-child interaction. *J Am Acad Psychiatry, 1,* January 1962.
19. Solnit, Albert J., and Provence, Sally A. (Eds): *Modern Perspectives in Child Development.* New York, International Universities Press, 1963.
20. Spitz, Rene: *The First Year of Life.* New York, International Universities Press, 1965.
21. Winnicott, D.W.: *Collected Papers.* New York, Basic Books, 1958.

# Chapter II

# FAMILY FACTORS IN LEARNING DISABILITY

ROBERT FRIEDMAN AND DAVID MELTZER

T HE family component of learning disorders will be discussed in this chapter under three headings: first, a review of the literature on family psychodynamics related to learning disability; second, some comments on the key issues of identification—self-esteem—separation, values, infancy, and adolescence; and last, the interplay between family dynamics and the external realities in the environment.

## LITERATURE

Investigations of the psychodynamics of learning disorders started from the premise that emotional illness (that is, the "sick" child) was a major causal factor. Initially only the child was studied, gradually the mother, father, and other children were added to the field of inquiry, culminating in a theory that to fully understand learning disability, the whole family must be taken into consideration.

Early psychoanalytic studies[2, 3, 26, 33] viewed learning difficulties as a fully internalized, unconscious conflict within the child. The parent, especially the mother, was consulted for historical data about the child in order to help the therapist better understand the child. Whatever changes in the home environment the analyst deemed necessary were suggested to the parents, but the parents were not themselves involved in the analysis. The analyst might see the roots of the learning disorder within the family system, but he dealt with this only by helping the child understand himself. For example, the analysis might reveal how early childhood difficulties in food intake would be connected with later problems in the intake of information, or uncover the relationship between early conflicts around toilet training and the later inability to store and give out learning material.

Another illustration from classical psychoanalytic theory was the Oedipal problem of the boy's fear of mastery that might be seen as competition with the father. The boy might fear castration or abandonment if he were to succeed in learning. Blanchard,[3] in her summary of early analytic thinking on the causes of reading disorders, included the following family-related factors:

1. Anxieties and conflicts arising from family relationships, such as sibling rivalry.

2. Rebellion of a child against a parent who has stressed reading success and for whom the child feels great antagonism. The child may retaliate against the rejecting, cold, or punitive parent by not learning.

3. Parental prohibition against "peeping"—an example of the disturbance of the exploratory function of the instincts, with consequent inhibition of curiosity. The parent who discourages development of autonomy often discourages exploration in which learning takes place through sensory stimuli—looking is particularly related to reading.

4. Traumatic experience, such as the loss or separation from a parent at the time of school entry or during the early school years.

5. The association by the child of school learning as a sex-linked trait; a boy who sees mother as very interested in learning while father seems indifferent about it may resist what appears as a basically feminine activity.

Pearson[26] contends that if this factor is not linked to a serious neurotic disorder, the learning problem can be solved by having the child instructed by a teacher of the same sex, who thus serves as a learning identification model.

Later, studies of mothers of children with learning inhibitions[6, 15, 23, 31] discovered that some mothers have extremely close bonds with and an intense fear of losing the special intimate relationship with a particular child. So long as this child does not learn, he will not lose his mother, will remain dependent on her, and be free from the anxieties of growing up. Sometimes these mothers will deliberately withhold information, creating a "family secret," or will unconsciously create a flagrant distortion of the family reality. For example, a child is required by mother to render special assistance to a sibling who is both intellectually and physically handicapped, yet is not permitted to comment on these handicaps and must pretend that nothing is wrong because the parents act as if the sibling's handicaps were nonexistent. This process sets up a model in which the child learns to play "dumb" at home and carries that role through in school. Learning in school, therefore, would require that the child change his relationship with his mother—resolving the school learning problem would require that the analysis work through the child's relationships with his mother.

Staver,[30] in her study of seventeen mothers of children with learning disorders, found that in addition to the school problem, all the children suffered from a great fear of separation and death and used helpless ignorance as a method of protection against these fears. The children's anxieties proved to be a magnified and all-pervasive version of the mother's more limited apprehensions. These mothers resisted separation from and the intellectual growth of their children, and used various maneuvers to promote poor school performance in their children, such as diverting the child from his homework and sabotaging the child's psychiatric treatment. Almost all of these mothers had suffered or were threatened by the loss of an important sustaining figure in their own lives and were deeply involved in unsuccessful attempts to satisfy their dependency needs. The importance of the child in warding off the mother's fear of abandonment can be inferred from the fact that sixteen of the seventeen mothers suffered accidents or illnesses during the course of their child's treatment, thus insuring that someone would have to care for them; the last mother withdrew from the study. A common defense mechanism in these mothers was the "learning problem" of not knowing or understanding various areas of their lives; for example, they were unable to remember painful details in their own lives or in their children's development. Their children also played important roles in their fantasy life. Several mothers used the child's "retardation" as an excuse for a highly sexualized relationship with the child under the guise that the child would not know.

As the importance of the parental role in the development of a child was increasingly recognized, the father was studied, individually or as part of the total family setting to determine his contribution to the learning disorder.[12, 13] As a result, he was included in the treatment program, usually on an individual basis. Two patterns appeared prominently when the father was studied. In the first, he regards himself as a failure and often will have an attitude of helpless resignation and low self-esteem. His wife and the children also hold him in low esteem. Usually, his job placement will be below his capabilities, and for this reason he is competitive with his son and unable to express pleasure or satisfaction in his son's achievement, often thwarting activities that could lead to his son's intellectual or emotional growth and maturity. At home, these fathers have a helpless, dependent relationship to the wife, who holds the position of authority and leadership in the family, a position clearly recognized by husband and children. A case illustration follows:

> Mike, aged eleven, suffered from a long-standing learning disturbance, which was gradually getting worse. He was obviously depressed and lacked friends. Yet his near-failing grades for the past semester did not motivate his parents to bring him for treatment. They were moved to seek treatment only after he was discovered stealing and wearing girls' underwear. In treatment, this behavior proved to be a repudiation and fear of a strong masculine role and an identification with his mother and youngest sister who seemed to be the powers in the family. Mike's father had not done well in school in spite of superior intelligence. After military service he worked for several small businesses, often under the supervision of his wife's parents. He, too, seemed chronically unsuccessful and depressed. He suffered innumerable minor and major injuries at work which seemed to be a manifestation of a strongly self-critical aspect of his personality. Shortly after Mike entered treatment, the father decided to open a small franchise food business; it ended in disaster, further lowering the father's self-esteem. Mike's mother was seen by the husband and the children as the stable and reliable parent. The wife's parents would often come to the financial rescue of the family.
>
> In Mike's individual treatment he became aware that like father, he was depressed, unsuccessful, and envious of the mother's competence, strength, and self-esteem. He became aware of how his father would allow him to avoid homework responsibility, but he was still not able to take responsibility for himself. In conjoint family sessions, father's incongruent messages about school and homework, as well as mother's passive acceptance of the situation, were discussed and changes instituted. As a result, Mike was able to form a firm attachment and friendship with his father for the first time. Mike's school performance increased to an acceptable level and he became involved in age-appropriate masculine sexual interests.

In the second pattern, father is a more successful and aggressive person and is the acknowledged authority figure in the family. Unfortunately, success and assertiveness only cover over a deep sense of inferiority and frustration stemming from early failures in life. The father's basic passivity is defended against by infantile aggressive, blustery overreaction—a reaction formation in which father acts the opposite of his unconscious wishes and feelings. In this kind of marriage the mother seems helpless and frightened of her husband's display of power and authority, but covertly she attempts to be the real authority. The son then becomes a pawn in and strongly affected by the parental power struggle, rejecting achievement as assertive, destructive, and hurtful. He assumes a passive, nonachieving role in which he both identifies with father's underlying personality structure and demonstrates the negative results of mother's infantilization and overprotectiveness. A case illustration follows:

Mark, age fourteen, was referred for treatment because of a total inability to learn. Although he received much remedial help at the special school he attended, he could not write his name or read the simplest books. In addition, his mother felt herself to be totally helpless in controlling his wild, impulsive, semidelinquent behavior. She argued continuously with her husband about the boy's behavior and complained about her inability to discipline him. Although father secretly enjoyed Mark's exploits, he imposed excessively harsh and unrealistic punishments, such as ordering the boy to stay in his room for a month. Father would then leave the implementation of the punishment to mother.

Although Mark's father claimed he wanted his school performance to improve, he did not carry out a plan to punish his son for not doing what little homework had been assigned by school. Father refused to participate in the initial evaluation of Mark, did not support a sorely-needed plan of intensive individual psychotherapy for the boy, and insisted that the mother come with him on trips which he knew would conflict with her appointments with the therapist.

The mother claimed to be tyrannized by and afraid of her husband, but always managed to get from him what she wanted for herself. Mark's father came from a poor family and he did not receive much education, yet he founded a very successful business. He employed many highly skilled and well-educated people whom he treated as if they were possessions to be bought and sold, thereby covering over his own lack of education. He stated many times that he went through a wild phase in his life and never needed education to succeed. Therefore, he considered his son's school performance and behavior as a transient phase, in spite of many professional opinions to the contrary.

In Mark's case, we see how his symptomatology revealed his identification with his father's negative attitude toward education and with his father's tyrannical, impulsive behavior. It seemed clear that for Mark to do well in school would be to feel alienated from his father and also to lose mother's involvement with his difficulties, their major area of interaction.

As a result of adding father's role in the etiology of learning disorders to the maternal influence, it became apparent, as in the case of Mark, that a family system develops in which school learning is negatively affected. Understanding the system supplied a fuller knowledge about the learning disorder.[14] It was also seen that while both parents may consciously want their children to succeed, they may unconscously undermine their children's performance and provoke revolt or negativistic behavior directed at teacher and school. These factors were described by Grunebaum *et al.*[13] in their study of boys with "neurotic learning inhibitions."

> *The boy's view of achievement, competition, and masculinity as influenced by the neurotic distortions of his parents.* The conscious attitudes of these boys toward achievement, competition, and masculinity reflect the internalization of the neurotic conflicts of their parents as they influenced the child's definition of crucial events in his own development. In general, the child's feelings about achievement are more rigid and primitive than those of his parents. Most of these children reveal an image of themselves as inadequate and incompetent in school. The range of self-defeating attitudes varies from views of the self as unable to achieve to a perception of schoolwork as useless. One child expressed the feelings that all his studying would be in vain and that he would "turn out to be a ditch digger." Another boy remarked: "There are a lot of things you can do, without learning how to read or write."
>
> These children do not feel consciously prohibited from learning by their parents. On the contrary, they feel that their parents are persistently, and sometimes angrily, demanding high performance from them. Their attitudes of discouragement are often colored by a near-conscious negativism related to the demands placed on them by the school and their parents. Their resistance shows itself in dawdling, in endless recopying, and in continual forgetting of books, homework papers and assignments. Thus, the child shows covert anger at his parents' ostensible support and encouragement, which he perceives as contaminated with hostility and depreciation. In the displacement

of this conflict to the school, the teacher and the schoolwork become the targets of the negativism and of the internalization of the parents' unconscious wish that the child not achieve.

Sperry *et al.*[29] reported similar findings but added that the fathers in their study identified with their problem children as being failures like themselves. She noted that the families studied had suffered much loss and tragedy, and also that the parents tended to exaggerate the needs, sensitivities, and fragility of other people. They found it difficult to say "no" and generally identified with a small, helpless needy person. They renounced their own goals and needs in favor of another person. The effect on the child and his school learning is expressed by Sperry[29] as follows:

> Not only do the parents encourage the child to follow their own pattern of giving up success to the other person, but in most of the families it is as if one or both parents had elected one of the child's siblings to serve as the bearer of aggression and the successful rival to our patient, as if the sibling were acting as an agent of the parents. In four families, this agent is a girl, whose aggressiveness represents less of a threat to either parent than a boy's aggressiveness would. In two cases, the agent is the patient's older brother who had early established a particularly close relationship with the mother. In the remaining case the child's problem occurs and is acted out directly in the triangular relationship with the parents without the intervention of a sibling.
>
> Many aspects of this pattern—the history of competitive problems in the family, the prominence of renunciatory behavior, the depreciated father image, the veiling of hostility but its manifestation through a sibling—are to be seen in the case of Benjamin H, aged ten.
>
> The father, a chemist in a small candy company, barely makes a living. After college, he had helped to support his family while his brothers went to graduate school. Mr. H has not received or requested a raise in five years and says, "If I found two dollars, I'd leave one for somebody else." As a child, he had had a terrifying experience in knocking out an older boy in a boxing match and thinking he had killed him. Mrs. H had an unsuccessful struggle with her mother during adolescence because her mother was determined that only the boy in the family should go to college. Benjamin's older sister had trouble in school at first, but was determined to succeed and did so. Both parents speak with admiring awe of her ability to take what is made available for her and to speak and act aggressively in her own defense. When this sister beats Benjamin, Mrs. H just walks out of the room, though she

recognizes that Benjamin will inevitably lose a fight or an argument with his sister. Benjamin is expected by his parents to share with his sister any money he earns or is given, to give gifts to a neighbor who is very severe with him, and not to express or even to feel any resentment toward two quite harsh teachers he has had. Mr. H regards himself as an abject failure and sees every aspect of Benjamin's troubles as being just like his own traits. At the same time, both parents also have genuine concern and sympathy for him; and Mrs. H is in addition not a little seductive as though Benjamin at ten were too young to experience anything but infant pleasure at getting into bed with her in the morning.

Meltzer [24] described the destructive effect of the "family secret" in the case of "Ron":

Ron, with a history of nonperformance in school, entered treatment at the age of seven because school had threatened to remove him from his regular class and place him in a class for the mentally retarded. Ron and his older brother were adopted. Ron's adoption was a desperate maneuver to save a disintegrating marriage. Although mother did not like the idea of adoption, she went along with it. The marriage failed immediately after the adoption was completed. Mother completely denied any feelings of anger or resentment toward Ron. These feelings expressed themselves, however, through her choice of clothes for him, clothes that were poor, ill-fitting, dirty, and drab. His attire made him appear as if he were a mentally defective waif; while his brother, by contrast, was constantly given expensive, stylish clothes. In addition, Ron's adoption was not made known to him but was known to the older brother, who used this "family secret" to blackmail Mother. In treatment, it became clear that Ron unconsciously sensed that he was adopted. He would constantly tell stories of treasures that could be discovered in the trash, bring mementos from garbage can pickings, and spend hours standing in the therapist's trash basket. It seemed that he was unable to verbalize his surmise about adoption to his mother, for that would force him to face his awareness of the second-class treatment he received. Also, Ron sensed that Mother did not want him to know about the adoption and that it was a forbidden topic in the family. Here, we can see how Ron's need to appear to not know and to suppress essential information led to a pattern of not learning (knowing). This pattern became global, and it was only through long-term treatment that learning could be resumed at school.

The final step in the unraveling of the family component of learning disorders involved the study of the whole family as a unit. Considerable interest in family-unit psychodynamics in the past two decades has evolved from two major sources; the rapid expansion in the utilization of family therapy as a treatment modality and the development of family communication theory, in particular the work of Jackson.[17] Some of the findings noted that in the neurotic or psychotic family, true feelings are suppressed or distorted, and relationships may be symbiotic, sadomasochistic, or mutually destructive in other ways. Roles are inconsistent and role-reversals are common; communication is a closed system of distortion, confusion, or double-binding. Not all of these characteristics are found in a single neurotic or psychotic family; however, the composite characterization described above describes a family system that is conducive to psychological distortion and/or pathology. The pathological family system contrasts sharply with its healthy counterpart, the well-functioning family, in which communication serves to meet the needs of family members, and permits the open expression of strong feelings (including love or hate, warmth or anger, happiness or sorrow, safety or fear, certainty or uncertainty). Such healthy communication facilitates internal role consistency within the individual and mutually enhancing interrelationships within the family. Too, family process and system are able to make constructive adaptations to needed changes as the family life cycle progresses. Satir[28] described the healthy family as an open system in which honest self-expression is encouraged, differences are viewed as natural, and open negotiation resolves such differences by compromise, agreement to disagree, or other transactions. Personal growth and need satisfaction are not at the expense of or destructive to the well-being of the other family members.

Drawing from family therapy experience, Brown[5] presented the family life cycle concept as a means of understanding the family unit. Brown pointed to phases of family development, each with its own tasks to accomplish and obstacles to be overcome, and described the stresses that develop when the family system does not allow a family member to progress to the next phase of the developmental cycle. In the first chapter of this book Brown elaborates on the school learning or behavior disorders that may be engendered by the failure of the family to resolve a life-cycle phase; for example, the inability of the parents to permit the toddler to develop autonomy could result in the inability of the child to learn in school unless he can be totally dependent on the teacher.

The effect of pathological family communication on learning as seen in the cases of Mark, Mike, and Ron described above can be decisive; however, the literature contains relatively few studies that focus on the family-unit aspect of learning disability.[4, 9, 11, 31] Friedman[9] interviewed fifty-three families from a heterogenous clinic population and analyzed the interview content. He concluded that family communication, role designations, conflicts, attitudes, and values play an important part in many school learning problems. Among the pathogenic factors found in Friedman's study were ambiguous, contradictory, and double-bind messages about achievement expectations, confusing communication patterns, and the focusing of family conflict in the school learning area. A full description of this review, including case illustrations, is found in Chapter 4 of this book.

The family's role in the genesis of a learning disorder can be a crucial one; the other side of the coin is the impact of the school difficulty on the family. A learning disability in one child can affect all members of the family and may alter basic family relationships. The school problem may be dysfunctional, or may fit in with the family system. If the learning problem is dysfunctional, as when it contravenes a family's high valuation of academic success, remediation may be welcomed. If, on the other hand, the learning disorder fits in with the family's need to have a "sick" or "failure" child, efforts at remediation may be resisted. Miller and Westman[25] describe the extreme case of reading disability as a necessary condition for the disturbed family's homeostasis, and give a dramatic example in which a rise in the son's reading level resulted in a parental argument in which father beat up mother and left home, and mother then became severely depressed. As a result, the child did not work in school and his ability to read deteriorated markedly—this enabled father to return, mother to lose her depression, and the family to continue as before.

Before leaving this section of the chapter it should be noted that most of the studies we have reviewed have dealt with intact, middle- or upper-class white families who have sought or accepted mental health consultation and intervention. Also, some of the investigators cited above have attempted to generalize from very small samples. Despite these limitations, the rich clinical data contained in the investigations reported are a valuable contribution to an understanding of the family factor in learning disability.

## SOME KEY ISSUES IN THE FAMILY-SCHOOL MATRIX

### Identification, Self-Esteem, and Separation

A baby is born helpless and totally dependent upon others for his survival. At first the child is not aware of this state of affairs, but as development proceeds and the child begins to see himself as separate from and dependent upon his parents, he begins to feel afraid and helpless. As a defense against these feelings, the child consciously and unconsciously models himself after the strong people upon whom he depends for his survival. This unconscious modeling through building a mental image of the other person is called identification. It is most important to understand that a child takes in not only conscious traits of the parents (the ones that the parents want him to have) but also the parents' unconscious motives, ideas, values, strengths, and weaknesses. Both are absorbed and used as a template against which the child measures himself. It is this process of incorporation that makes it impossible for a child to accede to a parental request to "do as I say, not as I do." Identification is the key to the passing life style, values, and attitudes in the fullest sense from generation to generation—"Like father, like son." The parent as a *model* for learning exerts powerful influence on the child's ability to learn in school. When the model is a poor one, learning difficulties can result.

A common element in neurotic families is low self-esteem. Low self-esteem fosters underachievement; school difficulties and low self-concept are mutually reinforcing. Several other factors enter into this picture; first, the tendency of identifications within rigid, neurotic families to be very resistant to change and therefore more potent than in the nondisturbed family, and second, parents with low self-esteem may discourage learning in the child because they fear the child who learns will soon leave them. The child gets the message that to learn— to compete with or eventually exceed the parent in accomplishment— may result in the loss of parental love. The child with low self-esteem, therefore, cannot take the risks needed to learn—the risk of failure, the risk of growing up and away from the parents he believes he needs to survive.

The process of identification does not stop at a certain age or include only the parents. Any important person can serve as a model and identificatory figure. Teachers, especially of the same sex, can often inspire a child to learn and rescue a student from certain failure; hence, the crucial need for more male teachers, especially in the beginning years of a boy's school career.

To review: through identification, parental attitudes lead to similar attitudes in children. Parents who feel unable to learn, who have low self-esteem often give rise to children who are unable to learn and have a poor self-concept. Children with low self-esteem cannot face the risk or endure the pain of learning. Parents who feel hopelesss and dependent and do not wish their children to learn and grow away from them will likely have children who will feel helpless and dependent and do not wish to learn and grow away from their parents.

### Values

The importance attached by the family to academic achievement can have a direct bearing on whether the child learns or fails to learn. The family may highly value achievement; the child may accept the value and be motivated to learn, or may reject the value and be prone to having difficulty with school work. A laissez-faire or indifferent family attitude toward school performance may contribute to inadequate skill development and low valuation of schooling; hostility toward education may predispose a youngster to resist strongly attempts to educate him.

On what does family attitude toward education depend? Social psychologists[21,32] have presented evidence linking family valuation of school to ethnic, religious, and socioeconomic background. The idea that education is the key that unlocks the door to the better life has usually been identified as a middle-class value. Middle-class values, however, are found in many working-class and upper-class families. The valuation of education by minority group parents has been underestimated. The stereotype that working-class or black, Mexican-American, or Indian parents are less concerned about the education of their children than their middle-class, white counterparts, a stereotype that has contributed to poorer educational opportunities for "disadvantaged" children, has been demonstrated repeatedly to be false. For example, demands for "community control" of the schools have become increasingly strong in minority communities in the major urban centers of the United States. In Los Angeles, concerned Mexican-American parents were able, through direct, activist pressure on the school board, to force elimination of the use of discriminatory intelligence tests that were instrumental in placing a disproportionate number of Spanish-surname children in special classes for the mentally retarded. It is becoming increasingly clear that negative feelings noted among some ethnic groups toward the school as an institution are caused primarily by the inability or unwillingness of the educational establishment to provide relevant, quality education for children in the "disadvantaged" areas. Underachievement and learning difficulties are concentrated, numerically, in the poverty and minority communities, communities where the inequality of educational advantage is seen in poor physical plants, limited curricula, and a rapid-turnover of less experienced teachers. Job discrimination and limited access to the higher echelons of business and the professions have created resentment toward and mistrust of the educational system that is viewed as maintaining the status quo. The recent surge of ethnic pride among blacks, Mexican-Americans, and Indians may result in family hostility toward a school that appears to negate the heritage of the cultural group, or denigrate its language. On the other hand, if minority-group families are part of a community that establishes "community control," their attitude toward (valuation of) school may change dramatically and be reflected in changed, higher motivation for achievement in the children from those families. Carter,[7] in his study of Mexican-American students in the Southwest stated "the crucial factor is not the relationship between home and school, but between the minority group and the local society."

The complexity of the issue of cultural attitudes toward learning is also illustrated by the interplay between class and ethnic factors; for example, the middle-class black families place more emphasis on academic achievement (and their children achieve significantly better) than black *or* white poverty families. Thus, a particular family's attitude about the value of school may indeed be conditioned by cultural factors. Stereotypes, however, should be avoided in evaluating that attitude.

## Infancy

Most of the literature on the family aspect of learning problems has dealt with the postinfancy child. With the advent of Head Start and other programs for "disadvantaged" children, there has been a resurgence of interest in the infancy period. Maternal deprivation, early stimulation, malnutrition, and "critical periods" for cognitive development have been the subject of a number of recent studies.[1, 8, 10, 16, 18, 19, 20, 22, 27, 34]

These issues are more complex than they appear on the surface. For example, the notion of the need for early stimulation of "disadvantaged" children who would otherwise start formal schooling with cognitive deficits has great common sense appeal. Wolff,[34] however, challenges the "critical periods" concept:

> The proposition that the child *must* learn—or at least be exposed to specific learning opportunities—at critical periods in his chronological development or else fail to reach his full intellectual potential is sometimes presented as a proved fact, although there is no persuasive evidence at present to support it.

Wolff states further:

> That the pathologic social and physical environment of underprivileged or ghetto children contributes to their learning disabilities is supported by ample evidence and hardly requires experimental verification. But whether stimulus deprivation during the critical periods of early childhood is responsible for scholastic failures is essentially unproven. To illustrate: we know with reasonable certainty that other factors specifically associated with social class affect these children and can play a significant causal role. In the first place, economically disadvantaged mothers whose children will later experience school failure have often had little or no prenatal and obstetric care. Furthermore the incidence of prematurity is far greater among these children than in the population at large; the mothers are more likely to be carriers of undetected chronic infections that may damage the central nervous system; malnutrition of fetus and mother are common; even the nutritional status of the mother during her childhood may influence the health and developmental potential of her children. The infants are therefore at a great disadvantage long before they encounter the impoverished environment to which they must adapt.
>
> In the second place, it is almost impossible, except in rare cases of "feral" children who are kept locked in closets, to create the extreme degrees of stimulus deprivation that are required in animals to produce significant central nervous system changes. In the third place, clinical observations indicate that children from "the culture of poverty" are usually not understimulated but exposed to an excess of chaotic and unpredictable stimulation; therefore they can neither assimilate nor respond properly to novel experiences in order to test the conse-

quences of their physical and social actions. If purely quantitative considerations were responsible for mental retardation, overstimulation would be a far more likely candidate than sensory deprivation.

The significance of the infancy period for later school adjustment is an issue that is not yet settled. Further empirical investigation is needed before firm conclusions can be reached.

## Adolescence

Studies of the family role in adolescent underachievement are in general agreement that the family can have a profound influence on school performance. Overprotection, infantilization, rejection, and displacement of parental strivings for educational accomplishment are among the familial factors that have been observed. Parents (and sometimes teachers) tend to view the low-achievement teen-age boy or girl as "unmotivated," "resistant," immature," "lazy," or "rebellious"; these labels can be viewed as the observable behavior that stems from the factors noted above. Poor school work may be a continuation of a pattern that began in elementary school or may be a more recent development. Sometimes teen-agers who did well in the earlier grades will show a marked drop in report card grades in junior, or senior high school (or college). This drop may occur as the young person begins to take a broader look at his identification with previously accepted goals and begins to challenge (openly or covertly) parental or societal values and standards. A rejection of "establishment" values of materialism and competitiveness and an abhorrence of ever-present war or threat of annihilation may result in the adolescent's dropping out of the establishment's school.

In our own experience, we have found that many adolescent underachievers fit into the following categories:

1. A long-standing decision to fail which resists all efforts at remediation.
2. A fear of growing up, usually carried over from childhood, that is accentuated as the adolescent backs away from the normal dependency-independency struggle typical of this age group.
3. Fear of competing with or outdoing a parent, particularly the same sex parent, and/or concern about loss of parental love or an unconscious fear of a resurgence of an Oedipal struggle

which may serve to keep the adolescent's achievement at a non-threatening level.

4. The establishment or maintenance of his own identity and the avoiding of a personality development dictated by distorted parental needs requires school failure.

5. The expression of a normal struggle for independence which seems to the adolescent to require a rejection of reasonable educational goals that parents have set for him. It should be noted, however, that at times parental aims may be either unrealistic, inappropriate, or may represent the projection of frustrated ambitions of the parent.

6. A specific example of the negative effect of chronic family conflict.

The list above is not presented as either complete or definitive, but rather as comprising some useful leads. Adolescence is a complex stage in the individual life-cycle and a fuller treatment of this topic is beyond the scope of this chapter.

## FAMILY INTERACTION WITH THE ENVIRONMENT

The etiology of school learning problems has proved to be an increasingly complicated and multifaceted issue; explanations labeled "lack of discipline," "laziness," "stupidity," or "neurosis" have in the long run proved too simple. Consideration of the family component of learning difficulties has also run the gamut from simple to complex. Early researchers, influenced by the psychoanalytic tradition, made intensive studies of the individual. Learning and learning difficulties were correlated with identification, lack of self-esteem, aggression, passivity, and intrapsychic conflict at all levels. Inborn sex differences, heredity learning styles, and the role of early stimulation were soon recognized as important additional factors. The field of view gradually widened to include interpersonal relationships—mother-child, father-child, and the special relationship of the child with the parent of the same sex. This trend led to a study of the family as a whole, which must be studied not only as a group of individuals dynamically interrelated in terms of needs, patterns of communication, and coalitions but also as a unit with its own internal dynamics, resistances, values, and customs.

A broader view, however, must take into account the fact that the family as a unit reacts to, and is in a dynamic relationship with the external world. A family's experience in the world, its opportunities, limitations, hardships, and satisfactions are shaped in part by factors of social class, race, ethnic, religious, and other cultural forces and conditions. An example of this interplay between the family and the external environment is the well-documented fact that a disproportionately high incidence of learning problems and underachievement is found in children from families who live in the "disadvantaged" areas. Too, changes in the environment, whether in the economic cycle or in social institutions like the school, affect the family in many ways, including motivation for or resistance toward school learning. A family mood of optimism or despair, a mood that carries over into the school environment, may result from objective conditions of economic stability or poverty, acceptance or discrimination, political power or powerlessness.

The family, in turn, has some impact on the environment around it, though to a rapidly decreasing degree in current society. Family attitude toward school can help determine the degree of interest and effort expended by the teacher and other staff toward the child. Hostility toward school, coming from the family through the child or through parent-teacher contacts, can predispose the educational establishment to make less than maximum effort to help a child who is developing a learning block. The warm interest, support, and cooperation from the parents of a child with a learning difficulty, on the other hand, increase the frustration tolerance of the child's teacher, up to a point! It is beyond the scope of this chapter to attempt a full treatment of the complexities of the interaction between the family and the external environment; it is clear that the objective conditions of life profoundly influence the family and have an effect on the child's learning.

## COMMENT

The global view of the child with a learning disorder can be conceptualized as a giant, dynamically balanced, interrelated series of mobiles. One group of mobile elements represents the child, with his inborn capacities, internal mental life, and the forces that affect the child from the environment. Another group of mobile elements comprises the family unit and the pressures exerted by family dynamics. The final elements represent those external realities that impinge on the family. Any change anywhere along this giant mobile affects all the other elements. However, the exact nature of the change that takes place is most difficult to determine in advance—thus the difficulty in predicting which children will have learning disorders. To illustrate this point, let us consider the case of Sam, a seven-year-old son of an aerospace engineer who has been unemployed for almost a year. Sam had some difficulty with reading in first grade, and is now resisting reading instruction. The impact of the external reality (layoff) on Sam's reading development would depend on many variables: father's attitude toward work relocation or job retraining, the effect on the marital relationship, the identification models of the parents, particularly father's, Sam's reaction to a family crisis, Sam's inner strengths and weaknesses, and a myriad of other factors. What the final outcome will be of the movement within the "giant mobile" is almost impossible to predict. It is certain, however, that there will be interaction between Sam, his family, and the unemployment, with possible implications for school success or failure. One of the outcomes for Sam could be that father's positive attitude and determination to overcome the problem created by the layoff may inspire Sam, through the process of identification, to try and overcome his developing problem in reading. This favorable outcome could depend, however, on the nature of *other* shifts within the mobile, shifts whose mathematical possibilities are almost infinite. For example, the value of father's positive identification model could be canceled by a flare-up of underlying marital tension produced by the layoff, which results in Sam not being able to concentrate in school, even though he would like to, because he does not have the ability to disengage himself from concern about the continual, loud quarreling between his parents. The possibilities of outcome described above in the case of Sam are only a tiny sample of the possible pool of reactions to a specific change in a mobile element. In evaluating the family aspect of learning disorders one must take into account an interactive *complex* of individual, family, and environment.

## REFERENCES

1. Birch, H.G., and Gussow, J.O.: *Disadvantaged Children: Health, Nutrition, and School Failure.* New York, Harcourt, Brace, & World, 1970.

2. Blanchard, P.: Psychogenic factors in some cases of reading disability. *Am J Orthopsychiatry, 5,* 1935.

3. Blanchard, P.: Psychoanalytic contributions to the problems of reading disabilities. In *Psychoanalytic Study of the Child.* New York, International Universities Press, 1947, vol. 2.

4. Brantley, D.: Family stress and academic failure. *Social Casework, 50,* 1969.

5. Brown, Saul L.: The family life cycle: perspectives drawn from family therapy, preschool through adolescence. Paper presented at American Orthopsychiatric Association Annual Meeting, Chicago, 1968.

6. Buxbaum, E.: The parent's role in the etiology of learning disabilities. In *The Psychoanalytic Study of the Child.* New York, International Universities Press, 1964, vol. 19.

7. Carter, T.P.: *Mexican Americans in the School: A History of Educational Neglect.* New York, College Entrance Examination Board, 1970.

8. Fraiberg, S.: Origins of Identity. *Smith College Studies in Social Work, 38,* 1968.

9. Friedman, R.: A structured family interview in the assessment of school learning disorders. *Psychology in the Schools, 6,* 1969.

10. Gewirtz, J.L. A learning analysis of the effects of normal stimulation, privation and deprivation on the acquisition of social motivation and attachment. In Foss, B.M. (Ed.): *Determinants of Infant Behavior.* Great Britain, Tavistock Institute of Human Relations, 1961.

11. Gilmore, J.V.: Parental counseling and academic achievement. *J Educ, 149,* 1967.

12. Grunebaum, M.G.: A study of learning problems of children: casework implications. *Social Casework, 42,* 1961.

13. Grunebaum, M.G.; Hurwitz, I.; Prentice, N.M., and Sperry, B.M.: Fathers of sons with primary neurotic learning inhibitions. *Am J Orthopsychiatry, 32,* 1962.

14. Hall, M.D.: Family relationships of latency-age boys with emotionally based learning inhibitions. In Helmuth, J. (Ed.): *Learning Disorders.* Seattle, Seattle Child Publications, 1966, vol. 2.

15. Hellman, I.: Some observations of mothers of children with intellectual inhibitions. In *Psychoanalytic Study of the Child.* New York, International Universities Press, 1954, vol. 9.

16. Hess, R.D., and Shipman, V.C.: Early experience and the socialization of cognitive modes in children. *Child Dev, 36, 1965.*

17. Jackson, D. (Ed.): Communication, Family, and Marriage, vol. 1 of *Human Communication.* Palo Alto, Science and Behavior Books, 1968.

18. Kallen, D.J.: Nutrition and society. *JAMA, 215,* 1971.
19. Kessler, J.: *Psychopathology of Children.* New York, Prentice-Hall, 1966.
20. Levenstein, P., and Stanley, R.: Stimulation of verbal interaction between disadvantaged mothers and children. *Am J Orthopsychiatry, 38,* 1968.
21. McClelland, D.: *The Achieving Society.* New York, Van Nostrand, 1961.
22. McGraw, M.D.: Major challenges for students of infancy and early childhood. *Am Psychologist, 25,* 1970.
23. Mahler-Schoenburger, M.: Pseudo imbecibility: a magic cap of invincibility. *Psychoanal Q, 11,* 1942.
24. Meltzer, D.: Unpublished manuscript.
25. Miller, D.R., and Westman, J.C.: Reading disability as a condition of family stability. *Family Process, 3,* 1964.
26. Pearson, G.: A survey of learning difficulties in children. In *Psychoanalytic Study of the Child.* New York, International Universities Press, 1952, Vol.
27. Pedersen, F.A., and Robson, K.S.: Father participation in infancy. *Am J Orthopsychiatry, 39,* 1969.
28. Satir, V.: *Conjoint Family Therapy.* Palo Alto, Science and Behavior Books, 1964.
29. Sperry, B.; Staver, B.; Reiner, B.C., and Ulrich, D.: Renunciation and denial in learning difficulties. *Am J Orthopsychiatry, 28,* 1958.
30. Staver, N.: The child's learning difficulty as related to the emotional problems of the mother. *Am J Orthopsychiatry, 28,* 1958.
31. Strickler, E.: Family interaction factors in psychogenic learning disturbance. *J Learning Disabilities, 2,* 1969.
32. Strodtbeck, F.L.: Family interaction, values, and achievement. In McClelland, D.C., *et al.* (Eds.): *Talent and Society.* Princeton, Van Nostrand, 1958.
33. Sylvester, E., and Kunst, M.S.: Psychodynamic aspects of the reading problem. *Am J Orthopsychiatry, 13,* 1943.
34. Wolff, P.H.: "Critical periods" in human cognitive development. *Hosp Prac, 5,* 1970.

*Chapter III*

# SCHOOL BEHAVIOR DISORDERS
# AND THE FAMILY

Robert Friedman

School behavior problems have been a constant cause of concern for school personnel, clinicians, parents, and the misbehaving children and adolescents themselves. The recent sharp increase in drug abuse at school, the mounting problems of vandalism, assaults on teachers and pupils in inner-city schools and the more open defiance of school authority have reflected similar developments in the larger society. Less dramatic but perhaps equally destructive problem behaviors of students have contributed to poor achievement, low self-concept, and the dropping out of large numbers of students. The problem is serious, and growing in magnitude.

To ascribe school behavior disorders to any single cause would be to ignore the reality of the complexity of human behavior and the rapid pace of change taking place in all facets of society, including the school and the family. This chapter will focus on one aspect of the problem—the family component of school behavior difficulties—with the recognition that all social behavior is multidetermined. I shall use the word "may" throughout the chapter in a deliberate attempt to remind the reader that correlation is not causation, that for example, while many delinquent boys have been found to have rejecting fathers, having a rejecting father will *not necessarily* either produce delinquency in the son or be a cause of delinquency if it should develop.

In this chapter we shall first review some psychodynamic and communication aspects of the family factor. Next, we shall examine the impact of family stress and disorganization on the child's behavior at school, and finally we shall look at some of the external environmental influences on the family.

## FAMILY DYNAMICS AND SCHOOL
## BEHAVIOR DIFFICULTIES

Most theories advanced to explain the relationship between the psychological climate of the home and the child's behavior describe the parent's personality as it influences the parent-child relationship. Bandura and Walters,[2] for example, point out the importance of the child's imitation of or identification with the parent model. Symonds[17] proposed the dimensions of dominance-submission and acceptance-rejection as the key to the impact of family living on the child. A two-sided schema, in which love versus hostility and autonomy versus control are interrelated psychological vectors, was projected by Schaefer.[15] While in theory the rejecting parent produces an aggressive child, the overprotective parent produces an anxious and immature child, the dominating parent will have a conformist child, and the submissive parent will have a defiant child, in practice these formulations and other schema do not work out as applicable generalizations even though they may be useful in an individual case study. Parents are not computers with programmed personalities. Parental behavior with a child varies with time and circumstance; a parent may be permissive with one child in the family and strict with another. A parent may manifest a basic feeling about the child in a variety of ways; for example, the rejecting parent may be punitive, neglectful, or overprotective. Parental trait combinations may cancel the potential negative effects of a single trait, for instance, the dominating but genuinely affectionate parent may not adversely affect school performance. In addition, Thomas, Chess, and Birch[18] point out that the child brings his own constitutional makeup and temperament to the parent-child interaction, and that the resultant match or mismatch with the parent's temperament can be a strong influence on the parent-child relationship and consequently on the child's behavior pattern.

The wide variety of behavior observed among the children of the same parents, a diversity that has not yet been satisfactorily explained by behavioral scientists, attests to the complexity of the effect of the home on the child's adjustment. We are not yet at the point where we can state with certainty what are either *necessary* or *sufficient* qualities in the psychological climate of the home for the promotion of the child's emotional health, and by the same token, we are not certain of what are the necessary or sufficient pathogenic factors that will create disturbed behavior in the child. Warmth, acceptance, respect, caring, and the granting of autonomy are qualities we see as desirable in the home; yet clinicians and educators see disordered children from homes with good "ratings" on these qualities and, conversely, children with surprisingly good mental health from homes with the absence of many of these qualities or with clear-cut family psychopathology. The point of all this is not that the study of parents and parent-child relationships will not reveal cause-and-effect, but rather that the study of the family of a child with a school behavior problem must be a careful one. With this caution in mind, some intrafamilial psychodynamic, attitude, communication, and system factors that *may* account for or contribute to a school behavior problem are listed below:

1. Conflicts in parent-child, marital, sibling or family-unit relationships are upsetting to the child; the upset is manifested in school behavior.

Chronic antagonism between parent and child can build up a reservoir of strong feelings which may spill over into hostile-aggressive behavior in school, particularly if there is little opportunity to express angry feelings at home. Sometimes, a child or adolescent brings with him to school much guilt about family relationship problems for which he feels responsible and may unconsciously seek punishment by acting-out in the classroom or playground. The child who is withdrawn at school may be exhibiting another kind of adaptation to excessive family stress. If a child is constantly at odds with siblings at home he may be unable to get along with his classmates.

2. Conflict and/or confusion around authority at home is carried over into school.

A harsh, punitive, or rejecting parent may instill in the child a hostility toward authority figures; this hostility may be expressed against the teacher-authority. If the child is engaged in a continual, unresolved power struggle with the parent, the child may test the authority of the teacher by misbehaving in an attempt to force a resolution of the child-adult authority relationship.

3. Parental overpermissiveness results in the child having inadequate inner controls, low frustration tolerance, and inability to brake impulsive action.

When the child at home gets what he wants when he wants it, has undivided adult attention most of the time, and has few (if any) limits set on what he can or cannot do, then the child will tend to behave accordingly at school. Establishing limits and controls for such a child may result in an abrasive encounter between child and teacher. On the other hand, a child or adolescent may subconsciously seek to have external controls imposed on him; misbehavior may be an attempt to have an effective authority step in and *stop* him.

4. An overly strict home environment may predispose a child to find behavioral release at school. The less strict school environment presents an opportunity for the child to "let loose"; the teacher may see this child as needing to test the limits of acceptable behavior.

5. Distortions, confusions, and double-binding in family communication patterns are expressed in unclear or permission-to-misbehave messages regarding parental expectations.

The spoken message from the parent may be "Do what the teacher says," but the child is confused because the parent is disinterested and is uncooperative with the teacher who complains that this child continually disobeys her. If the parent's overt, spoken message is "Follow the rules like a good boy," but the covert, unspoken message is "Only stupid people obey the rules," the child is in the double-bind position of displeasing the parent no matter what he does—he can be only good-but-stupid or smart-but-bad, and therefore the child is immobilized. Lack of response to class rules may be the result.

6. Negative feelings about the family's previous experience with a teacher, a school, or the "educational establishment" are picked up by the child and acted on.

The parent may identify with the child's resentful feelings toward school and may condone the unacceptable behavior. "I had trouble with teachers, too" may be stated by the parent in a combination of half-hearted apology for the child's actions and a partially disguised pride that the child is following in the parent's footsteps. Unsatisfactory experiences with the educational process may incline the family to be unsympathetic to the current difficulty school may be having with a child or adolescent.

7. The expressed family value is nonconformity; the child loyally identifies with the value and acts upon it by not conforming to school rules.

The teacher sees the child as unwilling to obey the rules and therefore a behavior problem; the parent sees the *teacher* as having a problem in not being able to accept nonconformist behavior.

8. Strong parental disagreement in regard to behavioral expectations or management is confusing to the child and leads to erratic classroom behavior.

Home standards that are contradictory or inconsistent may result in the child's nondeliberate distortion of class rules. A dominating father sets down strict rules for the child, but the mother reacts to what she considers to be father's undue harshness by nonenforcement or inconsistent application of the rules. The end-product may be nonadherence or inconsistent response by the child to school regulations.

9. The overall communication pattern in the home is confused and dishonest; as a consequence the child has difficulty in integrating information and behavioral guidelines at school.

When family members consistently do not mean what they say or say what they mean, the child is unable to trust the communication *process*. At school, the child may not be able to fully accept the rules, and motivation for learning is weakened.

10. The family scapegoat's deviant behavior in school gets him into trouble; the scapegoat role behavior is tolerated at home but cannot be accepted in school.

In disturbed families, the role of scapegoat fulfills a necessary and crucial function in the neurotic or psychotic family process; this role is not shed easily when the child comes into the classroom.

11. The child is encouraged to act out the parent's repressed wish to defy authority.

This is a more subtle and therefore less easily recognized dynamic. A parent may have a strong need to break rules or defy social norms but be unable to act on that need at this time in her life. The vicarious satisfaction that can be gained from the child or adolescent's defiance of school regulations may prompt a parent to give indirect or subtle encouragement for misbehavior. As an example, a mother "overlooks" the child's taking a beanshooter to school; the child is well aware that the mother knows this is a violation of the rule and that he has put it in his lunch pail. When mother is confronted by teacher with the child's having disrupted the class with beanshooting, she smiles inappropriately as she expresses agreement with the teacher's complaint.

The above list is not presented as a complete compendium but rather as an indication of factors that may be sufficient for or contributory toward a significant school behavior disorder. The factors do not always appear in "pure" form and the connection with the school difficulty may be complex rather than simple. For example, in the two-parent family there may be a combination of factors that impinge on the child—this combination may, depending on the particular set of parents, be additive or mutually canceling in its effect on the child's school behavior Also, the child's *perception* of family relationships may be more of a causative factor than the objective reality of those relationships.[1, 4, 16] Finally, it should be remembered that the school behavior difficulty may have a substantial effect on the family, with complications arising from a circular action-reaction. For instance, the school problem may be the "last straw" that brings latent family friction into open hostility, with the result that a shift in family relationships occurs, bringing additional dynamcs into play. In their study of the family scapegoat, Vogel and Bell[19] illustrate one kind of entanglement between family dynamics and school problems:

> While the functions of the scapegoat within the nuclear family clearly outweigh his dysfunctions, this is typically not the case with the child's relationship outside the nuclear family. While the family gives the child sufficient support to maintain his role in the family, the use of him as a scapegoat is often incompatible with equipping him to maintain an adjustment outside the nuclear family. This problem becomes particularly acute when the child begins important associations outside the nuclear family in relationships with peers and his teachers at school. It is at this time that many referrals to psychiatric clinics are made. While the child's behavior was perfectly tolerable to the parents before, his behavior suddenly becomes intolerable. While he may still be performing the role the family wants him to play in order to be a scapegoat, this comes into conflict with his role as a representative of the family. The family is thus in conflict between using the child as a scapegoat and identifying with the child because of his role as family representative to the outside. Both sides of this conflict are revealed most clearly in the one family which carried on a feud with the outside and alternated between punishing the daughter for her poor school behavior and criticizing the teachers and children in school for causing problems for their daughter. In nearly all of these disturbed families, school difficulty was a crucial factor in the decision to refer the child for psychiatric treatment. While the child's behavior was rewarded at home, it was not rewarded at school, and while the family

could tolerate the child's maladaptive behavior at home, when the school took special note of the child's behavior, this proved embarrassing and troubling to the parents.

## FAMILY STRESS AND DISORGANIZATION
### Family Stress

Clinicians and school guidance workers are well aware of the high incidence of family stress found concomitantly with school behavior problems. If the stress is temporary, for example due to arrival of a new baby, a difficult relocation, or short-lived loss of income, the school problem may be transient and may be resolved with or without intervention. However, if the strain on the family is chronic, the behavior difficulty may become entrenched and recalcitrant, and special intervention is often necessary. Discussed below are some common causes of family stress that may be related to a school behavior difficulty.

### *Separation and Divorce*

"He [or she] comes from a broken home" is a frequently heard comment when a child or adolescent gets into trouble. The comment may imply that the problem would not have arisen if the home had been intact. It is true that a large percentage of children with behavior problems come from families in which there has been divorce, separation, desertion of a parent, or remarriage and step-parent constellations including the mixed group of "his, hers, and ours" children. The word "broken," however, implies that the home has been damaged or destroyed, and the term "broken home" often carries the suggestion that the two-parent intact home is by virtue of its structural nature a better home than the "broken" one. The term "broken home," therefore, is a kind of cultural "put-down" of the one-parent family, a stereotype that does not take into account the many one-parent homes that provide a healthier psychological climate than many of their two-parent intact counterparts.

Separation or divorce usually creates, however, at least a temporary upset for the child; sometimes the upset remains over a long period of time and disrupts the child's functioning in many areas of his life, including school. Also, the absence of the same-sex parent can create difficulties due to lack of an identification model. The parent who tries to be both mother and father to children is placed in a difficult position, not only in the parenting function but also in terms of meeting his or her needs as an individual. The formation of the organization "Parents Without Partners" is a reflection of the need to discuss and solve some of the common problems that arise from separation and divorce. The unmarried mother has a particularly heavy burden in that societal stigma and the accompanying guilt are added to the other strains discussed above. Serious problems may arise in cases where the child is used by mother and father as a means of retaliation against each other, or if the child is burdened by guilt over the parent's separation, torn by divided loyalties, or becomes for the parent with whom he lives an object of excessive dependency and/or gratification. Separation anxiety may be more pronounced in the one-parent family; the child or single-parent's fears of separation and/or abandonment are intensified by the absence of the other parent. The child who is worried because of the illness, unhappiness, or temporary absence of the parent with whom he lives may be unable to concentrate on school studies or may express the anxiety through misbehavior.

The possible stress or trauma resulting from the disruption of the intact home cannot be ignored; the high divorce rate and increasing number of one-parent families is a fact of life. At the same time, hasty judgments about the effect of the "broken home" should be avoided.

### Family Structure Content, and Stress

The intact two-parent family is usually considered to be the most stable and desirable of the family types. While this generalization may hold up as a statistic, it should be remembered that family *content* can be a more decisive factor than structure. For example, the intact home may contain severe, chronic marital stress that is very disturbing to the child and his school adjustment. Clinicians and educators are familiar with parents who say, We stay together only because of the children; if the tensions cannot be alleviated, the children's best interests may not be served by maintaining the home intact. On the other side of the coin, there are significant problems inherent in the one-parent or step-parent situations. Also, grandparents or other relatives living in or close to the home can create intrafamilial stress. Two examples of living arrangements that may be experienced by the child as basically unstable are foster-home placement and the father-absent home wherein the mother has a procession of men living with her for a period of time.

## Alcoholism and Drug Abuse

The corrosive effect of alcoholism and narcotics addiction on family stability can be observed in divorce court proceedings, crime statistics, juvenile court hearings, or in the wreckage of a particular family under study. A parent's addiction to liquor or hard drugs, whether a "family secret" or out in the open, often has a devastating effect on family morale, finances, and relationships. The emotional strain on the family and/or the negative parent model may be sufficient explanation for a child's unacceptable school conduct.

## Crises

A family crisis can be precipitated by the death of a family member, the loss of the breadwinner's job, the desertion of a parent, and other traumatic events. Experienced teachers can recall instances of the sudden change in the behavior of a pupil, change that occurred simultaneously with clear evidence of a family crisis. Depending on the child's reaction to the crisis, behavior in the classroom may become hostile, aggressive, erratic, or withdrawn. The child may be unable to attend to schoolwork and may become fidgety and disruptive to class routines.

A special kind of crisis can be noted in many cases of "school phobia." "School refusal" would be a more accurate term for these cases, since the child does not have a fear of the school itself, but rather the child or the parent experiences acute separation anxiety. Separation anxiety may be linked to a parent's neurotic need to hold on to a child and the consequent failure of the child to develop individuation and autonomy. The prolonged illness of a parent, an imminent divorce, or other security-threatening situations may be involved. Frequently, it is the mother's fear of separation from the child that precipitates the child's balking at going to or staying in school.

The family's reaction to a crisis will depend on many variables. Availability of information and guidance, financial resources, coping ability, and support of relatives are some of the factors. Crisis may result in family growth and solidification, family breakdown, or in an intermediate outcome; school behavior may be a sensitive barometer of the family's adaptation to a crisis.

## Family Disorganization

The chaotic family has been aptly described by Feldman and Scherz[7]:

> Some families, often both socially and psychologically disorganized, appear to operate as though they were a family of siblings. There is little or no differentiation between the roles of the parents and between the parents and the children. There is confusion in marital and child-rearing roles. No one knows who is to do what, or which bed to sleep in. Often there are concomitant problems in the marriage such as delinquency or alcoholism. The parents give orders and rescind them whimsically; they assign responsibilities to children that are inappropriate for their ages; the parents fight with the children *like* children; and they feel helpless or overwhelmed by tasks that have to be carried out. These are families who have basic troubles with trust, self-control, and other aspects of identity. These kinds of persons generally have very serious characterological problems.

Although family chaos may occur at all socioeconomic levels,[10] it has been documented primarily at the lowest level.[11, 12, 13, 14] Malone and Pavenstedt and their co-workers[13] intensively studied families from the "hard-core" subgroup of the poverty strata. They described the pathological family environment of this subgroup, with its lack of predictability of emotional response, high degree of physical abuse and danger, and personal devaluation, and pointed out the adverse effect of this environment on the children's development. The impact on school adjustment was seen in the behavior of the children in the study-project nursery school:

> Certain qualities in the children and features of their learning difficulties seem particularly important. In the early months of nursery school there were a number of aspects of the children's play, behavior, and reactions that alerted us to the likelihood that learning would be a more difficult process for them than for an ordinary group of 3- and 4-year-olds. They were observed to be listless and inattentive. The children did not play much nor did they gravitate to the doll corner or the blocks; they only fingered the toys or puzzles for brief periods. They were readily distracted and often disrupted their aimless mechanical play to seek the attention of the teacher or a stranger who had entered the room. These youngsters showed little capacity for *focal attention*. Along with this, there was a low frustration tolerance and a tendency to discharge tension in diffuse motor activity. Although they were compliant and could manage to exert control for

fear of punishment, they found it difficult to control and modulate impulses under ordinary circumstances. They had difficulty in keeping out internal or external interferences, so that their concentration and attention span were low and their play and work were vulnerable to regression and disruption.

The tendency of preschool children from the disorganized poverty family to be impulsive, motorically oriented, and physically aggressive is discussed by Minuchin *et al.*[12] The communication patterns in disorganized and disadvantaged families are described by Minuchin as follows:

> The total amount of words—the vocabulary available in the family— is usually scarce. Not only are the parents limited in their verbal education, but they also tend to employ the best of their verbal equipment in situations outside the family. In the one-parent family, this trend has even more deprivational significance. The model of adults communicating among themselves is unavailable to the child. The role of verbal negotiation in solving interpersonal situations remains undeveloped, and the opportunity to sharpen capacities for abstract, relational thinking is largely unexercised. The parent's attention is absorbed in issues of inter-personal regulation, and he thus fails to focus attention on the continuity and development of themes. Specific subject matter in his family will rarely be carried to any conclusion. A small number of interactions around a topic is usually interrupted by a disconnected intervention of another family member. It is rare for more than two family members to participate in an interaction around a specific point. When another member intervenes, the subject usually changes. The family threshold for accepting abrupt shifts in content matter is much higher than that of most middle-class therapists.
>
> The result is a style of communication wherein people do not expect to be heard and in which they assert themselves by yelling. Conflicts do not have closure; there is faulty development of themes, a restricted affective range, and lack of training in the elaboration of questions to gather information. This style is perhaps adequate for the transaction of gross nurturing and power relationships, but is insufficient for dealing with chronic and more subtle conflicts, for this requires the search for, ordering of, and sharing of different or new information.

One can readily see from the above quote that children from these families may have problems in attending to school regulations as well as difficulty in abstract learning processes.

## EXTERNAL ENVIRONMENTAL INFLUENCES
## ON THE FAMILY
### Economic Factors

Financial status, job stability, economic cycle—these are powerful influences on family life. Money worries, unemployment, job relocation, recurrent recessions in the economy, welfare regulations, layoffs, displacement by automation, the seasonal fluctuations in the income of migratory workers—a complete list of economic factors would be a long one. Money problems as a source of family strain are reflected in the media advertising of loan companies, who offer quick and "easy" solutions to the harried head of the family. There is less public display of other aspects of economic status, for example the inherently discriminatory nature of poverty, which among other limitations and disadvantages consigns the child to schools that are inferior to their higher-income-level counterparts. Rapid teacher turnover, a preponderance of inexperienced teachers, inadequate physical plant, and reduced expectancy of achievement are characteristic of the inner-city school. The Coleman Report[5] graphically presents the school achievement differential based on income level. Poverty may also result in the child coming to school undernourished, in poor health, sleepy, or hyperalert to anticipated danger from an authority figure;[3, 13] these are conditions that could even negate the value of upgraded schools.

Another economic factor is mobility. Some families move frequently from place to place because of employment considerations. Mobility can have a detrimental effect on school adjustment for the child who has to make continual readjustments to different friends, classes, teachers, and school programs. Such children may have difficulty in establishing stable, meaningful relationships with peers and adults.

An economic issue that is receiving increasing attention is the welfare regulation that places a financial penalty on the family whose father remains in the home. The large percentage of father-absent poverty homes means that many poverty children have significantly reduced opportunity for positive identification with a male figure. This is particularly detrimental in the case of boys. Kallen[8] points out that welfare philosophy places parents in a dependent position which can undermine parental influence.

We have touched only very briefly on the economic factor. The overall impact on the social and educational development of the child is considered in a number of recent books.[3, 5, 6, 9, 12, 13] It is evident that despite compensatory education programs, the quality of educational opportunity available to the child is largely circumscribed by the financial status of his family. Economic factors are indeed a major influence on the child, the family, and the school.

## Socio-Cultural Factors

School behavior difficulties are found at all socioeconomic levels. Some children in affluent or middle-income communities, as well as in lower-income areas, disturb class routines, truant, defy authority, steal, and engage in hostile aggressive acts in and out of school. Higher-income level families are subject to many of the same strains as those of lower-income levels. Disorganized, chaotic families are found (though much less frequently) among the wealthy, and "cultural deprivation" can occur with the rich.[10] Excessive, destructive pressures for academic achievement that underlie some rebellious school behavior are found more commonly at the higher-income level. There are a number of considerations, however, that give the middle- or upper-class youngster an advantage in the outcome of school misbehavior. He has greater access to guidance clinics and other mental health services. His family values are more apt to coincide with the school's. The community in which his family lives has a greater voice in the conduct of school affairs, and his parents are typically better qualified to negotiate the educational "system." All of this tends to make his school behavior difficulties more likely to be resolved through school guidance or clinical treatment.

Cultural aspects of attitudes, values, and language that affect the education of children in the ghettos and barrios are receiving increased attention. Family attitudes toward the school in those areas are generally less positive than in other locations; this difference is based partly on legitimate grievances concerning past experience with the educational establishment's insensitivity to cultural differences. Many school systems have shown a lack of respect for the traditions, mores, or languages of ethnic minorities. This attitude contributes in turn to the lack of respect for school regulations that a minority group student may exhibit. A prime example of insensitivity has been the rejection of the Spanish language in the schools of the Southwest, which has created a major barrier between the school and the Mexican-American communities and has placed the Spanish-speaking youngster at a disadvantage. It is only recently that educational authorities have recognized the seriousness of the problem and have begun to make needed changes in curriculum, establish bilingual instruction and provide in-service training of school personnel in recognizing biases that teachers as well as children bring to the classroom learning encounter.

The damaging effect of discrimination in education based on ethnic or minority group membership has to a large degree cut across class lines. The *de jure* "separate but equal" segregated school systems in the South and the *de facto* segregation in the urban centers of the rest of the country have limited the amount and quality of education for Negroes and other minority groups at *all* income levels. Segregated schools are still a large fact of life, although their number is gradually decreasing because of integration prompted by the Supreme Court decisions of 1957 and the increasing pressure from a major section of the minority communities.

The socio-cultural factor in behavior and learning in school is a large and complex subject; we have touched only a few of its facets. Adding to the scope and complexity is the reality of the acceleration of social change, which will be discussed in the next section.

### Social Change and the Schools

To understand the family-school interrelationship in social context, we must take into account the powerful force of change. In primitive times, family and tribe were the child's school. As civilization developed, formal arrangements outside of the family were established to serve society's expanding needs. Today, some educators are questioning their broad role of *in loco parentis* (in place of the parent) and are suggesting a reversal of direction in which the home would assume a larger share of the responsibility for the education of the young. The institutions of family and school themselves are now being challenged in new and potentially far-reaching ways. Openness in living together without a legal marriage, communes, and a fixed-term renewable marriage contract have been offered as more desirable life-styles than the marriage-family-community arrangement we have accepted as traditional and correct. Critics of public education have made inroads into public consciousness; accountability, community control, the voucher system, and other major proposals to improve the quality and increase the relevancy of education are receiving serious attention. Basic changes in the family and/or school could result in either a working alliance or alienation. Change is inevitable, but the direction of change is difficult to predict.

The decade of the 1960's saw a dramatic intensification of the challenge to the social system and its values, a challenge coming primarily from the youth. A revitalization of critical thinking (one of the current goals of education) is one of the many positive outcomes of this development. There have been negative "side-effects," however, for example the use of drugs by school-age youth from elementary school through college. Erratic and sometimes bizarre behavior attributable to drug abuse is no longer a rare phenomenon in the classroom or playground. Another negative resultant is the increasing number of school dropouts; this is symptomatic of alienation among some young people. This disenchantment reflects the surfacing of the growing alienation felt by a large number of people in our society. A development in a different direction involves the reaction to the draft. The unpopularity of the war in Southeast Asia has created an unprecedented aversion to military service by young men. One unexpected consequence may be conforming behavior and academic achievement for the purpose of remaining in school long enough to get a student deferment!

### Crisis Factors

The process of social change can produce a crisis; integration of schools is an example of an explosive issue that has caused major confrontations between family-community and school districts. The bussing of children to achieve integration has produced conflict whose outcome is not yet determined. Political crises, war, and natural disasters have both direct and indirect effects on school children. Shock and acute anxiety reactions in their pupils were noted by teachers as an aftermath of the assassination of Presidents and political leaders. The earthquake disaster in the San Fernando region of Los Angeles in 1971 had as one of its aftermaths a sharp increase of sleeping problems in children as well as a good deal of restlessness, irritability, separation anxiety, and fear in the classroom. The prevalence of war affects youth not only directly via the draft but also indirectly by engendering in some young people the feeling that it is futile to acquire an education (or anything else) in a society that seems ready to self-destruct.

## COMMENT

In this chapter we have discussed family psychodynamics, stress and external environmental factors that may contribute to school behavior disorders. It should be noted that behavior and learning disorders overlap as categories and are also frequently found together. A child with a problem in learning often exhibits behavioral difficulties in the classroom, and vice versa. In Chapter 2 Friedman and Meltzer use the example of a mobile to point up the interrelationship of the factors in learning disorders. They conceptualize school learning disorders as a dynamically balanced series of mobiles, with any change in a mobile element affecting all the other elements. This formulation holds equally for school behavior problems. To illustrate, let us consider the case of Joan, a teen-age girl whose association with the "wrong crowd" had caused much friction between the girl and her mother over a period of many months. Previously, Mother and Joan had a reasonably satisfactory relationship. Joan was a well-behaved, good student. Joan's behavior in school deteriorated rapidly, however, as the strain between mother and Joan intensified and erupted into verbal war. Joan became irritable and restless in class, and began to truant. Her grades dropped markedly. Unexpectedly, father became seriously ill and bedridden, and a personal and financial crisis faced the family. At this juncture it would be difficult to predict the outcome in terms of school. Father's illness might result in further conflict between mother and daughter, with the school problem becoming exacerbated. A different possibility is that the family crisis might spur mother and daughter to put aside their differences over Joan's choice of friends in the context of a drawing-together turn in their relationship, thus enabling Joan to reverse her negative school behavior. These are only two of the possible outcomes. The psychodynamics of Joan and her mother, the marital relationship, further changes in the financial status of the family, and many other variables could affect the direction of the shift in the mobile. Clearly, the family-school matrix must be viewed as *complex*.

## REFERENCES

1. Ausubel, D.P.: Perceived parent attitudes as determinants of children's ego structure. *Child Dev, 25,* 1954.
2. Bandura, A., and Walters, R.H.: *Social Learning and Personality Development.* New York, Holt, Rinehart, & Winston, 1963.
3. Birch, H.G., and Gusow, J.D.: *Disadvantaged Children: Health, Nutrition and School Failure.* New York, Harcourt, Brace, & World, 1970.
4. Burchinal, L.G.: Parent's attitudes and adjustment of children. *J Genet Pyschol, 92,* 1958.
5. Coleman, J.S., *et al.: Equality of Educational Opportunity.* Washington, D.C., Superintendent of Documents, U.S. Government Printing Office, 1966.
6. Coles, R., and Piers, M.: *Wages of Neglect.* Chicago, Quadrangle Books, 1969.
7. Feldman, F.L., and Scherz, F.H.: *Family Social Welfare: Helping Troubled Families.* New York, Atherton Press, 1967.
8. Kallen, D.J.: Nutrition and society. *JAMA, 215,* 1971.
9. Lawton, D.: *Social Class, Language, and Education.* New York, Schocken Books, 1968.
10. Livermore-Sanville, J.: Deprived children of the upper socioeconomic strata. Proceedings of the Sixth Annual Conference for the Advancement of Private Practice in Social Work, 1968.
11. Malone, C.A.: Some observations on children of disorganized families and problems of acting out. *J Child Psychiatry, 2,* 1963.
12. Minuchin, S.; Montalvo, B.; Guerney, B.G.; Rasman, B.L., and Schumer, L.: *Families of the Slums: An Exploration of Their Structure Treatment.* New York, Basic Books, 1967.
13. Pavenstedt, E., *et al.* (Eds.): *The Drifters: Children of Disorganized Lower-Class Families.* Boston, Little, Brown, 1967.
14. Pavenstedt, E.: A comparison of the child-rearing environment of upper-lower and very low-lower class families. *J Orthopsychiatry, 5,* 1965.
15. Schaefer, E.S.: A circumplex model for maternal behavior. *J Abnorm Social Psychol, 59,* 1959.
16. Slyke, V.V., and Leton, D.A.: Children's perception of family relationships and their school adjustment. *J Sch Psychol, 4,* 1965.
17. Symonds, P.M.: *The Psychology of Parent-Child Relationships.* New York, Appleton-Century-Crofts, 1939.
18. Thomas, A.; Chess, S., and Birch, H.G.: *Temperament and Behavior Disorders of Children.* New York, NYU Press, 1968.
19. Vogel, E.F., and Bell, N.W.: The emotionally disturbed child as the family scapegoat. In: Bell, NW., and Vogel, E.F. (Eds.): *A Modern Introduction to the Family.* Free Press of Glencoe, 1960.

# PART TWO

# EVALUATING THE FAMILY ASPECT OF SCHOOL DISORDERS

*Chapter IV*

# STRUCTURED FAMILY INTERVIEWING IN THE ASSESSMENT OF SCHOOL DISORDERS

ROBERT FRIEDMAN

## INTRODUCTION

THE role of the family in school learning and behavior disorders, fully discussed in previous chapters of this book, has long been recognized. Despite this recognition, assessment of children and adolescents with school-related problems has not given adequate attention to the family aspect of the difficulty. The taking of a family history or the obtaining of a family drawing has been with few exceptions the extent of past diagnostic efforts in terms of family involvement in the school problem. Most frequently, attention is directed to the family after educational or therapeutic efforts are underway, or retrospectively in analyzing case material. However, comprehensive assessment of the family should be incorporated into initial diagnostic studies related to school problems, as standard practice.

The need for knowledge about family functioning is pointed up by the fact that the family is the first social unit, that patterns of socialization and learning are first acquired in the family setting, and that the parents of the child are indeed his first teachers. Attitudes toward and feelings about authority and the learning process, as well as family values regarding the importance of school, are taken by the child into the classroom. A positive *or* negative identification with the same-sex parent as a learning person is usually well-defined by the time the child enters school, and the quality of the working relationship between teacher and child can be strongly influenced by carry-over from the parent-child relationship. Thus, the impact of the family on

Part of this chapter was published as an article in *Psychology in the Schools.*[1]

school learning is considerable, and the need for pertinent diagnostic data is clear.

Direct observation of family interaction provides a more reliable basis for family diagnosis than individual test performance, questionnaire, or parent report. The object of this chapter is to present the goals of, the techniques for, and the experience with a one-session structured family interview which I have used in the assessment of children and adolescents with school learning and behavior disorders.

## GOALS OF THE INTERVIEW

The purpose of the structured interview is to determine the nature, extent, and etiological significance of the connection between the family and the school disorder. It is obviously impossible in one interview to gather all the vital information about the complex dynamics of a family, nor is it necessary to "cover all the bases" in order to get a useful diagnostic impression. It is feasible, however, to uncover those aspects of family relationships, communication, and values that are negatively affecting a child's or adolescent's school performance, and to accomplish this objective in a single structured interview.

Psychodiagnosticians are accustomed to looking for signs of neurosis or psychopathology when conducting interviews. The frame of reference of the interview described in this chapter, however, is the here-and-now of intrafamilial functioning, and the diagnostic focus is therefore restructured to concentrate on the *resultants* of psychodynamics as expressed in the family communication and relationship system that are revealed in the interview behavior. For example, the psychosexual forces driving a mother to infantilize a son are not considered germane as interview content, rather the emphasis is on discovering if a pattern exists wherein the mother's behavior (and son's cued-in response) serves as a brake on the boy's learning to cope with frustration, task demands, and problem-solving needs, with the result that problems arise in the classroom. Thus, when mother continually speaks for the child, shields him from responsibility for constructive participation in the session, or quickly gives answers to arithmetic problems the moment the child hesitates, the interview is considered to have produced diagnostically significant information when mother's behavior is linked to teacher's characterization of the child as having little frustration tolerance, short attention span, a tendency to give up quickly when balked, and as putting forth minimum effort in learning academic skills. What is looked for, then, is an *operational definition* of the family difficulty in terms of its effect on the school learning or behavior disorder.

The following aspects of the family yield relevant and important data, and are considered prime "targets" of the interview:

1. The quality of communication, with particular emphasis on role-cueing, double-bind messages, and confusion around expectations for achievement or behavior.
2. The roles of father and mother as models for identification with the learning process—the parent, particularly the same-sex parent, as an achievement model.
3. Conflicts in parent-child and family relationships.
4. Family attitudes toward school achievement and behavior, including indications of status needs, mobility strivings, and other culturally determined values derived from class, caste, race, ethnic, and religious factors.

The above list provides a general framework for conceptualizing the kind of material to be collected. The relevance of interview content can be evaluated as the interview progresses by noting whether it can be fitted into the frame. It should be noted that the relative importance of the categories listed above will vary from family to family—sometimes the intensive exploration of one aspect of the family makeup may be sufficient to establish the significant bond between the family and the school difficulty.

A key goal of the interview is to establish *specific* connections between family functioning and the school problem. It is my experience that the attempt to make explicit the links between the family and school performance helps to maintain a sharper interview focus and results in heightened involvement of family members in interaction with each other and with the interviewer. Moreover, a more meaningful and less easily discounted transaction occurs when the problem is delineated in operational terms. For example, if the interviewer has established that the parents permit the child to ignore their verbal requests during the sessions and to tune out most of the discussion, he *could* point out to the parents the generalization that they may be fostering negativism or immaturity, and that school performance would likely be adversely affected. It is more effective to elicit through teacher, parent, or child report, the fact that the child's listening habits in school are poor and that the child consistently does not follow directions in class, and to them make a specific tie-in between the classroom behavior, the parenting pattern, and the school problem.

## TECHNIQUES OF THE INTERVIEW

The basic technique in conducting the interview is the maintenance of the structure provided by focusing directly on the school learning problem. Content is limited, with rare exception, to the school issue. When the discussion veers away from the primary focus, the interviewer directively guides the family back on to the tract. Attempted diversions are not interpreted as resistance; instead, the interviewer continues to "zero in" on the verbal and nonverbal behavior that relates directly to the interview goals categorized in the preceding section. Repetition of or referring back to one of the questions listed below usually serves to pull the session back into the frame.

The use of a specific series of questions has been an efficient way of starting the interview—these questions are given below in the order they are usually asked:

1. *(to the parent)* "What do you expect of _____ in school?"
   *Note:* The answer to this question is often ambiguous, and if so, the question is repeated until a clear, direct response is elicited. This perseverance tends to give a structured "set" to the remainder of the interview.
2. *(to the child)* "What did mother (or father) say," or "What does mother expect of you in school?"
3. *(to the parent)* "Is _____ meeting that expectation?"
4. *(to the child)* "What did mother say?", or "Does father think you are meeting that expectation?", or "Are you meeting that expectation?"
5. *(to the parent)* "Are you disappointed that _____ is not meeting the expectation?"
6. *(to the child)* "Is father (or mother) disappointed about your not meeting the expectation?"
7. *(to the parent)* "How have you tried to help _____ with this problem?"

Not all of these questions are asked at all interviews, and the questions and their order of presentation can be modified according to the

issues being explored at the time. In addition, discussion can be directed to a communication issue itself. For example, if it seems clear that a
family member is not listening, the interviewer can focus on the in-
attention. If it appears that the child or parents are skeptical about an
answer, the interviewer may ask, "Do you believe what _____ said?"
Or if a parent has indicated that some specific change in the child's
school behavior is expected, the interviewer may ask the parents if
they really think the change will occur. Occasionally, the interviewer
will express doubt about a statement made by parents, especially
around the issue of expectations, in order to provide encouragement
for the child to verbalize his disbelief. The parent may say, "I want
him to do his best—if his best is C's, that's all right." With the interviewer's support, the child may be able to overcome fear of contra-
dicting his parents in public, and indicate that C's are *not* acceptable,
that B's or A's are the obligatory standard. Frequently, parents expect
and demand much more than they will express in the initial stages of
the interview. On the other hand, one needs to remember that the
*child* can distort and project his own high standards onto the parents.

## Content

There are a number of topics that are particularly productive in
the structured interview. Discussion of homework and/or report
cards, for example, usually yields significant diagnostic clues, and the
interviewer can ask about these topics if they do not come up spontaneously. The "homework hassle" is a frequent source of friction and
conflict in a family, and report cards can arouse intense feelings among
family members. It has been enlightening to discover the wide spectrum of parental reaction to report cards, ranging from almost total
ignoring of the card to intense rage. Some parents make a deliberate
practice of not discussing the card with a child except for a brief non-
committal comment. Others use the card as a veritable bill of indict-
ment in a one-sided "discussion." Children's fear of parental reaction
can result in their losing or hiding the card, changing the grades, or
in extreme cases—suicide.

Family *"educational history"* compared to the *value* the family
places on learning may provide useful data. By careful inquiry, one
can avoid making stereotyped assumptions about cultural values; for
example, the notion that parents of the working-class child consider

education to be less important than their middle-class counterparts. Also, parents sometimes describe their own school experiences, and this description is illuminating for the whole family as well as for the interviewer.

## Form

Interview form is flexible; the family may be seen conjointly for the entire sixty- to ninety-minute session, or in various combinations for part of the time. In addition to the conjoint session, the interviewer may wish to talk to the child alone, to the siblings, to the child and siblings together, or to the child and each parent separately as well as to the child with both parents together. An advantage of seeing one parent at a time with the child is that the interaction may be more intensive. Moreover, the parent may feel freer to state a position and to react more spontaneously at first with the spouse not present. Inclusion of siblings in partial-family subsessions can aid in uncovering family-system processes such as scapegoating or labeling. The subsessions follow the approach of limiting content to the school issue. Although useful, partial-family subsessions are not substitutes for seeing the family conjointly, since the exploration of family-unit communication, relationship, and system factors is essential.

The format of the interview has varied with experience, and format flexibility is the rule-of-thumb. As an example, it is advisable in a few cases to see the parents separately near the end of the interview in order to make some connection that is not appropriate to share with the children. Another variation is to conduct a brief homework or tutoring lesson with the parent as supervisor or tutor for the purpose of direct observation of parent-child interaction in an authority-related, task-oriented, and possibly conflict-laden situation.

## Treatment Aspects

The notion that diagnosis has therapeutic values is generally accepted in clinical practice. Some treatment gains both during and following the family interviews can be observed. It is helpful for children and adolescents to learn that they are not solely responsible for the learning or behavior disorder; even as their share of the responsibility is pointed out. Bringing into the open the "family secret" or the many feelings surrounding school learning can be beneficial to the child and the family. An attempt is made in the interview to get the family to make the specific connections between their functioning and the school problem with as little help from the interviewer as possible, partly as a means of pointing up their own potential for problem-solving. Occasionally, families become very active during the session and assume responsibility for making needed changes. In general, it is desirable to look for strengths as well as weaknesses and to try to make the family aware of the positive contributions they can make toward resolving the problem.

## *A Note of Caution*

The interview technique described in this chapter tends to place more emphasis on authority, confrontation, and directiveness than one finds in a less structured situation. For this reason, the interviewer needs to be aware of the greater potential for projecting his own needs onto the session or family, and for coming across as a blaming rather than as a helping person. In addition, the amount of guilt and upset that can follow a confrontation of parental and family-unit responsibility in contributing to the school problem points to a need for careful handling of feelings generated by the interview. In this regard, the designation of parents as potentially positive change-agents (in terms of specific ways the parents can improve the child's school situation) can allay guilt and alleviate upset. One of the values of making a direct link between family and school disorder is that specific ways of helping the child can then be described to the parents. For example, if parental "running interference" for the child leads to low frustration tolerance in learning, concrete examples of how parents can function differently in this area can be offered. If parents feel they cannot implement advice readily, the suggestion can be given that this inability could be worked with as a constructive step in aiding the child. As in any diagnostic procedure, one should be alert to the possible need for follow-up.

## SCHOOL LEARNING DISORDERS

My experience with the structured interview in the assessment of children and adolescents with school learning disorders is presented in two parts: (a) analysis of data obtained from the study of fifty-three family interviews and (b) summaries of four cases. I conducted the interviews discussed below over a two-year period in three settings: The Mental Health Development Center of Retail Clerks Local

770, AFL-CIO; the Southern California Permanente Medical Group, Department of Psychiatry; and private practice. The families in this study range from upper-middle class to lower-working class. Minority group (Negro and Mexican-American) representation in this sample is approximately fifteen percent of the total, and the ratio of boys to girls is four to one. All families were intact and lived in the Metropolitan Los Angeles area.

## Data Analysis

The material given below was obtained from my review of case files.* Diagnostic information was placed under nine categories dealing with family system, relationship, and communication factors. All data related to school learning fitted appropriately into this arrangement. It should be noted that there was some overlap between categories, and that many interviews yielded more than one critical factor. The number in brackets after each category heading indicates the number of times this factor was revealed in the fifty-three interviews.

### Factors

1. Double-bind messages were given by parents regarding their achievement expectations of the child [11].

Generally reflected in an I-want-you-to-do-well-but-I-know-you-can't kind of message, this factor was sometimes linked with parental cueing of a "damaged child" role. Examples in the case material of reasons given by parents to explain why a child could not meet their stated expectations included a visual problem, a mild heart condition, minimal brain dysfunction, "inability" of the child to achieve in the absence of the parent, and poor listening habits.

2. Communication between parent and child regarding (a) achievement expectations, (b) actual performance by the child in school, or (c) disappointments regarding performance was characterized by ambiguity and/or dishonesty [19].

"As long as he does his best" (but the standard is really "A"), "We'll be satisfied with C's" (when the expectation-demand is B or A), and "We don't care about grades—we want him to love learning" (yet censure or rejection have followed low grades on report cards) were frequently heard comments by parents that illustrate the poten-

---

*The analysis of interview content involved a subjective evaluation—the material is therefore not presented as objective research data.

tial for confusing or discouraging a child by this kind of parent-child communication.

3. Permission was given by parents to the child to fail, continue immature behavior in school, underachieve, avoid stress, act out resistance to the educational process, or passively resist school learning [18].

One frequently occurring pattern of family interaction was the infantilizing of the child, resulting in school problems of low frustration tolerance, poor listening habits, consistent (and sometimes massive) avoidance of the stress of learning, and weak task orientation. Lowered behavioral expectations as a result of the parent's viewing the child as damaged was noted in a number of cases, and some overlap of this factor with the double-bind message was apparent.

4. A significant discrepancy was evident between parental expectation of the child and the child's interpretation of that expectation [2].

Distortion by the child (academic goals as set by parents incorrectly perceived as inordinately high) resulted in resentment toward parent and teacher authority. The low incidence of this factor (2 cases) suggests that the children and adolescents in this study were accurate in assessing the level of parental expectation.

5. The same-sex parent represented a poor model in terms of learning-achievement [16].

Fourteen fathers and two mothers represented models of weak, passive, ineffectual approaches to environmental mastery. In the interview, these parents would often replicate the school behavior of the child; for example, not listening, memory lapse, plea of inability to understand, and other forms of passive resistance to learning-task demands.

6. Strong disagreement between parents was present, particularly in regard to expectations or management of the child relative to school learning.

Ineffectual or nonexistent structure around homework, divergent achievement expectations, and inconsistent rewards or consequences following school success or failure were produced by unresolved differences between spouses. As a result, the child was preoccupied, confused, and somewhat "frozen" in terms of utilizing intellectual ability in the school setting.

7. Overall communication in the family, as experienced by the child, was confused or dishonest [9].

The child verbalized lack of certainty regarding his actual level of performance, teacher expectations, or school standards. There was a tendency for the child to distrust or to be confused by information. The end-product of this factor was weakened or indifferent motivation for achievement.

8. Parent-child relationship difficulty was focused in the school learning area [14].

Strong, constant pressure from parents for high achievement accompanied by punitive or rejecting attitudes toward the child; and by contrast, a lack of communication between parent(s) and child about school (except when a poor report card stimulated rage reactions from mother or father) were two examples of conflict centered around learning. Resistance to or hostility toward authority transferred from parent to teacher was frequently the outcome in this category.

9. Achievement expectation communicated by the parent to the child was markedly inappropriate in terms of the parent's characterization of the child's ability [6].

Parental disappointment and children's fear of failure were linked as concomitants of this factor. Overlap with the double-bind message category was evident.

The tabular count of factor frequency in the fifty-three interviews was 101. In come cases, the information from the categories above seemed sufficient to explain the child's difficulty in school learning. With many families, however, the material fitted in with the results of other assessment procedures to lend weight to a multicausational view of the school difficulty. In total, the diagnostic data uncovered in these family meetings represented a substantial contribution to the understanding of the school learning disorders.

## Case Illustrations

Four of the structured interviews in this study are described below as examples of the kinds of interaction and material produced by this technique.

### Case I

The Harris family interview illustrated parental permission for the child to fail in school and the modeling by father of negative response to communication task demands as well as the repression of feelings aroused by frustration.

Sam Harris,* age nine, was reported by school to be achieving far below ability, unmotivated, and to have a short attention span, low frustration tolerance, and overall resistance to learning task demands. There was a history of prolonged absences from school (including a two-day hospitalization) accompanied by severe somatic distress but without clinical evidence of illness.

At the start of the session, father was asked what he expected of Sam in school, and the answer was "not any more than any other kid." In response to the repetition of the same question, he replied, "as long as he keeps up with the other kids." When asked whether Sam was keeping up with the other kids, father said, "some, yes . . . some no . . . not in everything . . . (the question was repeated) . . . "in general." Further query did not elicit from father a clear or specific comment regarding the severe disability in reading and arithmetic reported by school. Sam's comments about these issues were similarly evasive and ambiguous. Mother was asked about expectations and her answer was, "I want him to try hard and do his best," and when the question was repeated, with a request for specificity, Mrs. Harris stated heatedly, "I don't want him pushed." Father was then asked to have Sam read from a very easy book. What followed was much balking by Sam, pleading by father, and discussion and vacillation between them. Sam claimed he "forgot" almost all of the words in the book; his "forgetting" was replicated by a number of memory lapses by father during the interview. Finally, father stated that he thought Sam would "grow out of" the problem of not wanting to read, and then turned to the boy and asked him what he thought father should do to get him to read the sentence!

Confronting the parents with the infantilizing and anxiety-producing nature of the father-son tutoring session produced some intellectualized "understanding" by the parents, but Sam continued to control them through crying, somaticizing, or stubborn refusal to read. At this point, I decided to conduct a very brief tutoring lesson in arithmetic, with the intent of modeling firm structure and positive

*All names in this chapter are fictitious.

encouragement. Sam absorbed instruction readily and performed satisfactorily with a minimum of the "forgetting" that he had used ma-
nipulatively with father. Sam was asked to wait in the reception room
and some discussion ensued with the parents. Father was able to express his anger at Sam's balkiness, and said that his way of handling
anger with Sam was to suppress it and "give up or give in." The parents were able to see that Sam, too, held in much feeling and that his
behavior reflected a good deal of anxiety. The connection was then
made between father's model of repressing feelings leading to "give
up and give in," and Sam's repressed anxiety around task demands and
his consequent "giving up" in school tasks or "giving in" with an ineffectual performance. In addition, resistance to school learning was
linked to the many expressions during the interview of parental permission to maintain the current pattern of poor school functioning.
Finally, it was pointed out that Sam's response to the arithmetic tutoring sample gave evidence of potential for positive change.

### *Case II*

The diagnostic yield that can be obtained from the single question
about parental expectations was illustrated in the following condensed
verbatim excerpts from the taped interview with the Stevens family.
Donald Stevens, age seven and a half, was reported by school to be retarded in all academic areas and to be only tangentially involved in
school learning.

> THERAPIST. I'd like to know, Mr. Stevens, what you expect of Don-
> ald in school?
> FATHER. *(Nervous laughter)* I don't know—I expect him—to get by.
> THERAPIST. I'm really interested in hearing what you mean; what
> do you mean, you expect him to get by? I'm not sure I understand.
> FATHER. It means I don't expect any—I don't really care if he does
> brilliantly—I don't really care if he does above average—in fact, I'm
> not really upset, you know, that much, if he has a lot of trouble either.
> But I mean, I'm more concerned—I really don't think I can put pres-
> sure on him to get higher marks, but I am concerned about his read-
> ing because it's a key to other things in school. I'm concerned that in
> some way that we can bring him up to the reading level, let's say, of
> his age group. Not necessarily now, but, you know, before he's ten
> years old.
> MOTHER. I must say I agree—there's never any pressure on Donald
> at all.
> THERAPIST. I can certainly accept that. What I'm not sure I under-

stand though, is your saying you don't—I'm finding it hard to express what you said because it's a little bit confusing. Do you mean you just want him to be able to get through school?

FATHER. Well, what I'd like to see is if he's ten years old and reading up to his grade level. In other words, to me it's a long range thing—I don't expect overnight for Donald to be doing the work that perhaps everyone else in his class might be doing.

THERAPIST. Oh, I see. So you're not concerned if he doesn't do well; you're not concerned if he doesn't do average; but you are concerned if he hasn't learned to read by the age of ten. Am I saying this correctly?

FATHER. What I'm concerned about is—I hope that there should be some gradual improvement, so that, let's say, by the time he's ten he's doing adequate work in school.

THERAPIST. What do you mean by gradual improvement? I'm not sure what that means.

FATHER. I'm not sure what it means as far as reading, or as far as elementary school.

THERAPIST. What do you expect of Donald in school—today, this week, next month—what do you expect of him?

FATHER. Well, I *could* say I expect him to do whatever he can do.

THERAPIST. If you said it, would you mean it?

FATHER. Well, if he's not up to doing what the school considers passing work, I'm not concerned about that.

THERAPIST. You expect him to do what he can do? Well, what can he do?

FATHER. Well, right now he's—I guess he's below reading level of his grade, but you know that doesn't bother me that much; but if he has this kind of reading problem when he's ten years old—you know that's another—what?—two and a half years or so, then it becomes something of more concern to me.

THERAPIST. Would I be about right if I said that you're not concerned now, but you would be concerned if he's ten years old and he hasn't caught up in reading? Is that a fact?

FATHER. Well, no, I'm sorry—I'm concerned—I'm still concerned about Donald now, because I don't want those problems to occur when he's ten or eleven years old and not up to his reading level—I don't want those problems to occur. I'm concerned now.

THERAPIST. Is there any connection between your concern about what will happen by the age of ten in reading, what he's doing in school now, and what you expect of him?

FATHER. No, I can't really—I don't think I—right now, to me, I'm just letting him go to school without any pressure on him and so forth, so he can just go to school—whatever the teacher has to offer him that the atmosphere will be such that there will be some kind of improvement.

THERAPIST. Well, again I want to be sure I understand you. Are you saying that there isn't anything he is supposed to be doing in school about learning so he can be reading by the age of ten? That's what I think you said.

FATHER. Well, at school the teacher presents a certain amount of material—now what I understand—

THERAPIST. What do you expect him to do about this presentation of material?

FATHER. Well, if his reading problem is emotional—what do you mean, what do I expect him to do—what *can* I expect him to do?

THERAPIST. That's what I want to know. What do you expect him to do with the material that's presented in the classroom regarding reading?

FATHER. I don't know. I mean—what can I expect him to do? Can I expect—what can I expect as long as he has an emotional problem that's blocking his reading?

Later in the session, mother reported that teacher said Don responded in class to questions with evasive, vague, tentative answers, or with an answer to a different question. Don's verbalizations during the interview closely resembled teacher's description. Father, who became aware of his own tentative, qualified, uncommitted communication pattern, stated that observing Don's participation in the meeting made him aware of the model he was setting. After further discussion, Mr. Stevens was able to link his inadequate communication pattern with Don's school learning problems, and also could recognize the confused expectations and permission-to-fail message he expressed in the beginning phase of the interview.

### Case III

The meeting with the Lewis family provided some insight into the effect of a marked discrepancy between the parents' expectations of academic achievement and an adolescent's ability, as well as the negative influence of a "family secret." Mike Lewis, age fourteen, was reported by school to have a long history of poor classwork. School testing indicated he was of average intelligence. Comments by teachers revealed that Mike had a serious problem of inability to concentrate and also a tendency to become confused in mathematics.

At the beginning of the interview, Mike seemed depressed, preoccupied, fearful, defeated, and self-deprecatory. In talking about expectations of Mike, Mrs. Lewis was vague and preoccupied; her comments had a quality of missing the discussion topic target. Only after much repetitive questioning could she verbalize her disappointment in Mike's school work as being far below top quality. Further, Mrs. Lewis said that she did not believe Mike's obviously sincere statement that he wished he could do better. Mrs. Lewis' inattentiveness and apparent lack of sensitivity to Mike's feelings were pointed out. Mr. Lewis' position was that he had let Mike down by not whipping him more when he was younger, with the result that Mike did not grow up to be a good student. Father blamed mother for not putting more pressure on Mike for achievement, and stated that he was too busy to pay attention to how the boy fared in school. A long history of severe and violence-filled marital discord was then narrated by the parents, with much crying by mother in describing her feeling of total responsibility for father's alcoholism. It was revealed that the frequent quarrels between the parents (often concluded by violent assaults by father on the rest of the family) had driven an older son out of the home—a boy whose school record paralleled Mike's and who was now doing well in his job and in night school. As the interview progressed and the "family secret" (father's alcoholism) was brought into the open, Mike began to relax, concentrate, and make insightful contributions to the discussion. Mike had never been able to understand why his brother had done well after leaving the home, and in addition, had thought that he (Mike) was the cause of the parental discord.

Toward the end of the session, I asked the family to see if they could make any connection between what had taken place in the meeting and Mike's school performance. Mother said that she realized now that Mike's preoccupation in school and his lack of accuracy in arithmetic resembled her own mode of performance. Both parents were able to see that Mike's high degree of concern, guilt, and anxiety over the marital stress was largely responsible for his poor school work and that their very high expectations of him were not appropriate in view of his average ability. Mike accepted and seemed vastly relieved by these specific connections. He revealed that he had felt something must be wrong with him for father to have paid so little attention to him. Mike expressed much appreciation as the parents scaled down their expectations of him, and the interviewer pointed out that this change in expectation as well as the willingness of father and mother to share the "family secret" with Mike, could have a strong, positive effect on the boy's academic progress.

### Case IV

The Palmer family session illustrated the effect of double-bind messages and other parent-child communication-relationship difficulties on school achievement. Diane Palmer, age fifteen, had received consistently low grades throughout her school career, had been placed in remedial sections of her academic classes, and was currently failing mathematics. Teacher comments indicated Diane was frequently preoccupied or confused in class. Diane's sister, Patti, age thirteen, was a high achiever in school.

A brief sample work lesson with Diane prior to the interview revealed a very low self-concept and an attitude of utter defeat toward problems requiring manipulation of arithmetic concepts. In contrast, Diane worked very hard in arithmetic computation, an area she felt comfortable in. During this capsule lesson, Diane expressed her frustration in trying to understand explanations in arithmetic and her feeling of resentment at being rebuffed by teacher when she would try to get additional instructional help.

At the beginning of the interview, father described the family's valuation of school achievement as a "must" for their upward-mobility strivings. Mr. Palmer related that he spent many hours patiently tutoring Diane in arithmetic, but that it took "fifty repetitions" for Diane to understand. At first, Mr. Palmer said he expected Diane to pass arithmetic and stated that he had told Diane she could succeed if she tried. Skeptical probing of this expectation, however, enabled father to admit that he did not believe Diane could learn arithmetic. Mrs. Palmer felt it was a waste for father to spend so much time with Diane, declaring she wasn't sure if Diane could learn satisfactorily. Much general confusion was expressed by the family regarding Diane's academic capabilities and what should be expected of her. It was difficult for parents to see the connection between this muddle around expectations and Diane's confusion and defeatist attitude in school. Mrs. Palmer then expressed some concern about her relationship with Diane, characterizing it as a "silent war" that had replaced previously open hostility. Patti, who remained essentially detached during the meeting, contributed verification of the "silent war" relationship.

Toward the end of the interview, the parents were more honest about their opinion of Diane's school ability—finally and reluctantly calling her a "slow learner." However, neither parent overtly responded to Diane's bursting into tears as she recognized that her parents have not been able to fully accept her because of the slowness in learning. At this point, I outlined the connections between Diane's feeling of belonging in this family, the lack of recognition of her feelings, the mother-daughter conflict, the double-bind on expectations, and Diane's preoccupation, confusion, and defeatism in school. The parents were able to draw their own conclusion that this disagreement about the usefulness of home tutoring contributed negatively to Diane's efficiency in school. Father, who had taken the position at the start of the session that the problem was Diane's and not the family's, stated at the end of the interview that he and his wife needed counseling as a part of any program of help for Diane's school difficulties.

## *Discussion*

In the four interviews described above, a variety of techniques were employed and a diversity of information was collected. However, common threads could be found in the case material; for example, the importance of learning as a family value, and the distortions in communication involved in the attempts to implement that value. In all of the families, school learning served as a focal point for the expression of difficulties in parent-child and family relationships, and direct links were established between family function and the learning disorder.

## SCHOOL BEHAVIOR DISORDERS

Initially, the structured family interview was developed for evaluating school learning disorders. Later, the interview proved equally useful with school behavior problems, without any change in goals, technique, or format.* The family system, relationship, and communication factors described in a previous section of this chapter dealing with learning problems were also found in the school behavior interviews, and the negative effect of these factors on school behavior was as potent.

*I have found the technique applicable to behavior problems generally, whether centered in the school, home, or community.

## Case Illustrations

### Case I

Theresa Lee, age thirteen, had been expelled from two junior high schools for persistent truancy. She would either stay away from school for days or would go to school and leave soon after arrival. Theresa had not been a problem in school until she entered junior high school. An older brother and a younger sister were doing well, scholastically and behaviorally. Mrs. Lee, who had been separated from her husband for five years, had stated to a clinician that she had dropped out of school when she was thirteen. At another time she told the clinician that Theresa was "going to be just like me." I was asked by the clinician to conduct a structured interview for the dual purpose of assessing the truancy problem and evaluating the potential for constructive intervention.†

In response to my question "What do you expect about Theresa going to school," Mrs. Lee gave ambiguous responses which gave room for Theresa to avoid responsibility. When this was pointed out to the mother, she replied, "I'd tell her to go to school, but I know she'll leave." The question about expectations was pursued further until Mrs. Lee made a clear statement that she wanted Theresa to stay in school. As soon as mother made the unequivocal statement, she began to cry. Theresa quickly moved very close to mother, told her not to cry, and glared angrily at me. During the next few minutes, while the feelings of Theresa and Mrs. Lee were being discussed, mother and daughter entwined themselves around each other, not so much in a comforting manner as in a symbiotic embrace. This physical interaction gave an eloquent message about the nature of the mother-daughter relationship.

When I told Mrs. Lee that her expectations would be an important factor in determining whether the truancy pattern would continue, she became abusively angry. It was as if sending Theresa to school with a clear message to go and stay was the equivalent of sending her away from home, and that I was trying, in effect, to separate mother and daughter permanently. The intensity of this reaction indicated that the parent-child relationship was a deep one and that at-

†The structured family interview has proven to be a valuable collaborative consultation technique.

tempts to work directly on the truancy issue would not likely be successful.

## Case II

Martin Beck, age ten, was an intellectually gifted boy whose chronic misbehavior in school had led to a number of suspensions and expulsions. Verbatim excerpts from the tape-recorded interview with Martin, his mother, and stepfather follow:

THERAPIST. How can I help?

MOTHER. The school psychologist wanted Martin evaluated for medication. Now, I don't feel it's necessary—I feel it's because Martin is not being stimualted in the classroom by the teacher and the subjects; therefore that's why he gets into the trouble he gets into and I don't feel it's a medical problem; I feel it's a need for the training in school for the teacher to be the person responsible to stimulate Martin and discipline him while he is in the classroom.

THERAPIST. Mrs. Beck, could you describe the behavior that——

MOTHER. Martin walks in the classroom and tells everybody who he is and what he is and what he does and that it's going to be done his way.

THERAPIST. This is the behavior school objects to?

MOTHER. Yes, Martin's little problem, things don't go his way, he gets upset, very mad, belligerent toward teacher.

THERAPIST. What does he do?

MOTHER. Well, Martin has hit teachers and been expelled from school for physical abuse to the teachers. Not one occasion, but on two or three occasions—kicks, biting, hitting, what have you. Martin feels that the teacher deserves the treatment.

THERAPIST. Mrs. Beck, what do you expect of Martin in school?

MOTHER. I expect Martin to go up there and maintain good deportment with every one.

THERAPIST. I don't know what that means, what do you expect of Martin in school?

MOTHER. I expect Martin to go to school and behave himself.

THERAPIST. What do you mean, behave himself?

MOTHER. Not to agitate the teacher and the classroom—not to go up there and tell them who he is and how well he can do and how beneath they all are under him.

FATHER. He'll make statement like, I have an IQ of 148—he's very proud of this.

THERAPIST. What do you expect of Martin in school, I want to be sure I understand.

MOTHER. To do his studies without the talking, without the bragging, without the censuring of the teacher.

THERAPIST. Martin, what does mother expect of you in school?

MARTIN. To do my work.

THERAPIST. Mrs. Beck, was Martin listening to you?

MOTHER. Just now?

THERAPIST. When you were saying what you expect.

MOTHER. Martin heard what he wanted to.

THERAPIST. How do you feel about that—is that acceptable to you?

MOTHER. It's not acceptable, but I've learned to live with it because that's all Martin ever does, he does what he wants to do.

THERAPIST. If it's acceptable to you that he doesn't listen to you, then do you see any connection between that——

MOTHER. He doesn't listen——

THERAPIST. And how he listens then in school?

MOTHER. I know. I know what his behavior is from the first day he went to school, the problem he was going to have.

THERAPIST. What was the question, Mrs. Beck?

MOTHER. What he does for me and what he does for school.

THERAPIST. And is there a connection?

MOTHER. Sure there is.

THERAPIST. Can you tell me the connection?

MOTHER. He doesn't listen to either one of us.

THERAPIST. But what is the connection between you being his mother and what you expect of him right now in his listening and how he behaves in school?

MOTHER. No, I can't comprehend the question.

THERAPIST. OK, let's try again, what do you expect of Martin in school?

MOTHER. To behave—to do his work and behave.

THERAPIST. Martin, what does mother expect of you in school?

MARTIN. To do my work and behave myself?

THERAPIST. What does she mean, "behave yourself"?

MARTIN. Be good.

THERAPIST. What does "be good" mean?

MARTIN. Be nice.

THERAPIST. What does "be nice" mean?

MARTIN. I don't know, really.

THERAPIST. I don't know either, Martin, I don't know what mother means. Mrs. Beck, what do you expect of Martin in school?

MOTHER. I expect him to pay attention, not to correct the teacher in front of the entire class, be called on and answer, and other times to sit there and work.

THERAPIST. Martin, what does mother expect of you in school?

MARTIN. She just said to not correct the teacher, but I don't correct the teacher.

THERAPIST. What else does mother expect of you in school?

MARTIN. To work and to listen—but I do that.

THERAPIST. Mrs. Beck, was Martin listening to you then?

MOTHER. Yes, he was listening.

THERAPIST. Does Martin, in school, do what you expect of him about not correcting teacher, and listening, and behavior?

MOTHER. No.

THERAPIST. Martin, does mother think you listen in school, don't correct teacher and listen?

MARTIN. No, but I—

THERAPIST. Does she think you do that?

MARTIN. No, but I do!

THERAPIST. But does mother think you do?

MARTIN. Do what?

THERAPIST. Listen?

MARTIN. No.

THERAPIST. Mrs. Beck, how do you feel about the fact that Martin says you're wrong? That he does listen? That he doesn't correct teacher?

MOTHER. Well, because too many times I've had the teacher or principal call me to school because of the problem that had happened in the classroom that day—his not listening, and his not behaving, and his correcting teacher in front of the class.

THERAPIST. Mrs. Beck, are you disappointed in Martin's behavior in school?

MOTHER. Not in his grade achievement, the academics, but in his behavior problem, yes.

THERAPIST. Are you disappointed in his school behavior?

MOTHER. Yes, I am.

THERAPIST. Martin, is mother disappointed in your school behavior?

MARTIN. Yeh, but I don't know why.

Mother's message to Martin, as stated above, blamed the teacher for the problem and denied her own as well as the boy's responsibility for the difficulties. Interestingly, one of Martin's teachers had commented that if she attempted to discipline him, he would say, "You'll hear from my mother."

Mr. Beck expressed clear and appropriate expectations of Martin during the session. However, he placed the blame for the problem on the teacher, who did not know how to control children, and on mother, who always undermined his authority with Martin.

The interview made it clear that the decisive factor in Martin's school problem was the permission (almost encouragement) he received from parents, particularly mother, to continue his unacceptable behavior. It was also evident that the model of denial of responsibility set by the parents was being faithfully followed by this boy, in school.

## Case III

Louis and Joseph Kaplan, eight-year-old twins, were referred by school because of behavioral difficulties. The boys were in different classes, and both teachers reported that they were disruptive and demanded an inordinate amount of attention. Louis was described as erratic, at times presenting no problem, at other times getting up from his seat, walking around the room, and talking out of turn. Joseph's teacher stated that he was restless, had trouble staying in his seat, did not seem to understand class rules, and insisted on constant and immediate praise for his academic efforts.

At the beginning of the interview, Mr. Kaplan was visibly angry and insisted on expressing his frustration at his inability to get the boys to perform household chores. When asked about his expectations of the boys regarding the specific task of taking out the trash, Mr. Kaplan explained his strong conviction that Louis and Joseph did not need expectations spelled out for them, that they should know what to do, when to do it, and how to take turns in sharing task responsibility. Further discussion elicited the following:

1. Expectations regarding the boys' behavior at home were high, but were couched in ambiguous terms. Trash was to be taken out when the can was "full," but the meaning of the word "full" was explained by the parents in vague, somewhat contradictory terms; the method to be used in rotating tasks between the twins was equally obscure.

2. Mother was inconsistent in her discipline of the boys and would enforce a rule only if necessary to avoid a confrontation with her husband.

3. Father was punitive, spent little time with the boys, and did not provide any clear direction for the social growth of Louis and Joseph to complement his high (and sometimes inappropriate) standards of conduct.

4. The parents had fallen into the trap of lumping the twins together as "they," and found it hard to separate them for discussion purposes. This lack of individuation was perplexing to the twins, who sat tense and fearful throughout the interview.

Mother was able to see the connection between family functioning and the problem behavior at home, and also accepted my comments regarding the carry-over from the lack of direction and the vague, unrealistic expectations at home to the unsatisfactory and/or erratic conduct at school. Mrs. Kaplan seemed to grasp the connection between the lack of structure and the confused and confusing parenting at home and the continual demand by Louis and Joseph for attention and structure at school. Both parents agreed that the boys should be treated as individuals, not as a "they." Father, however, seemed to be baffled by the session, even though he acknowledged the possibility that the family communication model could create upset and confusion in the twins.

## Comment

In the three cases described above, the family component of the school behavior problem was the decisive determinant. The session with the Kaplans uncovered a behavior disorder manifested in both school *and* home—a frequent finding. It should be noted that since the twins' father felt so strongly about the home chore situation, I made an exception in not focusing directly on the school complaint; what emerged in interview content made it possible to draw the home-school parallel.

## SUMMARY

In its basic orientation the approach described in this chapter is qualitatively different from the interview in which one looks primarily for the psychodynamics or pathology in the family and its individual members. The latter approach concentrates on such issues as displacement of marital discord; problems in expression of aggression, hostility, or curiosity; frustrated parental ambition projected onto the child; or difficulties in identification or dependency. In the structured interview, one looks for the *operational resultants* of these dynamics in terms of family process.

Focusing on the family aspect of the school problem provides a structure in which specific connections can be made between family functioning and the school difficulty. Uncovering these connections not only provides significant and often critical diagnostic data but also opens avenues for involving the family in constructive intervention.

## REFERENCES

1. Friedman R: A structured family interview in the assessment of school learning disorders. *Psychology in the Schools, 6,* 1969.

*Chapter V*

# THE INTEGRATION OF INDIVIDUAL AND INTERACTION TESTS IN FAMILY EVALUATION

## Mortimer M. Meyer

In view of the importance of the influence of the family on a child's development, much effort is being invested in studying such relationships. The variety of methods for such investigation is reflected in a recent publication by Straus[3] which lists over 300 published techniques between 1935 and 1965. One general method is that of psychological testing, which is the topic of this chapter. Of the many published tests, some have been devised specifically to tap the area of family relationships; whereas others, although established as tests for individual evaluation, lend themselves well to providing insights about families. It is not possible to discuss in this chapter all the tests available. For those who would like to have additional information, a bibliography of tests is appended to this chapter. This presentation is an attempt to illustrate the use of psychological tests for family evaluation, employing both the tests of family interaction and the tests for individuals. Although it is recognized that siblings are a part of family relationships, only the relationship between father, mother, and one child will be evaluated. This limitation has been adopted as a practical measure. The evaluation of the three major relationships will illustrate the basic approach. Although the chapter does not deal with the problems of appropriateness of test selection, the reader is reminded of the necessity of taking into account the total background of an individual as test selection is made.

To understand the family it is necessary to understand both the characteristics of the individual members of the family and the characteristics of their interactions. Thus, tests for both family and individual are included. To achieve the detailed understanding of an individual, it is desirable to use a group of tests, or battery, rather than one alone. This conclusion is based on the recognition that no one test is comprehensive enough to provide such understanding. Enough varied tests must be used to obtain an adequate sampling of the various areas of functioning of the person. The composition of the test battery will vary according to specific situations, but some generalizations can be drawn and are presented here. The tests for interaction study of the family will be presented later.

The development of the test battery was in part related to the concept of adequacy of sampling, but also was associated with developments in psychological theory wherein the concept evolved that within a person motives of which he was unaware might be at least as important in his behavior as those of which he is aware. Correspondingly, it became apparent in testing that certain kinds of tests lend themselves more readily to understanding the unconscious motivation and characteristics of the person, and others more readily gave insights into understanding the more conscious, overt behavior. A frame of reference developed in which a test battery consisted of tests which were highly structured, semistructured, and unstructured. The dimension of structure refers to the degree to which a test task has or does not have a high degree of specificity. Structured tasks tend to be close to the concept of "right" and "wrong" answers and permit the individual to use those responses which have been relatively prescribed by the general environment. Thus, for the most structured tests, the tasks are quite specific with little opportunity for the subject to make an individual interpretation of the task. An illustration of this is in the intelligence test. When the question is asked about how many months in the year, the answer is expected to be the prescribed answer and no individual variation, despite explanations, is acceptable. Thus, this test is more like demands of those everday, routine situations wherein activities are relatively repetitive and follow established formats rather than requiring or permitting personal decisions. On this basis, the child's performance on an intelligence test provides an opportunity to observe how he performs in everyday situations that are highly organized.

For the most part, unstructured tests have tasks which are vague, unfamiliar, and require that the subject contribute much to the interpretation of the task itself. The more the test requires the individual to use his own ideas and imagination in responding to the task, the less structured is the task situation. This lack of structure forces the individual to use his own resources, thus permitting the individual style of responding to be more apparent. There are also tests which are semistructured, that is, not as highly prescribed as the intelligence test nor as vague as the totally unstructured test. Thus, tests can be classified at three levels in accordance with the degree to which they are structured. It is usual to design a battery of tests to have representation at all three levels. Such a sampling provides an opportunity to evaluate whether the individual is able to cope efficiently with and without the support of external structure to guide his responses. Where ineffective coping occurs, the sampling provides the means to learn what degrees of structure are necessary to the individual's effectiveness. For example, this type of analysis could help to explain why a child who knows the subject matter may respond effectively at one time and respond in a totally confused manner at another time. The problem for this child is not knowledge of the subject matter but the circumstances in which it is presented. For such a child, it may be that when he is presented with a formal, well-structured test, he is at ease. When he is presented with a task such as writing a composition for which a highly specific topic has been assigned, he may be able to proceed without difficulty. When he is assigned the task of writing a composition totally of his own choosing, however, he becomes confused and impotent. In this presentation, the Wechsler was used as an illustration of a structured test, The Family Relations Indicator Test as a semistructured test, and the Rorschach as an unstructured technique. Family Relations Test, I.E.S. and Draw-a-Person were added to round out the sources of information, but clearly these do not represent the total possible pool of tests from which one can draw. For the interaction family evaluations, two newer techniques were used. The first is the Consensus Rorschach and second is the recently revised Family Relations Indicator. When each of these tests is discussed, a more detailed description will be offered.

Inquiry is often made as to the contribution that psychological testing can offer where careful clinical interviewing is available. Since psychological testing is based on the use of accumulated data, objective comparisons are possible to a degree that is not possible in the usual clinical interview. In addition, the indirect approach of testing often makes available information which is so unavailable to the individual's conscious process that it is not accessible in the clinical interview. The testing, by itself, does not allow for the kind of inquiry, the kind of flexibility, and the observation of interpersonal relationship which the unstructured clinical interview provides. Thus, the two approaches supplement each other most helpfully.

The information below is selected from a detailed study of parents and child. The family is intact and consists of parents; the identified patient "Johnny," who is a ten-year, 10-month-old boy; and a two-year-old girl. The family is Caucasian with a low-middle-income status. They had been referred by the school, and the parents described the complaints as follows: "Learning skills far below age and grade level. Does not try to learn. No confidence in ability. Poor self-image."

Only a relatively small amount of the data available is used here since the purpose of this presentation is to illustrate and discuss how tests may be used to gain insights into family interaction and its effects on a child's development. The WISC was administered only to Johnny. The other tests were administered individually or to the parents and Johnny as a group in accordance with the specific test. The responses were then scored and evaluated to learn the characteristics of each individual and the way in which his characteristics influence the family relationships. With such information it becomes possible to understand how each parent influences the child's development and how the relationships between the parents may affect the child. Where possible, the analysis is then related directly to the complaints. A more detailed analysis of a single case has been presented by Eiduson, Meyer, and Lucas[2] elsewhere.

## RORSCHACH

The Rorschach records are considered first because they afford opportunity for inferences about basic characteristics of the individual. The Rorschach is an instrument in which the individual is presented with a series of ten ink blots in a specific order. The blots vary not only in their shape, but also in terms of the presence of chromatic and achromatic color. Some cards have only achromatic colors, others have chromatic colors, and some have both. Both the chromatic and achromatic cards have various shadings within the colors.

The cards are presented with minimal instructions about the task so that the individual's fantasies will be stimulated yet affected as little as possible by immediate external sources. As mentioned earlier, this procedure, because of the ambiguity of the task and the lack of precise resemblance between ink blots and real objects, requires the individual to respond in terms of his own concept of the task and blot resemblance. Judgment of the individual's functioning is based both on his use of the blot characteristics and the fantasies with which he responds. Analysis of the use of blot characteristics takes into account the style in which such aspects as color, shading, and form are used. In addition, it is noted whether or not life-like qualities are projected into the images created as responses. This information helps understand the richness of the personality development; the areas of potential functioning which are not being used; and the psychological areas in which special kinds of deviation have taken place. The content of the fantasy is used in very much the same way that dynamic interpretation of free association is done, but with the added opportunity to compare the fantasies of each individual with those which have been accumulated in the research literature. It is often said that the Rorschach provides opportunity for understanding the unconscious motivation of the individual. This statement is made on the basis of the fact that free association, with its opportunity for understanding motivation, plays such an important part in the analysis of the Rorschach protocol. Unlike the structured situation, the individual cannot rely on a learned response or a prescribed one as a means to conceal his own individuality. Instead, although he is responding to a standard stimulus, he must react with an image that is his own individual creation.

The capacity for emotional involvement as revealed in the Rorschach is discussed first because there is general agreement that such capacity and readiness to be emotionally involved is an important ingredient for mental health as defined in our culture. Such capacity clearly underlies a child's readiness to relate to teacher and peers. The inability to relate to teacher and peers will certainly interfere with the learning process.

In Johnny's Rorschach responses there is no use of the color, which suggests that he is quite resistant to permitting himself emotional involvement with others. The Rorschach responses given by father indicate that father sees emotional involvement as representing either a markedly unpleasant, aggressive process or as putting oneself at an early dependent level. Mother, in turn, gives responses suggesting that for her, emotional involvement with others is a poorly defined, infantile kind of relationship. Thus, neither parent seems to have been able to integrate effectively emotional involvement with others as part of their character structure. It is not surprising, therefore, that such parents would be unable to provide the child with a deep emotional relationship or the experience of gratification from such involvement. Their immature needs are more likely to put them in the position of wanting from others, without being able to give. Their difficulty in this sense would not be limited to their inability to give to the child, but would undoubtedly have to be evident in their relationship to each other. Each would be looking to the other as a source of gratification, rather than to the relationship as an opportunity to have an integrated emotional exchange.

The Rorschach protocols can be reviewed from another point of view. In contrast to the basic characteristic of emotional involvement with others is the individual's attitude toward his own inner experience which in turn affects his feelings toward others. All three members of the family tend to be very unaccepting of their basic drives. Both father and son, taking age into account, have a very similar pattern. There is a tendency to try to achieve higher social values at the price of denial of their own urges with resulting inner tensions. With mother, this push is not quite so evident, and she manifests less tension. Looking at all three records, and once again taking age differences into account, Johnny's protocol shows a striking resemblance to that of his father as contrasted to that of his mother. The favorable aspect of the male child identifying with the male parent is present. There is also, however, indication that as part of this identification, Johnny is incorporating father's need to deny basic inner needs. It is believed that as a result of such denial the constructive channeling of aggression may suffer. This explanation could account, in part, for Johnny's lack of constructive, aggressive perseverance at tasks and drive for achievement as noted in the complaint "Does not try to learn."

## CONSENSUS RORSCHACH

The Consensus Rorschach is a relatively new manner of using the Rorschach approach. The same cards are used and, in general, the same unstructured situation is established. Instead of administering the cards to a single individual, the cards are administered to a small group whose interaction is to be studied. It may be, as in this case, a family or it may be a small group of individuals whose work requires close interaction. The possible variations are many. The task assigned requires the group to come to an agreement, or consensus, on one response per card. The details of the interaction as the group functions to achieve consensus, as well as the specific responses, provide the basis for insight into the group's dynamics. Trends such as the respect for individual ideas, need for dominance, need for submission, conflict areas, and the character of affects are likely to emerge.

As one notes which family member was the originator of the agreed-upon responses it is readily evident that they are divided between father and son. Mother is never permitted to have her idea accepted, although there are moments when all three have spontaneous agreement.

It is striking to note further that no agreed-upon response of this family group involves color. This observation supports the previous inferences about the likely failure of these people to be able to relate effectively to each other emotionally. In fact, the evidence points to an avoidance of such involvement. The importance of this confirmation lies in the fact that in this family's interaction, whatever drive there is for emotional involvement is not carried over into the interaction itself. Instead, there is the apparent pattern of introversiveness which we see reflected in Johnny's development. This reflection of parental patterns in Johnny indicates the importance of family interaction on a child's personality development. In this family, despite the parental capacity for emotional involvement, the parents convey their own limitation to the child because they cannot use their capacity effectively in the relationship with Johnny.

Major conflicts expressed by the parents in this interaction situation are in the areas of dependence versus independence; male-female relationships and identification; and morality in terms of "good" and "bad." Their uncertainties have led to a fear of anything unexpected, so that when any family member expresses anything unanticipated and thus threatening, the others tend to exert pressure to distract or to have the individual change or surrender the original reaction. Their reactions communicate to Johnny a sense of his parent's doubts and distress which places Johnny in a position of uncertainty. His uncertainty in relation to his parents causes him to behave impulsively and with poor control. Thus, it appears that although, as pointed out earlier, Johnny is trying to restrain impulsiveness, his attempts are not successful when his parents are unable to support his efforts. The reason for this lack of success is clarified in his responses to the I.E.S. Test, which is discussed later. A further effect of a flagrant parental rejection of one of Johnny's contributions, one which happened to be a highly original one, is to stir up his persisting, negative response to a point where his responses appear bizarre and the parents are unable to guide him into more efficient reaction. With original thinking being discouraged and negativism being reinforced, difficulty in the classroom is again a logical outcome.*

## THEMATIC TESTS

Moving from the Rorschach to thematic material provides an opportunity to observe expression in a form that allows the individual more awareness of the implications of his statements because emotions and actions are attributed to relatively realistic figures and in relationships or lack of relationships between them. In this frame, the motivations inferred from such material can generally be considered closer to awareness than those inferred from the Rorschach. The tests of this type are many and varied. This variation is not only in the style of the test, as evidenced in the contrast between the Thematic Apperception Test, The Make-a-Picture-Story (MAPS), Blacky Test, and Family Relations Indicator, but also in terms of adaptation to age as seen in The Children's Apperception Test which was designed for children from approximately three to ten years of age, the Michigan Picture Test designed for children from eight to fourteen, the Symonds Picture-Story Test designed for adolescents, and the Thematic Apperception Test for children and adults.

*The author wishes to express appreciation to Fred Cutter, Ph.D., a leading initiator in the Consensus Rorschach technique, for his help. He graciously permitted his interpretations of this family's consensus protocol to be quoted freely.[3]

## FAMILY RELATIONS INDICATOR

The Family Relations Indicator was chosen because it is designed to produce thematic material with specific organization to allow for information about interaction within the family. The test consists of a series of forty pictures showing the various combinations of father, mother, son, and daughter in a variety of situations. The situations have been carefully selected to be typical of real experiences which are likely to occur in a child's life, such as trying to get father's attention when he is reading a newspaper, and observing a younger sibling getting a great deal of attention. The subject is asked to tell something about the situation and where appropriate, specific questions may follow. The responses are then analyzed in terms of a formal structure of the relationships within the family, and in terms of the psychodynamics which can be inferred. Analysis of the specific records in this family indicates that Johnny tends to be highly protective of his fantasies in that the thematic material is not only limited, but relatively impersonal. Although it may be that he is being protective in relation to the examiner, experience suggests that in his case it may be not only protective from the examiner, but also that repression has been instituted so that he, himself, need not have much awareness of his motivations and attitudes. From what he has expressed, it seems that he views his father and mother as somewhat angry people, and that mother in her relationship with father is seen as neglectful of her responsibility to provide nourishment for father. Johnny feels that both parents are demanding of school performance at a level which he cannot achieve. In his fearfulness of the angry, demanding parents, he would prefer to retreat to a younger developmental level.

Father's responses suggest that he sees both mother and son as demanding too much. This inference is congruent with the interpretation made from the Rorschach that father is more likely to seek support than to be able to give it. Such a view indicates father's feeling of not being able to fulfill his role of father to Johnny, as a giving person. There is indication, further, that father may have some awareness that Johnny finds it difficult to get his attention. Johnny, in response to father's lack of attention, feels that support is not forthcoming and undoubtedly does become demanding, as mentioned by his parents, in his attempts to elicit the parental support a boy needs. Father feels, in addition, that Johnny does not live up to his expectations. Thus there would seem to be a struggle between father and son in which each feels the other is failing to live up to his obligation.

Inspecting mother's stories, it is worth noting that she, like Johnny, has a very limited record. In addition, she is so uncomfortable with negative comments which she makes from time to time that she then reverses herself and tries to undo these comments. Such behavior would certainly be confusing to a child and create uncertainty in what is expected of him. She draws a picture of father as a stern, scowling man who nags at her and who has developed the technique of not listening. The clinical interview confirms the father's use of this technique, and its effect on Johnny's attitude to mother may well be represented in the findings in the Consensus Rorschach where he joins father in "not listening" to mother's contributions. Such a technique, if generalized to other women and to the classroom, could further explain the complaint that Johnny "Doesn't try to learn." Mother feels that father is not carrying his share of the burden, and that father will listen to Johnny, but not to her. The "divided house" seems quite evident. Reviewing the three records, it is clear that there is very little positive, supportive relationship expressed by any of the three, which confirms earlier inferences. It was noted that Johnny's mode of dealing with the situation is to move toward a younger level. Using a retreat approach is clearly antagonistic to growth and undermines motivation to learn and acquire more mature skills. With such an attitude, it is again not surprising that the complaints involve "Learning skills far below age and grade level. Does not try to learn. No confidence in ability. Poor self-image."

## FAMILY RELATIONS TEST

Although the Family Relations Test is a distinctive technique in style, it can be used as representative of a group of tests whose structuredness is far greater than that of the TAT, but not quite so predetermining of answers as the intelligence test. The questions are quite direct, but there is some room for choice in reply. Techniques such as the Sentence Completion and Story Completion can also be grouped into this category. These tests give the individual opportunity to be directly aware of the implications of the questions and their answers. Thus, inferences made from these responses can be considered as reflective of material which the subject consciously accepts.

This is in contrast to material from the Rorschach, wherein the subject has so little opportunity for awareness of the implications of his responses as to make inapplicable the inference of conscious acceptance of the implications. It should be recognized that conscious acceptance of material does not necessarily mean comfort with or approval of it. Ambivalence about a relationship may be consciously accepted and yet be the source of much discomfort.

The Family Relations Test is a technique which can provide further information about the child's relationship to his family. This is a technique in which the child selects from many figures those which best resemble the members of his immediate family, including himself. Attached to each paper figure is a box with a slot that serves as a container for cards which will be read to the child. There are approximately seventy cards which have statements of positive and negative feelings about the individuals in the family and statements of feelings from the family toward the child. These are read to the child, and he distributes them to the various figures which he has assembled. One additional figure is provided. It is called "Mr. Nobody." The child places in this box those statements which he does not wish to assign to anyone. This arrangement permits him to deny the presence of a particular feeling. The statements are obvious in their content and the child makes the choices openly in the assignment of the statement to the various figures. Therefore, the child is aware of what he is communicating, and his pattern of responses can be interpreted as the way in which he consciously wishes the examiner to view his family relationships. The distribution of Johnny's scores indicates that he denies completely that he has any negative feelings toward his parents or they to him. What is equally striking is his indication that he experiences his relationship to his mother as almost negligible. Although he does not show an especially marked involvement with his father, he describes it as being one in which each has a positive feeling for the other. It is noted further that he experiences his sister as the person with whom he has an intense and highly ambivalent relationship.

Such a pattern of scores can be cause of concern about his future development. He manifests a pattern in which his relationship to the two feminine figures in his family are represented as either minimal or as intensely ambivalent. Without examining its meaning in depth, but to indicate further the possible significance of this pattern, one response which Johnny made during the Consensus Rorschach takes on added significance. He saw two men kissing, but no women in warm relationships. The response disturbed his parents, especially father. While the concept of two males kissing could be a source of discomfort to an adult, it is also noteworthy that such a degree of closeness expressed by his son would be an intrusion into father's attempt to avoid close involvement. At this point, it is noteworthy to recall that in the style of interaction on the Consensus Rorschach, it was essentially father and son who dominated the situation and mother who was left out. Thus, there is a child who fundamentally wants closeness to his father as represented by the response to the Rorschach, but who feels that such expression must be inhibited, as expressed on the Family Relations Test. This conflict is enhanced by the fact that the family pattern is one in which he is unable to turn to his mother for the closeness which he cannot fulfill with father. Since the development of a comfortable sense of self is dependent upon wholesome, intimate relationships with the parental figures, it is appropriate to infer, on the basis of the information from the Family Relations Test and previous material, that Johnny is experiencing considerable difficulty in the development of such a sense of self. Thus, once again we can see a factor which contributes to the complaint, "Poor self-image." A poor self-image is quite destructive to readiness to learn. In view of the character of the difficulty, his tolerance for women teachers is likely to be extremely low. If it is indeed correct that Johnny must avoid involvement with feminine figures, the learning difficulty in the usual classroom where women teachers prevail is further exacerbated.

## I. E. S.

The I.E.S. Test (Id, Ego, Superego) is specifically adapted to inquire into the functioning of these three structural aspects of personality as described in psychoanalytic theory. The I.E.S. Test Manual[1] states that the test "is designed to give measurements of the relative strengths of impulses, ego, and superego, and to estimate the effects of impulse and superego forces upon ego functioning." An understanding of the way in which the three structures are integrated provides insight into the degree of efficiency in channeling impulses into acceptable behavior. Additionally, such understanding provides opportunity for discerning whether id drives or superego or both are the crucial factors in creating inefficient coping.

There are four subtests in the I.E.S. The Picture Title section requires the individual to give a title to each of twelve pictures. From his responses, the inferences are made about "the degree to which the subject can accept impulses and superego pressures as belonging to himself and the degree to which he can integrate these aspects with his more objective judgment." The Picture Story section is made up of thirteen sets of cartoons in which two or three cards begin a story. The individual must complete the story by choosing an ending from one of three provided. From these responses, deductions are made about the "subject's conception of the outside world." Also revealed is the individual perception of reality. The Photo-Analysis section uses nine photographs of men placed on a large card with a series of questions. The individual must choose one of three responses to each question. Interpretation of these responses is for the purpose of understanding "how the subject would like (consciously or unconsciously) to function if he were free to behave in a manner of his own choosing." The Arrow-Dot Test requires the individual to draw a line from the point of an arrow to a dot, but with prescribed restrictions about coping with obstacles in the way of the shortest path. It is believed that his responses will reflect his style in daily life in coping with restrictions of impulses. It is a simple test to administer. The advantage of the I.E.S. is the highly focused information it can provide. For this discussion, the term "conscience" as a factor in shaping behavior will be used as representative of "superego." "Impulse" will represent the "id" wish for immediate gratification, and "ego" will represent that internal process which takes all the varying incoming information and internal wishes and tries to find a suitable integration of both.

If we examine father's responses, the general trend represents father, again, as someone who tends to deny himself immediate gratification and to set conscious control and conscience on a high level of priority. He has, as indicated by conscience pressures, a strong wish to do right. At times, he finds it difficult to push aside his own gratification and to come to an effective resolution of the push of conscience and his own wishes. Mother's responses indicate that she, too, would like to push aside impulses for gratification and is somewhat critical of herself that she may be more impulsive than she should be. Unlike father, her way of dealing with these impulses is to try to use rationality as a means of control rather than the dictates of conscience. Both apparently agree on the desirability of denying impulse gratification as much as they are psychologically able.

When Johnny's record is interpreted, it is noted that he emulates his parents in trying to push aside his impulses so that he clearly has gotten their message, although he actually would like to indulge himself. Here it becomes evident that there is unresolved ambivalence about giving up his impulse gratification to the extent demanded by his parents. Any parental "doubt or distress" eradicates for him the parental support to gain impulse control, and impulsiveness breaks through. Thus, he finds himself in conflict and seems to have conscious feelings of badness and lack of worth. He deals with this by trying to project the impulsiveness as being part of others and tends to deny his own impulse needs. He tries to deal with the conflict by meeting the demands of conscience. He seems to have taken in both parents in the sense that he experiences the demands of conscience as he has learned it from father and tries to use his mother's mode of attempting to ignore the demands of conscience and trying to live by rationality. In the process, there is evidence that his conflicted feelings create a distorted perception of others in which they are highly impulse-indulgent to a degree that he is not permitted.

## DRAWING TECHNIQUES

The Draw-A-Person technique was also administered to all three family members. This is only one of many approaches to using drawing as a means of gaining understanding of the individual. These techniques are more structured than Rorschach or thematic approaches, but less so than intelligence tests. Questions are sometimes added to the drawing task to expand the fantasy production, or the subject may be asked to make up a story about his drawing. A variation of the Draw-A-Person is that which asks for a drawing of the entire family. Another is the House-Tree-Person, which includes questions and elicits fantasies about the drawing in an organized manner. Still another is the Kinetic Family Drawing technique, which requests the drawing of the family with each member in the act of doing something. A variety of inferences are made from the drawings and associated material, depending on which technique has been used. Inferences can be made about self-concept, about images of the psychological position in the family hierachy, and sense of body integrity and function. For Johnny, the Draw-A-Person, rather than a family drawing, was chosen because other family interaction techniques (Consensus Rorschach, Family Relations Indicator, and Family Relations Test) had been used, and also because it seemed desirable to obtain a comparison of individual self-concepts. Thus, each member was asked to draw a person, and when the sex of the figure drawn was determined, he was then asked to draw a figure of the opposite sex. Each one drew first a figure of his own sex.

If we turn first to father's production, we see that he had done something most unusual. His drawings were so large that it took two sheets of paper to accommodate the full length of both the male and female figures. Such a size is extremely unusual, regardless of the age of the individuals involved. One of the major characteristics inferred from the size of the drawing is the individual's self-evaluation.

A large figure indicates an extremely high self-evaluation, which in a case like this suggests considerable compensation for underlying feelings of inferiority. The way in which father achieved the two-page drawing is also significant. Most individuals, when given a sheet of paper, accept this as the limits set within which they must work. Father simply reached out and took another sheet without comment or question. The inference can be drawn that when his self-estimate is involved, he may tend to ignore the usual limits and be oblivious to the reactions of others. As noted in the clinical interview, such seems to be his behavior to his wife and possibly to Johnny as well. The quality of the drawing was excellent. Some of the secondary aspects, such as the vague, inadequate drawing of the feet and hands point to the presence of considerable insecurity, which would tend to support the inference that the size of the figures was compensatory for feelings of insecurity. When we compare his drawing of the male and drawing of the female, we see that although both are large, the female is certainly taller and more imposing. We, therefore, raise the question whether his sense of inferiority may not be related to feelings of inadequacy in relation to women. In the clinical interviews, his attitude toward his wife, at least, suggested very definite compensatory feelings in his manner of treating her as if she were of little significance. This was also observed, as pointed out above, in terms of his behavior during the Consensus Rorschach. Father's need to magnify his own importance certainly must make Johnny feel that he can never measure up to father and father's standards. This effect on Johnny may well be contributing to the behavior which his parents interpret as a "poor self-image" and to Johnny's conclusion that it is no use to try.

Inspection of mother's drawings show that she remained quite clearly within the given situation, although the figures she drew were a little larger than the average. Both figures were fairly clear and did not rely on the sketchiness seen in father's figures. The feet for both figures were well drawn, particularly those of the male, who was drawn to represent a man of fairly powerful frame. Interestingly, mother, in her drawing of the male, managed to achieve a striking similarity in facial characteristics to her husband. The female figure is relatively dainty and clearly feminine, but by no means weak.

Examination of the figures drawn by Johnny permits a noteworthy observation. They were not only small in themselves, but both of his drawings were one-half the size of figures drawn by mother, and by measurement approximately one-sixth the size of those drawn by father. This representation tends to be supportive of the inferences previously made of Johnny's feelings of inadequacy. Thus, the question of the degree of vulnerability and inadequacy which he feels in this triangular relationship must be raised. The drawing of a male reflects an image of the male as rigid, constricted, and poorly defined. His drawing of the female shows a figure far more powerful than the one he drew of the male. In these drawings, Johnny is again showing an identification with father, as well as his difficulties with father. Johnny identifies with father's feeling of inadequacy in relation to women. It is as if Johnny's identification with father is more with father's inadequacies rather than strengths.

## WISC

Only Johnny was given a test of intellectual functioning. The Wechsler Intelligence Scale for Children was used. Although intelligence tests have as their purpose that of estimating intellectual functioning, they provide additional information from a clinical frame of reference. As indicated earlier, these tests deal largely with objective material requiring objective, standard answers, rather than creative ones which call upon individual, personal resources. As described earlier, Johnny's responses to this test allow an opportunity to infer how he deals with everyday situations for which he can use prescribed patterns which avoid revealing the self. It is also possible to examine his pattern of answers within the test itself, to see whether his intellectual functioning is generally successful or whether particular areas sampled show impairment. The WISC was chosen as the intelligence test to be used because it is organized to provide opportunity for analysis of areas of functioning. The WISC has two sections. One section (Verbal) consists of five subtests, all of which are administered verbally and require verbal responses from the child. The second section (Performance) also contains five subtests, but in these, with slight exception, the child responds through activities, rather than verbally. The combination of the two sections, plus the variety in each section, permits not only a good sampling of the child's intellectual functioning, but also an opportunity to have greater insight into varied levels of functioning. With Johnny, for example, the functioning on the Verbal scale was at the average level, whereas his achievement on the Performance section was at a definitely superior level of functioning. Such children are likely to have difficulty in school, since their most effective functioning is not in the verbal modality in which teaching and learning usually take place in our culture. If we look within the subtests scores, we find that his lowest score is on arithmetic. This is not surprising in a child who is having school difficulty. His next two lowest scores are on tests which deal with social situations. One test deals with those kinds of social situations which have relatively prescribed forms of behavior; and the other, situations where the child must make his own judgment. Although his scores on these are only slightly lower, it is noted that both of these are not quite up to the average of his scores, so that they represent for him a lower level of functioning. Interpretation of these two lower scores could be that his social development is lagging behind other aspects of his development. This lag is congruent with the observation on the Family Relations Indicator that Johnny prefers to function on a younger level. This aspect of immaturity may be contributing to his lack of readiness to learn from his environment.

## SUMMARY

Summing up the material as it relates specifically to Johnny and his learning problem, we can make the following statement: Johnny's difficulty is clearly not one resulting from inadequate intelligence, but we do see that his intellectual functioning is not efficient. The inefficiency is in the verbal area which is quite detrimental to the learning process, since most teaching at his level is through verbal approaches. His motivation to learn suffers from two directions. The first is his defensive need to remain at a younger level. Here, the familial interaction, especially with father, seems to play a vital part in that he experiences father as unapproachable and therefore unavailable as a comfortable model, and also as setting and living by such high standards and values as to be totally discouraging to Johnny. This problem is accentuated by the fact that he cannot turn to mother for encouragement because she is both a derogated individual and one with a self-image that provides no support for him. The second direction in which his motivation to learn probably suffers is from his tendency to reject females. Teachers in elementary school are usually females and thus are likely to have more difficulty in engaging him in a learning relationship. This difficulty is furthered by his general attitude of avoiding emotional involvement which is often the crucial aspect of the teacher-child relationship as a factor in the learning situation.

The complaint of Johnny's "poor self-image" can be understood additionally, as reflecting a real detriment to learning. The child who thinks of himself as inept and stupid manifests this belief in his behavior. This manifestation will be expressed in poor school work. In addition, his attitude toward himself expressed in this behavior will cause others to treat him in accordance with his manifest poor self-concept. In this way the results of his attitude serve to reinforce his beliefs in his incompetence and a vicious cycle is established.

The use of interaction techniques to understand family relationships and their effect on the school child is a most useful approach. The richest and most helpful information, however, cannot be achieved by investigating either the interaction or the individual dynamics alone. As illustrated in this chapter, it is possible and most enriching to integrate the findings of testing of an individual family member with testing of the family as a group. The addition of the individual testing makes understandable the motivations and needs which lie behind the behavior evidenced in interaction approaches such as the Consensus Rorschach.

In this particular case where the concern centered around the learning situation, the detailed study revealed not only the individual and family group factors contributing to the problem, but also the effect of the problem on the family. Unlike many other symptoms, a child's learning failure, even when unaccompanied by behavioral disruptiveness, is generally a cause for impairment of good family relationships. School failure carries with it visible evidence that brings upon parents societal disapproval, which is in turn passed on to the child so that a vicious cycle is established in the relationship of school to parent, parent to child, and child back to school. This cycle is seen in Johnny's situation. Father, in particular, experiences Johnny's failure as a disappointment of which Johnny is directly or indirectly made aware. This awareness reinforces Johnny's sense of inadequacy which handicaps Johnny further in his school work, and the difficulty grows. In this case, we have been able to trace the initiation of Johnny's school problem and have readily observed how it became reinforced. Even were the etiology not observable, the effects on family interaction can be noted. For these reasons, the evaluation of learning difficulty as only a cognitive problem is viewed by this author as incomplete in understanding Johnny's distress and planning for its remedy. If more than surface manifestations are to be evaluated, it is essential that there be included information concerning the needs and motivations of each member of the family, the relationships within the family, and the behavior of the family as a group.

## REFERENCES

1. Dombrose, Lawrence A., and Slobin, Morton S.: The I.E.S. Test. *Percept Mot Skills*, (Monog. Suppl.) *3*, 1958.
2. Eiduson, Bernice T., Meyer, Mortimer, M., and Lucas, Winafred B.: Contribution of psychological testing of parents to the understanding of the child. *J Proj Tech*, 27, 1963.
3. Straus, Murray, A.: *Family Measurement Techniques: Abstracts of Published Instruments*. Minneapolis, U. of Minn. Press, 1969.

# BIBLIOGRAPHY

## General

Hirsch, Ernest A.: *The Troubled Adolescent.* New York, International Universities Press, 1970.

Palmer, James O.: *The Psychological Assessment of Children.* New York, John Wiley & Sons, 1970.

Rabin, Albert I. (Ed.): *Projective Technique in Personal Assessment.* New York, Springer, 1968.

Rabin, Albert I., and Haworth, Mary R.: *Projective Techniques with Children.* New York, Grune & Stratton, 1960.

## Bender-Gestalt

Koppitz, Elizabeth: *The Bender-Gestalt Test for Young Children.* New York, Grune & Stratton, 1964.

Tolor, Alexander, and Schulberg, Herbert C.: *An Evaluation of the Bender-Gestalt Test.* Springfield, Charles C Thomas, 1963.

## Blacky Test

Blum, Gerald L.: A study of the psychoanalytic theory of psychosexual development. *Genet Psychol Monagr, 39,* 1949.

## Draw-A-Family Test

Burns, Robert C., and Kaufman, S. Harvard: *Kinetic Family Drawings.* New York, Bruner/Mazel, 1970.

Koppitz, Elizabeth: *Psychological Evaluation of Children's Human Figure Drawings.* New York, Grune & Stratton, 1968.

## Draw-A-Person Test

Koppitz, Elizabeth: *Psychological Evaluation of Children's Human Figure Drawings.* New York, Grune & Stratton, 1968.

Machover, Karen: *Personality-Projection in the Drawing of the Human Figure.* Springfield, Charles C Thomas, 1949.

## Family Relations Test

Bene, Eva, and Anthony, James: *Manual for the Family Relations Test.* Windsor, Berks, England; National Foundation for Educational Research, 1957.

## Family Relations Indicator

Howells, John G., and Lickorish, John R.: *Family Relations Indicator* (Manual). London, Oliver and Boyd, rev. 1967.

## I.E.S.

Bortner, Rayman, W.: School subject preference and the structure of value systems. *Percept Mot Skills, 20,* 1964.

Dombrose, Lawrence A., and Slobin, Morton S.: The I.E.S. Test. *Percept Mot Skills, 8,* 1958.

Golia, George A., and Roback, Howard B.: I.E.S. arrow-dot performance of institutionalized delinquents and adolescent patients in a mental hospital. *Percept Mot Skills, 21,* 1965.

Herron, William G.: I.E.S. test patterns of accepted and rejected adolescents. *Percept Mot Skills, 15,* 1962.

### Make-a-Picture-Story Test (MAPS)

Shneidman, Edwin S.: Manual for the make a picture story test. *Soc Proj Tech Monogr 2,* 1952.

### Michigan Picture Test

Andrew, Gwen, Hartwell, Samuel W., Hutt, Max L., and Walton, Ralph E.: *The Michigan Picture Test* (Manual). Chicago, Science Research Associates, 1953.

### Rorschach

Ames, Louise: *Child Rorschach Responses.* New York, Hoeber, 1971.

_____: *Adolescent Rorschach Responses.* New York, Hoeber, 1971.

Beck, Samuel J.: *Rorschach's Test.* New York, Grune & Stratton, Vol. I, 1949; Vol. II, 1949: Vol. III, 1952.

Halpern, Florence: *A Clinical Approach to Children's Rorschachs.* New York, Grune & Stratton, 1953.

Klopfer, Bruno, *et al: Developments in the Rorschach Technique.* Yonkers-on-Hudson, New York, World Book Company, 1956, Vol. I.

_____: *Developments in the Rorschach Technique.* Yonkers-on-Hudson, New York, World Book Company, 1956, Vol. II.

_____: *Developments in the Rorschach Technique.* New York, Harcourt, Brace & Jovanovich, 1970. Vol. III.

Ledwith, Nellie: *Rorschach Responses of Elementary School Children: A Normative Study.* Pittsburgh, U. of Pittsburgh Press, 1959.

Schachtel, Ernest G.: *Experimental Foundation of Rorschach's Test.* New York, Basic Books, 1966.

### Sentence Completion

Rabin, Albert I., and Haworth, Mary R.: *Projective Techniques with Children.* New York, Grune & Stratton, 1960.

### Thematic Apperception Test (TAT) and Children's Apperception Test (CAT)

Bellak, Leopold: *The Thematic Apperception Test and Children's Apperception Test in Clinical Use.* New York, Grune & Stratton, 1954.

Haworth, Mary R.: *The Children's Apperception Test: Facts About Fantasy.* New York, Grune & Stratton, 1966.

Henry, William E.: *The Analysis of Fantasy,* New York, John Wiley & Sons, 1956.

Murray, Henry A.: *Thematic Apperception Test Manual.* Cambridge, Harvard Press, 1943.

_____: *Explorations in Personality.* New York, Oxford Press, 1938.

Murstein, Bernard I.: *Theory and Research in Projective Techniques, Emphasizing The TAT.* New York, John Wiley & Sons, 1963.

Murstein, Bernard I. (Ed.): *Handbook of Projective Techniques.* New York, Basic Books, 1965.

Rabin, Albert I., and Haworth, Mary R.: *Projective Techniques with Children.* New York, Grune & Stratton, 1960.

## *WISC*

Glasser, Allan J., and Zimmerman, Irla L.: *Clinical Interpretation of the Wechsler Intelligence Scale for Children.* New York, Grune & Stratton, 1967.

Wechsler, David: *WISC Manual.* New York, Psychological Corporation, 1949.

# PART THREE

# INTERVENTION: CLINICAL TREATMENT

*Chapter VI*

# STRUCTURED FAMILY-ORIENTED PSYCHOTHERAPY FOR SCHOOL BEHAVIOR AND LEARNING DISORDERS

ROBERT FRIEDMAN

SCHOOL-RELATED problems are the most common complaints parents bring to clinical settings. The purpose of this chapter is to present the rationale for and the experience with a range of psychotherapeutic interventions in which treatment is structured around the school problem and its family component.* Approaches discussed include (a) individual therapy in which family attitudes, values, and feelings about the learning process and school adjustment are actively brought into the content of the treatment by the therapist, (b) parent-tutor therapy in which the parent becomes the primary change-agent, (c) concurrent treatment of child and parent(s), and (d) conjoint family therapy.

Emphasis on the family component of the school problems stems from a recognition that the family, both genetically and in an ongoing way, has a powerful effect on the behavior of the child in school. In a previous publication,[2] I stated:

> The need for knowledge about family functioning is pointed up by the recognition that the family is the first social unit, that patterns of socialization and learning are first acquired in the family setting and that the parents of the child are indeed his first teachers. Attitudes toward and feelings about authority and learning process, as well as family values regarding the importance of school, are taken by the child into the classroom. A positive *or* negative identification with the same sex parent as a learning person is usually well defined by the

*Part of this chapter was published as an article in *Child Welfare*.[1]

133

time the child enters school, and the quality of the working relationship between teacher and child can be strongly influenced by carryover from the parent-child relationship.

The rationale for structured family-oriented therapy is based on the view that the values, goals, models, dependency and authority relationships, and interpersonal dynamics found in the home tend to reproduce themselves in the school milieu and thus are prime determinants of success or failure in school adjustment. The emphasis placed on the family component of the school behavior or learning disorder reflects my conviction that one must deal with the familial aspect of the problem as an important, and often crucial factor affecting the outcome of a treatment program.

## SCHOOL FOCUS

A number of modalities can be employed in focusing on the link between the family and school conduct. Structuring the therapy around the school difficulty itself has definite advantages. Education has a culturally determined high level of family ego-involvement. School adjustment is concrete, visible; changes in performance are relatively easy to measure and verify. For the child, school learning and behavior involves a critical area of ego-functioning, and therapy gains can set off a chain reaction leading to positive reinforcement for desired changes in other areas of the child's life. This reinforcement and the ego-enhancement from school success can make the durability of the child's therapy gain not so dependent on the continuance of the progress made by the family unit or parents. In addition, concentrating on the educational area eliminates the need for the "transfer of learning" or "spread of effect" that is necessary when therapy does not focus on the school issues directly. Also, active participation by parents in the treatment program often results in improved home-school relationships. Finally, although the family may have a stake in maintaining the school difficulty, parents are often less threatened by and more willing to participate in family-group, conjoint, or parent-child sessions when treatment is focused directly on the school issue rather than on neurotic patterns or marital discord.

It is possible of course, to deal with the family aspect of a school difficulty without working directly on school issues. For example, the successful treatment of the same-sex parent may produce a different, more positive model for the child to identify with in terms of achievement motivation. Family therapy not centered around educational issues may resolve parent-child relationship problems, thus improving the child's functioning in all areas, including school.

In a few cases, a family-school focus in therapy is either contraindicated or of doubtful utility. Miller and Westman[6] document the possibility that the resolution of a school learning problem can so jeopardize the psychological stability of a family as to be intolerable. Also, one occasionally sees a family where finding, building on, or developing strengths is almost impossible; where the family members do not, and cannot be taught how to communicate with each other. Further, it must be noted that some parents may refuse to or cannot become involved in the treatment process. There can be other unusual circumstances that make it not feasible or desirable to introduce the family-school aspect of the problem into therapy content.

## FOUR MODALITIES OF TREATMENT

### Individual Therapy

The first approach is individual psychotherapy, in which parental attitudes, values, and feelings about the learning process and school behavior norms, as well as intrafamilial problems negatively affecting school adjustment, are actively brought into the content of the treatment by the therapist. A family "educational history" often reveals that one or both parents have had school experiences similar to the child's current difficulty. The influence of the parent's school history on the child's adjustment in the educational setting can be considerable. For example, the father who resented being pushed for achievement may resolve to spare his son the same ordeal, and lean over backward to avoid pressuring the boy. This policy can undermine the child's motivation or may appear to the child as lack of interest. The mother whose parents virtually ignored her school problems may resolve to be a good mother by never letting up on the demand for high performance, thus defeating her intentions. Upward-mobility strivings on the part of parents may lead them to expect high performance from a child with average abilities. When parent or family attitudes and values about education are interfering with the developmental growth of children, the therapist's task is not just to bring the issue into the open, but to understand how difficult it may be for a parent to give up or modify the family value, and patiently to help parents modify this important aspect of family goals. As it becomes clear that disturbances in family relationships are having direct and serious consequences on school adjustment the therapist introduces the conflict into the therapy for the specific purpose of helping resolve the school problem.

### Case Illustration

The Sally Kent* case is an example of a complicated family situation that served as reinforcement for a pattern of underachievement and made it necessary to bring the family component of the school problem into the individual treatment of the child.

Sally Kent, age twelve, was referred by parents because of underachievement. She was reported to be very shy in school, would freeze during tests, was afraid to ask a teacher a question if she did not understand the work, and became panicky if a teacher looked at or stood near her. There was a long school history of poor work and timidity. At the start of Sally's school career, in first grade, there had been three significant events—the parent's divorce, a molestation, and entry into a very strict parochial school environment.

Psychological tests were administered as part of the evaluation of the problem. An individual test of intelligence indicated that Sally was functioning in the low end of the average range. Assessment of personality revealed that the girl had a fear of relationship with people and a wish to delay her maturity and development. In an interview, Sally stated she was embarrassed when called on in class, felt "weird" when the teacher looked at her, was afraid she would be laughed at and teased, and felt she was "dumb" in certain things. Sally's behavior during the evaluation reflected her anxiety and the tendency to try to manipulate adults as a defense against that anxiety.

A session with Mr. and Mrs. Kent disclosed that Sally, the only child of Mrs. Kent's previous marriage to John Martin, visited her natural father and his new family once a week, and also spent a month each summer with the Martins. These visits had apparently become a bone of contention between the two sets of parents. The Kents felt that the contact with the Martins was very upsetting to Sally, and Mr. and Mrs. Martin, when seen separately, blamed Sally's difficul-

---

*All names in this chapter are fictitious.

ties on the poor parenting she received from the Kents, claiming the girl was happy only when she was with them. Adding to the family complexities were the maternal grandparents, who frequently tried to interfere in the management of Sally, and the coincidence that Mr. Kent's first wife and Mr. Martin's second wife were sisters.

Individual therapy for Sally was chosen as the treatment modality, with the agreement that the two sets of parents could be involved as needed. Initial focus of therapy was on Sally's fear of closeness with people, her immature regressive behavior in the face of developmental demands, and the resultant low school performance. Desensitization to the fear of teacher attention was carried out as a conditioning process, with role-playing used to help Sally relax in recitation and test-taking situations. When Sally's tenseness and withdrawal in interpersonal relationships were explored, it was learned that this pattern was continually reinforced as result of her being used as an arena for the unfinished business of antagonisms between the divorced mother and father. The use of Sally as a psychological football served to maintain a personality development that was interfering with productivity in all areas of development.

Since it was clear that some of Sally's family experiences were negatively affecting her school achievement, I decided to involve the parents in a number of sessions. First, Mr. Martin was seen alone, and then with Sally. His infantilizing and over-affectionate behavior, as well as the girl's manipulative use of her mother in trying to terminate the weekend visits, was brought out. Father's wish to have the girl live with him, Sally's guilt at leaving her father after the weekend, and the girl's concern that father may feel she doesn't love him if she wishes to leave, had all resulted in the visits becoming a stressful experience. For example, Sally would call her mother and get her to find an excuse to end the visit (a manipulation mother fell into readily), but would feign crying in order to give father the impression that she was unhappy at leaving him. This issue was largely resolved through ventilation of the feelings of father and daughter. Mrs. Kent was seen with Mr. Martin at the end of this session and they agreed to plan the visits so that decisions regarding frequency of visits as well as details about the time for ending the stay would be worked out in advance by the adults. At another session, Mr. and Mrs. Kent were interviewed and the unrealistic nature of step-father's high expectations of Sally for academic achievement was discussed. Mr. Kent's upward-mobility strivings had caused him to exert much pressure on Sally and his own child for top grades. The individual intelligence test results were shared with the Kents, and Mr. Kent agreed to scale down expectations in the light of Sally's barely average academic ability. At the same time, Mrs. Kent responded to her husband's complaint that she was too soft on Sally by agreeing to set up a more effective structure for homework responsibility.

A conference was held with both sets of parents, and I recommended some easing up by Mr. Kent and Mrs. Martin and some tightening up by Mrs. Kent and Mr. Martin, in an effort to provide more consistency in management of Sally by the four adults involved. All agreed to resist grandparent's attempts to interfere. Encouragement of social activities for Sally and supervision of the homework routine were accepted as working goals. I stressed the importance of direct communication between the adults involved in order to avoid manipulation by the girl. It should be noted that these sessions were not intended to remove long-standing antagonisms between the parties, but rather to forge a working alliance with the significant adults in Sally's life. Fortunately, the Kents and the Martins were able to put aside some of their differences in the interests of helping the girl.

As Sally gained confidence in her relationship with me, she began to relax, assert some independence, and raise for discussion boy-girl issues of concern. As her need to manipulate parents decreased, Sally began to relate more honestly to her feelings; she began to socialize more with her peer group and made friends at school. Teacher reports indicated the beginning of a change toward less fearfulness in the classroom and some improvement in her academic work. At this point, I decided to enlist the support of the school counselor, Miss Banks, as another adult with whom Sally could establish a "safe" and constructive relationship. This perceptive woman permitted Sally to move slowly in establishing rapport in line with the girl's degree of readiness, and after a few months Sally would occasionally drop by Miss Banks' office on her own initiative. In addition, the counselor persuaded Sally to enroll in a public speaking class. Another step was to ask Sally to assist another therapist with a group of five-year-old children. Sally's participation with the group was minimal but meaningful. Over the next six months there were ups and downs with grades but a steady though slow improvement in terms of class participation and social outgoingness. Visits to the Martins became less frequent and not so emotion-laden. At the end of the school year, Sally had pulled all her grades up and was registering social peer success. Issues within the family were faced more openly by Sally as she became more comfortable with herself as a person. Although disinclined to dig deeper into herself than the presenting problems of school and family, Sally was able to understand the connection between her personality development and the school difficulties. I accepted the girl's view that the goals of therapy had been reached, and termination was planned and carried out. There had been a total of twenty sessions.

## Parent-Tutor Therapy

The second approach to be reviewed is the parent-tutor modality in which the parent is considered the primary change-agent.* The stimulus for the development of this approach came from the fact that in many years of working with children with school problems, a number of unexpected treatment failures were noted that could be grouped in a single category—the child's difficulty was principally due to identification with the inadequate, ineffective learning-model of the same-sex parent.

Since the school difficulty was being unwittingly perpetuated by each parent contact, a method had to be devised for simultaneous modification of the inadequacy in parent and child. The technique consists of bringing the parent into the therapy hour as an observer of or participant in a tutoring session. The therapist may model or explain a constructive tutoring approach with the child, and comment on the reaction of the child and/or parent. The therapist may thus be more gentle or more demanding than the parent has been in the past, depending on the need. Rich opportunities for reflection and interpretation of feelings can present themselves. When the parent is asked to assume the tutor role, the therapist takes a "back seat" but may respond to the interplay between parent and child with meaningful silence, nonverbal cues, or verbal comments about the feelings, transactions, or concrete results (success or failure of the "tutoring").

*David Meltzer, M.D. contributed to the description of this modality.

### The Role of the Therapist

In utilizing the parent-tutor modality, the therapist must determine what the child *can* do in contrast to what the child is typically *willing* to do in school learning or behavior. A sample lesson may be conducted by the therapist to verify his perception of the *child's* ability to benefit from constructive tutoring. On occasion, the parent is asked to observe the therapist in the role of tutor in order to give parents concrete evidence of the child's readiness. The parent is also assessed in terms of readiness and ability to follow through with the approach. The tolerance of the child and parent for anxiety and stress as well as the readiness of the parent to take interpretations and direction from the therapist must be taken into account. This evaluation enables the therapist to have confidence that what he asks of the parent and what the parent asks of the child is realistic and fair. The therapist "votes" the child competent to accomplish the task, conveys that confidence to the parent and child, and encourages the parent to join in the "vote." The therapist models a fair but nonyielding expectation to the parent in an attempt to get the parent to model the same expectation for the child. The therapist's basic role with the parent is that of a supportive coach. If the parent tries to assume a stance of over-dependency on the therapist, however, the therapist rejects that stance and asks the *parent* to assume responsibility. The therapist gives only as much help to the parent as is truly needed, and expects the parent to follow suit with the child.

Giving *support* to the parent is crucial, and it is often necessary during the therapy hour to see the parent alone for a time. The confrontation with the child can arouse strong feelings, and the parent may need to ventilate anger or frustration directed at the child or therapist. When the parent seems to be uncertain, confused, or wavering, discussion without the child present may be necessary. Also, the therapist may wish to share some interpretation, suggest a tactic, or discuss some issue that is not appropriate for the child to hear, and will ask the child to wait in the reception room for a while. In addition, if the participating parent's spouse has some disagreement with or lack of understanding of what is taking place in therapy, the husband or wife can be invited in to observe or to talk with the therapist. Sometimes the parent will take the initiative in asking for time alone with the therapist, and the therapist grants this request since he has "voted" the parent (and the child!) to be competent and must back up this "vote" with both conviction *and* support. In a sense, the therapist gives to the parent so that the parent, in turn, has something to give to the child.

Occasionally, the therapist may leave the room and ask parent and child to work out some problem in private. This approach may be followed up by suggesting that the "tutoring" take place between therapy sessions as "homework."

An illustration of the therapist's coaching role is given in the following verbatim exchanges between Carl Barnes, Carl's father, and the therapist:

> CARL. (*reading from a book*) This man was Hudgin, Hudgin, Hudgins——
>
> FATHER. Hudgin*s*—has an "s" on it.
>
> THERAPIST. Mr. Barnes, did you think he might not have seen that "s"?
>
> FATHER. Well, perhaps he did or he didn't put it in, because he said the word before he put the "s" in it, before he did it I broke the word up into two syllables, put the syllables together to form the word and then he didn't put the "s" in it—I waited to see if he was going to put the "s" in it.
>
> THERAPIST. My suggestion would be that if he doesn't seem to see it or put it in, that you ask him to look at it again and ask him to find it, rather than you find it for him, you might stop him and say, "Look at it again"—try that kind of technique.

(In another session, Carl was asked to use the dictionary to look up a word that he could not read. The dictionary, with its simplified sounding key, becomes a tool for giving more responsibility to Carl to figure out difficult words.)

> FATHER. Are you just sitting here, are you really trying to find the word?
>
> CARL. Trying, but I can't.
>
> THERAPIST. (*reflecting feelings*) If I tell my father I can't maybe he'll believe me.
>
> THERAPIST. (*after a long pause*) If I wait long enough, maybe father will forget that I figured out where that word is and that I really can get it. His patience won't last, I think.

It has been observed that with passive-resistant children like Carl, interpretations such as "It's hard to grow up," "it was easier when

Dad gave all the answers," or "you're wondering how come father isn't giving in and telling you what the words are, like he used to" can serve to stimulate verbal or nonverbal response from the child.

### Case Illustration

The usefulness of the parent-tutor modality for treating behavior problems as well as learning difficulties is illustrated by the case of Matt Perlman. Matt, age nine, was referred because his consistently disruptive classroom behavior had brought him to the brink of expulsion from school. Matt had been a severely disturbed, prepsychotic youngster and had undergone psychotherapy with a child psychiatrist for two years. He had made good use of individual treatment, which was terminated concurrently with the referral from the psychiatrist. Behavior in school, however, had not shown the same improvement that the family had observed at home and in the neighborhood. Learning difficulties had also persisted despite individual tutoring.

I decided, after discussion with the psychiatrist, to begin treatment with joint interviews with father and son.* Mr. Perlman, an engineer, was a precise, legalistically argumentative man with a rather rigid personality. He was distanced from his feelings (including his genuine concern for Matt), and had permitted his wife, an immature and very insecure woman, to exercise almost all of the parenting function in the home. Unfortunately, Mrs. Perlman experienced much guilt over her illness during Matt's pregnancy, and had therefore infantilized the boy and was unable to set limits or control him. Much of father's limited contact with Matt consisted of Mr. Perlman's engaging in lengthy intellectualized pleadings or temper outbursts, but without any follow-through regarding problems at home or school. The school principal's threat to expel Matt had upset father, who was now willing to consider some meaningful participation in a therapeutic endeavor.

In the first parent-tutor session, Matt was mildly hyperactive, nervous, and tense, but attentive to the psychological transactions taking place. I had spoken to the father on the telephone in advance of the meeting, had indicated the direction that therapy would take, and had gotten verbal agreement from Mr. Perlman regarding his active participation. Father was, therefore, somewhat "geared up" for the encounter, but nevertheless began to make excuses for his son's school

*The reasons for the choice are discussed in a later section of this chapter.

behavior as soon as the problem was discussed. After much vacillation, Mr. Perlman finally expressed a clear expectation that Matt was to conform to the teacher's rules during the one hour he was permitted to attend school. These rules were spelled out in detail. Matt did not say much during the hour, but gave nonverbal cues that indicated he did not think father would back up this expectation. When I asked father how he would know whether Matt had obeyed the rules at school, Mr. Perlman revealed his prior lack of attention to reports from teacher and mother regarding Matt, and accepted my suggestion that he check with school every day to determine whether his expectation for Matt was being met. Significantly, as father's determination to follow through mounted, Matt verbally expressed his understanding that father did indeed mean business. It was agreed that therapy would be conducted on a twice-weekly basis.

At the second session, Mr. Perlman reported that he had visited school every day to check on Matt's behavior, that Matt was conforming satisfactorily, and that school had acceded to his request to keep Matt in school for a full day. Much of the discussion at this meeting dealt with the feelings of father and son about the heightened and more positive interaction between them. In the following two sessions, Matt revealed his striking ability to sense the degree of resolve of father's commitment to the change process. When this resolve would weaken, or when father demonstrated ambivalence about Matt's ability to conform in school, Matt was able to point out most accurately this change in father.

Matt's classroom behavior showed steady improvement, and father avoided the inconvenience of visiting school by having Matt report to him by telephone after each school day. Weekly written statements from teacher to father confirmed the gains being made. Matt, in turn, clearly was enjoying father's involvement, and noticeably began to relax.

Frequency of sessions was reduced, after one month of treatment, to once a week. Most of one therapy hour was devoted to a discussion with father alone. Mr. Perlman related his unhappy and difficult childhood experiences—including the death of his mother when he was five years old, the lack of close relationship with his cold and self-centered father, and his moving out of the home when he was eighteen—in the context of conveying to me his concerns about Matt's character development, in particular Matt's apparent lack of caring about anyone. It was apparent that therapy had reawakened childhood memories for father. Mr. Perlman could not openly admit to the sad *feelings* connected with childhood, however, as he had strongly repressed both the affect and the importance these memories had for him. It was evident, as Mr. Perlman talked about his past, that his lack of knowledge about how to be an effective father (as well as his strong tendency to relate to me as a father-figure) had its roots in his emotionally impoverished early life experience. Although it was hard for father to talk about feelings as such, he would frequently ask to come into the office without Matt at the beginning of the session, in an attempt to get *something for himself* out of the therapy. When I gave to Mr. Perlman (modeling warmth and caring), father gained something he could then give to (model for) his son. This helped remove the barrier to the development of an effective father-son relationship that had been created by Mr. Perlman's identification with his own emotionally distanced father.

As treatment continued and Matt's behavioral gains solidified, it was no longer necessary for Matt to call father each school day. Teacher continued, however, to send home with Matt periodic written reports. Frequency of treatment was reduced to biweekly meetings, and the focus shifted to Matt's reading problem, with father assuming the tutor role. Mr. Perlman moved quickly in taking and maintaining a firm stance with Matt, and did not permit himself to be manipulated by his son's efforts to get more help from him than was necessary. Matt tested father's resolve with angry explosions and loud ultimatums, but gradually gave in as father demonstrated his ability to withstand the boy's anger and to avoid the temper outbursts that had characterized the past sporadic efforts father had made to help Matt with homework. Matt would occasionally proclaim in a very loud and strident voice that he "will absolutely not" do the work father gave him while actually performing the tasks with vigor and skill. At one point, father rebuked the therapist for inadvertently supplying a cue to a word that Matt was struggling to get!

Matt's report card at the end of the semester showed dramatic improvement in his academic subject grades, including reading. He was elected a class officer, and father and son expressed mutual pleasure at the changes taking place. As the new semester began, father's interest and involvement waned, and consequently Matt's performance dropped. Therapy was then focused on father's weakening resolve, and Mr. Perlman managed to get back on the track sufficiently to convince Matt that he was not abandoning his involvement in the boy's school adjustment. The last two therapy sessions were spaced over a three-month period, and treatment terminated shortly before the end of the school year, with Matt doing well in both behavior and learning. Father and son described their relationship in the final meeting as new, more satisfying, and carrying over into areas of contact between them other than the school issue.

### Treatment Process

The objective of involving the parent in the session is not to teach the parent how to be a tutor but rather to facilitate therapy. The *parent* assumes the major responsibility for modifying the child's behavior by becoming an *effective* parent. The therapist serves as a catalyst.

The change process is conceptualized in the following sequence:

1. The parent is asked to make a commitment to active participation in the treatment of his child. This commitment must be based on a genuine concern for the child in order for the parent-tutor modality to be effective.

2. The parent is confronted with his unconscious acceptance of the child's nonproductive behavior, and the ambivalent nature of the messages he has been giving to the child is pointed out, clarified, and worked through.

3. The therapist elaborates for parent and child a clear, unequivocal, but realistic expectation about what each can do in terms of specific behavior, thus setting up a task requiring interaction.

4. The parent confronts the child with the now-unambivalent demand for change, this produces an intense encounter as the child reacts to the task presented. Since the parent-child conflict is centered on a concrete, resolvable problem, change is facilitated.

5. The therapist's active participation as coach to the parent and interpreter of feelings to parent and child is reduced as the parent assumes more responsibility for the therapy. The *parent* is in charge.

### Advantages

Parent-tutor therapy produces vibrant interactions and evokes strong feelings. The intensity of the experience in identifying and/or interacting with both his child and the therapist often rekindles the parent's own conflicted school experience, allowing for potential parent change which is then reflected in the child. Other advantages of this treatment approach are the following:

1. A more immediate and heightened involvement of parent and child in the therapeutic effort.

2. A "face validity," common sense appeal, and a transactional impact that is difficult for the parent to depreciate or ignore.

3. A direct concentration on a critical aspect of ego functioning, enabling any appreciable change in the parent model to produce significant improvement in the child.

4. The obtaining of diagnostically important information about the kind of learning model the parent represents, the degree of stress that may permeate the homework scene, and possible provocation by the child as part of a family system.[2, 3]

5. The creation of opportunities for educating or giving permission to parents to take a stronger, more effective stand around the learning or behavior issue involved or to ease up on pressures being applied, thus directly modifying parent-child interaction, bringing fears and feelings into the open through verbalization of the stressful ongoing parent-child confrontation, and relieving parental guilt by involving mother or father in a potentially helpful encounter with the child.

The latter possibility can be of particular value in getting fathers who are emotionally distanced to become more involved with their sons. It can also be useful for guilt-ridden parents to see and acknowledge the *child's* contribution to the problem.

## Concurrent Treatment

The next modality to be discussed is concurrent treatment of child and parents.* This approach is particularly useful when parents or family have a vested interest in maintaining the negative school behavior or learning disorder. Just as in severe mental disorders, where a member of the family is "chosen" to encapsulate the family disorder and maintain the family's desperately needed balance, one child is often "chosen" to express, poignantly, the deepest conflicting

*Faye Tolmach, M.S.W., contributed to the description of this modality.

stresses within family members. This is the binding and stabilizing force in such families and becomes the responsibility of the unsuccessful child, who loyally carries out his function. Thus, the family, in spite of its disappointment and concern over the school problem, has a major stake in its continuance.

If more than one therapist is involved with the family, close liaison between therapists is essential in dealing with interlocking family disturbance. Comparing, clarifying, and utilizing the co-therapist's impressions serves to illuminate the way in which family members affect each other. Simultaneous setbacks, plateaus, or improvement can be observed. Parallel developments in the material produced, as well as in stages of treatment, are occasionally seen, as in the case of "Stuart Smith" described below. As therapy progresses, it may be possible to discern whether the parent will be able to gain and use insight into his need to make the child fail. If such a change is not possible, the goal is to help parents alter the most damaging aspects of their behavior. Treatment for the child may be focused in the school area, as in psychoeducational therapy,[4] or may be a more traditional psychotherapy. In either case, it can be helpful for the child to have some understanding of what drives the parent to behave in ways that negatively affect his school conduct or achievement.

A major advantage of concurrent treatment is the opportunity to work in depth with the resistances parents may have to positive change in the child. If this resistance is strong, treatment of only the child will not suffice.

### Case Illustration

The basic features of the concurrent treatment modality are seen in the work with the Smith family. Stuart, age eight, was referred because of poor academic achievement, disinterest in school work, and very low self-concept. From the parents' description of him, it seemed that the boy was dependent, isolated from his peers, and full of guilt. Mr. and Mrs. Smith stated that the cause of Stuart's problems was brain damage incurred during an incident of measles at age two. There was one other child in the family, Pam, a bright and high-achieving six-year-old.

Complete medical and psychological work-ups were ordered. The testing revealed that Stuart was above average in intelligence and had no demonstrable organic pathology. His personality was described as "characterological passive-aggressive pattern with the aggressive component well-defended against, which often gives the appearance of resigned passivity." Pending further study of Stuart's school difficulties, the parents were engaged in separate and conjoint treatment with a clinical social worker. During this period it was determined that both mother and father were experiencing serious emotional difficulties centering around a long history of repression of anger and related to current unfulfilled ambitions and disappointments with themselves and each other. The deep disappointment over father's career failure was pervasive, with father constantly berating himself, and mother criticizing this self-depreciation. Although mother appeared to defer to father repeatedly, she seemed in actuality the more decisive and capable parent. The Smiths' parenting model was characterized by weak and inconsistent discipline combined with an excess of intellectualized discussion with the children about feelings. They seemed unable to distinguish between that aggressiveness which would help motivate Stuart and that which might destroy him. On the one hand, they were disappointed and angry at his poor motivation; on the other, they unconsciously discouraged his achievement. Depression was evident in both parents.

Individual sessions with mother revealed that she wished to return to her psychiatric nursing career, maintained a fixed idea that Stuart was brain damaged and therefore should not be pressured in school work, and assumed the blame for his problems. Mrs. Smith believed that she had permitted Stuart to "regress" after the measles episode and that her inadequacy as a mother had inflicted the boy with "minimal cerebral dysfunction." Further probing of this irrationality elicited the fact that Mrs. Smith had assumed the blame, as a young girl of six, for a fall which resulted in brain damage in an infant sister, and had never permitted herself to resent the responsibility given her at this age for her sister's care, turning her anger inward and experiencing much guilt instead. Not only did she appear to displace her anger upon herself and use her son as punishment; she also seemed compelled to repeat the traumatic experience with him. In addition, Mrs. Smith had known and loved only damaged males. Her father was a brutal and ineffectual alcoholic; her first husband died in a tuberculosis sanitarium, and her present husband was a passive, inadequate failure. Although the dominant person in the family, Mrs. Smith was afraid to assert herself openly, was constantly on guard against any "rejecting" comments, attempted to "reason" with the children or "interpret their motivations." She denied her deep disappointment about her husband's career failure and expressed a conscious wish that Stuart might be stronger and more successful. In practice, her interaction with Stuart around homework was very defeating. She sympathized with his "inability" to grasp the work, permitting him to give up trying after a few minutes. She intellectualized with him about his "short attention span," "poor retention," and "perceptual problems." When Stuart would occasionally express genuine and appropriate dissatisfaction with his school work, she tried to cheer him up or encourage him in more active or creative prsuits.

Mr. Smith, a low-paid clerk, was continually preoccupied with past failures in his career as a painter. He had shown great promise as a young man, was offered important scholarships, but bad luck, recurrent hysterical paralysis of the hands (for which extensive medical investigation revealed no organic basis), and frequent poor judgment prevented his ever succeeding at critical junctures. At the time treatment began, he still spent his spare time at the canvas, but rarely completed a painting. It seemed clear in therapy that he was unable to surpass his own father, toward whom Mr. Smith felt both anger and guilt. He tried to be unlike his own father, who he described as "cruel, like a Prussian sergeant," but in this effort he was forced to become passive and ineffectual, abdicating leadership in the family to his wife, and subjecting the children to his continual despair and self-preoccupation. Mr. Smith volunteered his feeling that Stuart was just like him. Father had very little to do with Stuart's homework or school responsibilities, adapting an attitude of pessimism toward the boy. However, unlike his wife, he revealed in the course of therapy an ability to separate himself from his projections onto Stuart and eventually tried to give the boy permission to succeed.

Several months after the parents' treatment had started, I conducted a psychoeducational evaluation of Stuart, using sample work lessons in lieu of formal testing. It was quickly established that Stuart's reading was satisfactory but that he had some difficulty with arithmetic. There did not seem to be any organic component or perceptual lag in the learning area. What did emerge was a clear pattern of very strong passive resistance to full involvement with the learning process. A surface cooperative, conforming, and pleasant manner was utilized by Stuart to defend against and deflect attention and pressure away from anxiety-producing learning task stimuli. Overall emotional and social immaturity was observed, as well as an underlay of mild depression. Under the facade of resigned ineptitude, however, a genuine spark of motivation did exist—Stuart was himself beginning to be uncomfortable about his poor achievement in the classroom.

It was decided that I would initiate psychoeducational therapy with Stuart, on a once-a-week basis. The therapeutic stance was an open, direct, and persistently unyielding confrontation of the resistance. Learning-task demands were increased until the bedrock of the resistance was reached. Meanwhile, this clever and creatively manipulative boy attempted to use verbalizations about feelings as a device to avoid the expression of genuine emotion, particularly anger. Stuart would try to trap me into a discussion of the dynamics of the interaction, would often yawn, claim he was sleepy, or daydream for long periods of time. My approach, however, was intended to reach Stuart initially on a nonverbal, visceral level rather than on the verbal, cognitive level, and it said in effect, "You can do this hard work if you try, and I expect you to try." There were many sessions in which very little was said, but in which there was much transactional content.

After a number of months, some minor success in learning how to do arithmetic word problems was registered, but reversion to discouragement or self-defeating tactics was consistent. At the same time, Stuart had made a strong identification with me as a learning-authority person. He had accepted my sole interpretation regarding his ambivalence toward growing up and succeeding in school work, and was able to express some anger at my tactics and at himself for being a failure.

Concurrently, mother had been making some progress in her therapy and began to see Stuart's repressed and misdirected anger as her own. Although she remained unconvinced that Stuart was not brain damaged, she began to recognize the psychogenic components of her son's learning problem. Mrs. Smith was not able to express directly her own hostility but did complain about her role as housewife and took some steps to finish her interrupted career. She returned to part-time nursing and began working on an advanced degree.

At this point, I asked mother to sit in on some of Stuart's therapy sessions to observe the process. Mrs. Smith maintained her skepticism about Stuart's ability to do the work presented, even when Stuart told her clearly that he could handle it if he wanted to. Finally, in the sixth shared session, she could no longer ignore the evidence of Stuart's ability to work well if he was not resisting, and began weeping profusely, expressing for the first time her anger at his lack of effort—crying, "I'd like to yell at you or give you a good whop." In the next session, Stuart asked his mother to be more firm with him, and refused to accept her reply that she could only reason with him. He pleaded spontaneously and with genuine feeling, "Don't be so gentle with me, make me do it, yell at me, spank me even, if you don't I'll never learn, I'll never grow up." In reply, Mrs. Smith was able to tell Stuart about her own childhood experiences with anger and violence and how this made it very hard for her to be firm or to express anger now that she was a parent. Mother identified this problem as her own, and not Stuart's. The clinical social worker and I maintained close contact at this juncture, sharing experiences after each therapy session, and Mrs. Smith was able to express in her own therapy (as a parallel development) the anger she felt toward me for confronting her with the nature of the boy's difficulty. Her conviction about Stuart's brain damage was also weakened as she discussed with her therapist the evidence she had witnessed of Stuart's ability to do the work. This understanding helped reduce her guilt about Stuart, permitting more investment of herself in her career advancement.

Mr. Smith had managed by this time to separate his projections about Stuart from reality sufficiently to take an active part in the boy's therapy. This development made it possible to employ the parent-tutor modality, and father was asked to come to Stuart's sessions and assume the role of tutor.* Having established in his own treatment a tentative goal of resuming his artistic career, he was able to give verbal encouragement to his son to do the work presented. In saying to Stuart, "You're in command" (meaning "You can affect your own destiny as I am beginning to see I can affect mine"), father

---

*The father-son interaction is an example of the simultaneous modification of a weakness in father and son in the course of parent-tutor therapy conducted in the context of the concurrent treatment of parent(s) and child.

was translating his own therapy gain into useful modeling for his son. Mr. Smith was able to show mild aggressiveness in asking Stuart to dig into the work, and the boy's pleasure at this change in father was translated into a real effort to succeed. At the end of this session, it was suggested that father spend ten to fifteen minutes a day working on arithmetic with Stuart—not to serve as a crutch, but to give only the help really needed. More tutoring sessions followed, with father continuing to serve as a positive identification figure. Although Mr. Smith spoke in a soft and gentle manner, his firmness in rejecting the boy's attempts to avoid the stress of the task surprised everyone, most of all father himself. He commented, in a semiapologetic way, "You have to be like a Prussian." In one of the parent-tutor sessions, father described his memory of his own father, who had been very strict about making him work for hours at a time on troublesome arithmetic problems. He verbalized his insight (gained by discussing his experience as a parent-tutor with his therapist) about Stuart's past learning difficulties, relating them to parental overprotection and pessimism. Mr. Smith could see how the boy used parental or teacher anxiety about his learning to manipulate and control his environment. Father told his therapist how clearly he could see the similarity of Stuart's problems with his own, and stated his determination to help his son avoid career failure. As a result of father's involvement, Stuart began to solidify some of the gain in arithmetic skill. In parallel fashion, father managed to complete several paintings. Mr. Smith continued at home to provide constructive tutoring with Stuart, not accepting the boy's willingness to fail, and expressing directly to Stuart his confidence that he could indeed succeed if he tried. The tutoring sessions with father seemed to be the turning point in Stuart's therapy. He began to be more aggressive in his individual sessions and his resistance became more overt and obvious; he would throw his pencil down, aggressively tear up his paper, or insult me. Stuart reported that father had taken over from mother as the authority-parent with him. He was able to stay with a difficult task at times, persevere, and despite much griping, mobilize his intellectual resources for the solution of difficult arithmetic word problems. School and parental reports confirmed our impression that he was becoming more successful in school and with peers. Perhaps the best gauge of positive change was his own comment, "It's easier to learn like a baby, but I want to learn like a man."

Several family sessions were then held, and the ambivalent nature of parental-expectation communication was explored. Father recognized that his tendency to give permission to Stuart to slough off homework that did not interest the boy stemmed from attitudes that dated back to his own school experience. Mother continued to give intellectualized explanations of why parents cannot be firm. The parents had told Stuart that "only a spanking will make you learn," but they did not spank, bringing an accusation from Stuart about this double message that parents did not really care about him. Father finally (and angrily) told Stuart he was old enough to work without spanking, and this seemed to please the boy.

The social worker continued to deal with the parents' personal frustrations and their effect on Stuart, but there were many low points for the Smiths in the months that followed. Father experienced some disappointments in his attempt to regain his art career and finally had to abandon this hope. He did not, however, permit his own disappointment to crush him as it had in the past, and I was able to point out to Stuart the model father was setting in not letting hardship and defeat get the best of him. Stuart accepted this challenge and began to consolidate some of the gains he had made into an aggressive stance toward learning. Work at school improved to the point where all grades were satisfactory, and effort toward achievement was consistently above average. Stuart asked for much less crutch-type help from therapist or father and assumed some initiative and responsibility in the learning area. The boy's success seemed to bolster father and help him through a very difficult ego-deflating period where he had to again take a menial work position. Mother was by now thoroughly engrossed in her own career advancement and was able to adopt an "it's up to him" attitude toward her son. About two years after the beginning of treatment, mother and father withdrew from therapy, and Stuart was terminated several months later. A follow-up interview with the parents by telephone, four months after termination, revealed that father was unhappy about his job situation, mother was experiencing some difficulty in completing her graduate work, and family financial and morale problems were continuing to be quite troublesome. Stuart, however, was continuing to improve in school, was beginning to express himself aggressively in play with peers, and was openly expressing anger toward his competitive sister. The probability that Stuart's therapy gain would hold up, barring complete collapse of father or the family unit, seemed good.

In reviewing the Stuart Smith case, parallel developments with parent and child can readily be traced. The key role the concurrent parent therapy played in the boy's improvement can also be discerned. The parent-tutor sessions with father and son are described above as the turning point in Stuart's therapy; it should be noted that two important developments in the parents' treatments made possible the use of this modality. First, mother was able to meet some of her own needs, enabling her to back away from the intensity of her destructive role with her son, at the same time permitting father to move closer to the boy. Second, Mr. Smith gained enough strength through adopting a more aggressive stance in terms of his own career wishes, to deal firmly with the self-defeating behavior he saw mirrored in his son.

## Conjoint Family Therapy

The last modality to be discussed is conjoint family therapy in which the family is seen as a unit for most of the sessions. Occasionally, individuals or family-member combinations are seen separately, but this is held to a minimum.

Conjoint family therapy has been adequately described in the literature, with a number of points of view represented in current clinical practice. Our discussion here will be limited to family-group treatment focused on a school issue which stresses events and developments at school and their repercussions in the home. Specific treatment goals include identifying situations negatively affecting school adjustment, establishing open and clear communication within the family about the problem, and the finding and building on family strengths that can provide leverage for changing school behavior.

Some advantages of this approach are the following:

1. There is first-hand elaboration of the family aspect of the difficulty.

2. There is less opportunity for distortion in communication, both in terms of therapy content and ongoing events.

3. Changes and resistances within the family are more easily observed and interpreted.

4. Since the family is directly engaged in a learning (therapy) endeavor as a unit, interaction with the therapist can provide op-

portunities for observing family attitudes toward a teacher-authority.

5. Identification of the presenting complaint as a *family* problem can take the onus of complete responsibility away from the child or adolescent and place it in a more realistic context.

6. The family, in a sense, is a kind of school, and changes in the social learning context of the family unit may transfer more readily into the social context of the school milieu.

## Case Illustration

The Bob Gardner case illustrates the conjoint family method. Bob, fourteen years old, was a ninth grade, junior high school boy whose behavior had placed him, after a number of suspensions, in danger of expulsion. Bob was severely retarded in academic skills and had a long school history of nonconforming behavior. He frequently disrupted classroom activity through minor disturbances, and many students had reported his inappropriate, immature conduct on the playground. Psychological testing revealed that Bob was infantile, emotionally constricted, severely anxious, and depressed. Intelligence was reported as average. The school counselor had observed signs of regression, including the bringing of toys to school in an attache case.

Bob had been a soiler up to the age of twelve and had been a continual source of worry to the parents. An older brother, now married, had been an outstanding athlete and an average student. The parents had sought help many times for Bob's long-standing school problems, but the difficulties persisted. Mrs. Gardner presented the complaint as a crisis in which this middle-class family would lose its community social prestige should Bob be permanently excluded from the public school. Since the complaint was presented as a *family* problem, I decided to begin treatment with the conjoint modality.

At the first session, Bob barely spoke in a whisper, stared at the floor, and withdrew from the discussion. He slowly became more involved as the sessions progressed and the following dynamics were uncovered:

1. The mother's infantilization of the boy and father's having virtually renamed his son "Stupid" combined to maintain Bob's basic feeling of inadequacy.

2. Father and son were in an alliance that incorrectly charac-

terized mother as neglecting the home and being an alcoholic, a nag, and more interested in community affairs than her family.

3. The "family secret" regarding father's heart condition—a condition distorted by the family into a life-and-death need for father to avoid stress—was used (a) by the father to justify distancing himself from Bob and his problems, (b) by the mother as a weapon to keep the boy in line, and (c) by the boy as a rationale for trying to conceal from parents the seriousness of his school problems on the basis that this knowledge could kill the father.

4. There was severe marital discord over management of Bob.

5. The father shut out from his consciousness the affective significance of ongoing events.

Frank discussion of these dynamics constituted the first phase of treatment, involving six sessions. The relationship between family process and Bob's school behavior was delineated and stressed; for example, the connection between mother's infantilizing, father's distancing of feeling from action, and the boy's consistently immature behavior. This phase of treatment was followed by the attempt to develop some understanding and acceptance of the feelings generated (though previously denied) in all family members as a result of Bob's school problems. It was also helpful to correct some of the distortions of fact, communication, and individual characterization. For example, the therapist obtained father's permission to telephone his physician, and thus learned that the heart condition was not serious and did not require avoidance of family stress. Mr. Gardner then agreed to make an office visit to the physician, with Bob, so that the boy could hear the diagnosis first hand. The school was cooperative in lowering behavior standards for Bob to the bare minimum of acceptance and was patient in waiting for improvement.

The next step was to work toward establishing some cooperative effort between the two parents on expectations and management, while weakening the father-son alliance that had established the pattern of casting mother in the role of the "heavy." In view of the marital dissatisfaction and the resistance of both parents to making changes in their parenting function, the therapist decided to see the parents individually for one interview each. In her session, mother stated that dinner was a very unpleasant occasion, with either fruitless bickering between or cold withdrawal by family members. She further complained that her husband avoided stress by hiding behind the news-paper and ignoring her. She put the blame for Bob's problems on her husband, contending he was not strict enough with the boy. At the same time, she related, in a critical way, a number of instances of fa-ther beating Bob. As a woman prominent in community social affairs, Mrs. Gardner described her husband as being very charming and out-going at social functions of her organizations, but the opposite when they were home alone. In essence, she wanted more attention from him; she declared herself the injured party in terms of neglect.

In the interview with Mr. Gardner, he complained that his wife neglected his needs, did not give him a chance to relax after work, nagged constantly, and was domineering. His demands on both wife and son seemed perfectionistic, a quality this man was aware of only as a virtue in his executive position. His description of Bob as a boy who bullied or pestered other children provided an opportunity to discuss the forms that demands for attention can take, and how meet-ing needs more adequately can help reduce nagging. In a conjoint session, the parents were able to ventilate enough of their mutual dis-satisfactions to permit some suggestions for compromise aimed at ameliorating the unpleasantness at home. I proposed that mother stop the constant nagging, in return for more attention from her husband. The parents were also asked to agree on a few basic rules of manage-ment regarding Bob's homework and bedtime. Agreement on these proposals did not come easily, but it did materialize and was carried out. At the next family session, two weeks later, the parents reported that things were going better at home and that dinner time was less tension-filled. Mother stated that father was communicating with her, and father was pleased that they did not talk about Bob continually and said the "atmosphere" was better. One could observe at this point a more amicable feeling between husband and wife, and also sense that Bob was pleased with the changes taking place.

I then proposed a deal: mother would reduce her nagging and cut down on her before-dinner drinking; father would try to tune in on what was happening with Bob and stop undermining mother as an authority figure, and Bob would keep his school behavior within bounds. Skepticism was expressed by all family members regarding their ability to live up to such an agreement, but they finally agreed to try. Bob's spontaneous comment was, "We'd all be depending on each other." In an attempt to model a constructive dependency relationship, I asked the Gardners to call me every evening for the first three days to report on how the deal was working out. The family called faithfully, and noted, to their surprise and pleasure, that they were individually and collectively keeping the bargain. This telephone contact tapered off and finally was dropped as the agreement was incorporated into family process. The therapist pointed out to the family that Bob had not had a positive dependency relationship and that this unfulfilled need had mirrored the family's status in its previous lack of constructive interdependence.

Encouraged by the family's progress, Mr. Gardner began to take a more active interest in Bob's school adjustment, permitting mother to back off from her infantilizing role. As the home situation improved and the family gained some confidence in its ability to function in a better way, Bob began to deal with the reality of meeting graduation requirements and the subsequent transition to high school. He became more involved in the external environment, began to look for an after-school job, and worked with his father on a minibike engine. Bob was able to maintain sufficiently acceptable behavior and school work in the next six months and was graduated.

Treatment was terminated at this point; there had been a total of twenty-one sessions. Although many family and individual problems still remained unsolved, the Gardners had benefited by the conjoint family modality sufficiently to make important changes that resulted not only in Bob's staying in school but in the reversal of his drift toward regression and withdrawal.

## DISCUSSION

### Selection of Modality

An important factor in the success or failure of psychotherapy is the choice of treatment approach. Considerations that influenced the choice of modality in the four case illustrations in this chapter are discussed below.

Sally Kent needed more individual therapy experiences in desensitization and developing a close relationship than could be provided in a family therapy setting. None of the four parents involved was so neurotically fixed in his relationship with the girl that the needed change could not be effected by brief, directive counseling; therefore, concurrent treatment was unnecessary.

With Matt Perlman it was felt that continued individual psychotherapy would not improve the school situation because (a) Matt was not able to overcome in his therapy the legalistic, argumentative, and illogical denial of responsibility for misbehavior, (b) the identification of Matt with father's negative model was both strong and resistant to modification, and (c) Mr. Perlman would not make himself available for participation in Matt's treatment. Neither conjoint family therapy nor concurrent treatment was feasible, since father would not become involved. The parent-tutor modality, on the other hand, was less threatening to father, the timing fitted in well with Mr. Perlman's real concern about the threat from school to expel Matt, and the concrete and specific nature of parent-tutor therapy goals was compatible with father's legalistic and precise personality traits. The structure of parent-tutor therapy could force contact between father and son under circumstances that could produce some spontaneity in the father-son relationship and lead to a constructive confrontation.

Concurrent treatment of child and parents was the treatment of choice in the Stuart Smith case because of the combination of the deeply entrenched neurotic problems of Stuart, mother, and father. Individual therapy for the boy could not have succeeded in the face of the mother's intense need to keep the boy as he was, and the father's poor identification model, lack of involvement with the boy, and aura of pessimism. The parent-tutor modality could not have been used with the Smiths as the sole treatment approach; this method could be employed only after much work had been done with both parents. Family-group treatment of the Smiths as the primary modality was not practical in view of the powerful resistance to change and the emotional vulnerability and fragility of both parents.

In the Bob Gardner situation, conjoint family therapy was chosen as the modality for beginning treatment because the complaint was presented in a family context. This approach was maintained throughout the course of therapy for several reasons. Bob's parents, both in their fifties, were not interested in probing themselves beyond the minimum necessary to relate to the family-unit aspects of the school difficulty, and therefore concurrent treatment was not feasible. Individual treatment of this withdrawn, severely disturbed youngster would have been a long process, with doubtful prognosis and much less chance to provide motivation for change in school or life adjustment. Family therapy was able to engage this boy actively in the treatment process at an early state through the frank exploration of the disturbed family relationships. As a result of shifts in parenting, Bob began to receive some of the basic psychological nurturance he had missed in his early development. The changes in the Gardner family gave Bob concrete and fairly dependable reasons for coming back into the environment and modifying his self-destructive school behavior.

While change of modalities in the course of treatment may be appropriate, and though combination of approaches (as in the Stuart Smith case) may be necessary, careful consideration should be given at the *start* of therapy to the family members as individuals as well as the family as a unit in the choice of treatment modality.

## Treatment Content

In reviewing case material, one finds a number of specific events that tend to exacerbate family tensions around school-related issues, for example, homework, the report card, the first day at school, a warning about or an actual suspension for misbehavior, or an unexpected or unpleasant telephone call from school to parent. These events are usually brought into the treatment situation without any effort on the part of the therapist. However, there are some issues that may not intrude so obviously, yet can be of paramount importance. The question of vocational choice, even at the elementary school age, can be creating covert or open family friction.[5] A child or adolescent may resist, through developing a learning or behavior disorder at school, a vocational goal set for him by the parents. Another instance of a "behind the scenes" causal factor in school difficulties is the self-fulfilling prophecy of a family for educational failure that can be generational in time and pervasive in character.

Listed below are some additional key aspects of family-oriented psychotherapy for school problems:

1. The importance of including the father in the diagnostic and treatment process cannot be overstressed. Although some mothers try to convince the therapist that the husband is unavailable, most

fathers can be involved. Further, if father is not involved, prognosis for therapy with a boy is poor.

2. Permission to change for the better, given by parent(s) to a child, is often an important treatment goal.

3. Resistance to change within a family needs careful consideration by the therapist. In rare instances, a school-related problem may be necessary to maintain family homeostasis.[6]

4. A child or adolescent can be chosen as the family scapegoat for parental guilt or failure, and once chosen can find it hard to escape from this assigned role.

5. The school adjustment of siblings can be an important factor in the family's view of a child's school difficulty. Parental expectations of similar achievement from children of widely divergent abilities, sibling rivalry expressed in destructive comparison-competition, and the identification with and imitation of an older child whose school behavior was notoriously disruptive are some illustrations from my case files of the direct negative effects of this factor.

6. It may be necessary to alter the family's overall communication model before changes can be effected in communication about specific school-related issues.

## CONCLUSION

Structured family-oriented psychotherapy is effective in terms of both improved school performance and the transfer of gains to non-school aspects of functioning. It can be adapted to varied points of view in the clinical spectrum, from behavior modification through psychoanalytically based therapy, and can be employed in long-term treatment or in short-term limited-goal therapy. In school situations deemed a crisis, the school-problem structure and the family focus lend themselves well to the immediate handling of issues perceived by the family as directly related to the complaint, and to a therapeutic ambition limited to the level and extent of intervention acceptable to the family at the time.

## REFERENCES

1. Friedman, R.: Structured family-oriented therapy for school behavior and learning disorders. *Child Welfare, 49*, 1970.
2. Friedman, R.: A structured family interview in the assessment of school learning disorders. *Psychology in the Schools, 6*, 1969.
3. Friedman, R.: A rage-reduction diagnostic technique with young children. *Child Psychiatry Hum Dev, 1*, 1970.
4. Friedman, R.: An educational psychologist in a psychiatric clinic. *Children, 14*, 1967.
5. Friedman, R, and Wallace, M.: Vocational choice and life goals. In Buhler, C., and Massarik, F. (Eds.): *The Course of Human Life.* New York, Springer, 1968.
6. Miller, D.R., and Westman, J.C.: Reading disability as a condition of family stability. *Family Process, 3*, 1964.

*Chapter VII*

# THE FAMILY APPROACH TO PSYCHOEDUCATIONAL TREATMENT IN THE PRESCHOOL SETTING

FRANK S. WILLIAMS

Preschool children with learning or psychological disturbances have been generally shortchanged by most existing models for assessment and educational treatment in this country. Some of the pertinent literature, as well as site visits to many centers, suggest that most preschool systems are caught up in unilateral emphases.

At one extreme, there is the utilization of primarily educational and operant-conditioning approaches; and at the other extreme, psychosocial and psychological approaches. It is unfortunate that those who work primarily in psychiatric centers often do not fully utilize educational and behavioral approaches, whereas those who work in primarily educational centers often tend to neglect familial and intrapsychic dynamics.

## THE PSYCHIATRIC MODEL VERSUS THE EDUCATIONAL MODEL

Many preschool psychiatric centers are staffed by professionals with a keen awareness of a child's anxieties; with knowledge of the relationship between those anxieties and the interruption of normal learning and social development; and with appreciation for the reciprocal effects between familial interactions and a child's psychologi-

Some of the programs and clinical studies described in this chapter were, in part, performed at the Julia Ann Singer Preschool Psychiatric Center, Department of Child Psychiatry, Division of Psychiatry, Cedars-Sinai Medical Center, Los Angeles, pursuant to a grant from the U.S. Office of Education, Department of Health, Education, and Welfare. However, the opinions or points of view expressed herein do not necessarily represent official Office of Education position or policy.

cal and cognitive states. Unfortunately, those who function solely within a psychiatric model often neglect and lack basic knowledge and skills in the areas of structured curriculum, language development, perceptual-motor retraining techniques, and behavior modification approaches.

On the other hand, in those centers primarily staffed by educators, one notes a deficit in sufficient appreciation for familial dynamics which perpetuate learning and behavior disorders, as well as a deficit in knowledge regarding the relationships between a child's intrapsychic life, his classroom activities, and his peer relationships. In many centers primarily reflective of an educational model, the stress is upon *academic achievement* as the top-priority objective for helping children attain competence and parental support. Relatively little attention is paid, therein, to the child's potential for intimacy experiences and the development of his empathic relationships with other children, and with adults. Again, by way of contrast, psychiatric centers often stress the child's empathic social reciprocity and human warmth experiences at the expense of neglecting academic achievement and curriculum prescription.

Although varying degrees of behavior modification occur in most treatment modalities, whether in a psychoanalytic approach or an immediate type reward-reinforcement approach, clinicians in psychiatric centers often sacrifice potential gains in their reluctance to explore more structured simple reinforcement techniques. This is particularly shortsighted in cases of severely autistic children. The basic attentiveness essential to the learning process and to communication development may not be attained with these very disturbed psychotic children, in spite of much work with their families, and with individual analytic and anaclitic approaches. Simple positive reinforcement and "timing-out"* techniques often facilitate that basic attentiveness necessary for further development in such disturbed youngsters. Again, noting extremes, I have seen certain centers so devoted to a strict operant-conditioning approach that familial factors perpetuating and reinforcing behavior were totally neglected. Here the emphasis is primarily upon working with children in operant condition-

---

*"timing-out" is a behavior modification technique in which the teacher or therapist turns away from and ignores the child, immediately following unwanted behavior on the part of the child.

ing, reward situations without sufficient attention to the training of their parents to do the same.

At the Julia Ann Singer Preschool Psychiatric Center—the primary prevention arm of the Cedars-Sinai Department of Child Psychiatry—an attempt is made, within a family-centered model, to provide children with a combined approach attending to psychological and educational needs. Within the three major areas of direct parent involvement—family demonstration therapies, parent education groups, and parent participation as "staff-partners" in the classroom—observation, demonstration, and discussion concentrate on strengthening both the child's educational and psychological capacities, as well as helping parents to interrupt their own interactions which perpetuate faulty cognitive and psychological development.

## DIRECT FAMILY INVOLVEMENT—RATIONALE AND EXAMPLES

Family approaches with children who have been unrewarding (educationally and socially) can provide the parents with an opportunity to experience success, thereby reducing their chronic sense of helplessness. Training parents in operant-conditioning approaches alone often falls short of desired goals when the "behavior modifier" does not have an awareness of, and does not utilize confrontation regarding *familial dynamics* which perpetuate behavioral symptoms. I recently observed an example of the effects of long-term operant conditioning with a seven-year-old autistic girl, which had begun when she was five. The objective of the training was to rid her of her crippling oppositional behavior, both at home and in the classroom. Her teachers worked with her, using candy and a great deal of warmth and praise as rewards for cooperation, and "timing-out" for rebellious, defiant behavior. While sitting with the girl's mother and grandmother behind the one-way mirror, I noted that they were both extremely aware of and in tune with the teacher's operant-conditioning techniques. It was of further striking note, however, that mother and grandmother consistently commented with "How cute!" each time the girl engaged in rebellious activity, such as throwing the ball in a direction opposite to the group's explicit playing area. Had this particular staff had more training in family-interviewing techniques, and the concomitant understanding of familial "cueing" mechanisms, it would have spotted and dealt with this family's tendency to cue rebellious behavior. Instead, one could surmise in this case that the familial cueing must have been going on at home, but without the advantage of a one-way mirror to block out the subtle but definitive reinforcement of this child's oppositional behavior.

Psychosocial approaches, whether eclectic or psychoanalytically oriented, have often dismissed the value of behavior modification techniques, perceptual-motor retraining approaches, language stimulation, and systematic curriculum prescription. Social learning, corrective emotional experiences, and the human warmth approach, all need to be sufficiently developed in a child at the same time one helps him master motor coordination problems and visual-motor deficits.

## A Combined Approach

The case of Billy, a four-year-old seen with his family at the Julia Ann Singer Preschool Psychiatric Center, offers an example of an approach which combines educational and psychological models, as well as an illustration of the many ways in which parents can be actively and directly involved in the total treatment approach in a preschool setting. Billy initially appeared as a child with atypical development, some mild neurological deficit, and definitive autistic features. He was extremely hyperactive, had limited eye contact, was not toilet trained, had a five-word vocabulary, and continually engaged in head-banging, rocking, and routinized twirling of objects. During the nine months that Billy and his family were involved at the Center, Billy attended the *therapeutic nursery school* in which his mother functioned as a teacher's aid, initially—and later as a "staff partner." A *staff partner* functions as both a teacher and a trainer of other parents. Major emphases in the classroom, for Billy, were limit-setting and techniques for increasing eye contact and attention span. The mother was also involved in observing an educational therapist utilizing *perceptual-motor retraining* techniques with Billy. This involved helping him with his poor eye-hand coordination; drawing lines from one picture on a page to another; and the putting together of simple puzzles. A *behavior modification* approach was utilized to help reinforce his successes in the perceptual-motor retraining activities. Billy's mother learned to warmly praise his successes and ignore his failures. She eventually took over Billy's perceptual-motor retraining, and has remained at the Center as one of our key trainers of other parents, volunteers, and paraprofessionals. Billy's mother and father also participated in a three-month *family demonstration therapy*. In these weekly sessions, mother and father observed the therapist communicating with Billy around feelings of anxiety, sadness, frustration, and anger. They learned that their child could communicate feelings in spite of his limited vocabulary. They further learned, via observation and participation, how to elicit more meaningful and increased language production from Billy. During the family demonstration therapy, there was an opportunity for the parents to observe physical restraint and limit-setting, geared toward modifying the child's hyperactive behavior. At night, mother and father participated in a *parent-education group*. The emphasis in this group was upon child growth and development. In the parent-education group, Billy's parents learned to recognize when his behavior was appropriate to his age and when it was not. They further learned when it would be appropriate to make demands of him, and when demands would produce frustration and regression. When Billy was ready to leave our Center, he was talking like a magpie, expressing anger directly, was toilet trained, and ready for a regular nursery school in the community. Both of Billy's parents have continued to be active *parent alumni* at Julia Ann Singer. His mother, in addition to teaching other parents and paraprofessionals perceptual-motor retraining techniques, also serves as a co-therapist for one of our parent-education groups. Like many of our parents, she represents the Agency at professional conferences related to children with emotional or learning disabilities. Billy's mother reflected upon the value of active and meaningful parental involvement, one day, when she said: "They made us feel that we were capable, that if we wanted to do something, we could. We once thought Billy was superhyperactive. My family used to say it was all right, that he was all boy and all that, but I knew something was wrong when we brought him to Julia Ann Singer because he was four years old; he couldn't talk; he couldn't sleep; and he wasn't even potty trained. We really know Billy now, and know how to help him."

When parents are not directly involved in assessment and in corrective efforts to change perpetuating forces, I feel they remain dependent, helpless, and guilty. The unspoken message they receive from the professional staff often implies, "You are the 'heavies' who

have crippled your child! Stay away! Don't *sabotage* the treatment!"
The case of Billy dramatically presents the value of parents as therapeutic agents. Direct family involvement in preschool programs offers
a broader diagnostic field, as well as an opportunity to enlist parents,
siblings, and grandparents in the implementation of those corrective
approaches which bridge the gap between educational and psychological models. Family members, when seen together with an educationally or emotionally handicapped preschool child, usually display interactions and attitudes which foster nonlearning, noncommunication,
and impedence to cognitive and psychosocial growth. Interactions and
attitudes which perpetuate deviant or delayed development can be
noted and presented to the family in constructive ways—as points of
challenge to the family, in their efforts to help one of its members.
The utilization of playback video tapes offers an excellent nonthreatening tool in sharing with parents areas for desired change. As an example, during a series of *home visits* with a family, the video camera
could record a situation in which a mother and father laugh aloud or
smile broadly each time their hyperactive, rebellious three-year-old
boy disrupts a game or academic lesson with the teacher. We can then
show the parents that segment of the tape, asking them to observe the
timing of their smiling, as well as the glance from their child indicating his perception of their nonverbal cues which point toward the per-
petuation of his rebelliousness. It can then become an implied or
explicit family task in subsequent interviews with the teacher or therapist and family to avoid such cueing. When such an approach is carried out in an atmosphere of respect for rather than condemnation of
the parents, one notes an enthusiastic parental and staff vitality, in
which progress and therapeutic comradeship, rather than guilt and
defensiveness, prevail.

Unfortunately, the more traditional child guidance model, in which
the child is seen by a psychiatrist or educational therapist, and the
parents are seen separately by a psychiatric social worker, does not
foster such therapeutic alliances. In many ways it fosters, instead, a
sense of guilt, overattention to the parents' psychological problems,
and feelings of failure and impotence in relation to their child. Involving parents directly in family-interviewing approaches offers an
immediate opportunity for the parents to correct pathogenic inter-

actions, thus validating their own capacities to change and become effective.

## FAMILY THERAPY INTERVENTION IN COMMUNICATION DISORDERS OF PRESCHOOLERS

Much of the pioneer work in family communications systems has been related to very disturbed young adults and adolescents. Ambiguities, double-bind communication patterns, and other transactional distortions have been described as triggering and perpetuating schizophrenic thinking and psychotic behavior in young adults or older adolescents.[5, 6, 8] In our family studies at the Cedars-Sinai Department of Child Psychiatry during the past nine years, my colleagues and I have tried to learn about family dynamics and communications development involving very young preschoolers.[9] In our empirical explorations, we have observed, and attempted to alter, familial forces which can perpetuate symptoms such as elective mutism, hyperactive inattentiveness, autistic withdrawal, omnipotent oppositional and aggressive behavior, and other distortions of normal cognitive and psychosocial development.

In a family-demonstration therapy session, the therapist can observe such familial forces, point them out, offer corrective alternatives, and then encourage the parents to institute those corrective alternatives. For example, when an electively mute child is asked a question by the therapist, and one of the parents quickly responds with "Don't be silly! She won't talk! She never talks to strangers!", this cueing mechanism can first be pointed out by the therapist. He may then suggest ways by which the parents can actively encourage trust for adults outside the family. As a hyperactive child runs from one parent to another during a family-demonstration therapy session, bombarding them with activities, toys, and words, the therapist often notes how the parents, in their desperate attempts to help, often speak at the same time; contradict each other, and give a multitude of directions, compromises, and alternatives to the child. The therapist is in a position to demonstrate calming physical holding, as well as methods of presenting simple, clear directions, instructions, and encouraging suggestions to the child. In such family demonstration meetings, parents have an opportunity to observe, for example, how the therapist or teacher actively and intrusively stimulates an autistically withdrawn child to make eye contact and produce language, without either physically hurting the child or suppressing the child's autonomy. Parents who have been frustrated by the withdrawn, noncommunicative state of their autistic child are often surprised how easy it is to elicit eye contact and some minimal verbalization with simple tickling, arm-holding, and face-holding techniques. When a controlling oppositional child aggressively controls and directs his parents to give him all he wants, when he wants it, without the frustration of delay, the therapist can point out how the parents' acquiescence to such demands reinforces the child's social inappropriateness. The therapist can demonstrate ways of encouraging social reciprocity, meaningful language, and other signs of human contact in the child, in relation to meeting his needs and wishes. The parents can further be encouraged to try out similar patterns of corrective interaction with the child, in an attempt to foster their own feelings of strength and capability.

I should like to stress the value of such active involvement of parents in the ongoing education and therapy of their children. Although child guidance clinics and special schools for emotionally disturbed children have long encouraged involvement of parents in therapeutic ways, it is only recently that schools like the Julia Ann Singer Center have moved in the direction of enlisting parents as "allies," compared with the more traditional model which had involved parents primarily as dependent receivers of help. A training program for the parents of very young mentally ill children has been described by Doernberg *et al.*[4] in relation to some work at the League School for Seriously Disturbed Children, in Brooklyn. At the League School, the approach to parents is related to the problems of daily living and reflects a staff conviction regarding the competence of parents to affect their child positively. This emphasis is similar to the one at the Julia Ann Singer Center in that it encourages a cooperative endeavor between parents and professionals "building on the strengths and health of the parents in effecting growth and positive change in the behavior of their mentally ill child."[4]

### Disordered Parent-Infant Communication Patterns

Many professionals (teachers and clinicians alike) and parents are simply not aware of the degree and range of both receptive and expressive communication capacities for modeling available to and present in very young children. Tasem, Augenbraun, and Brown[9] have described family interviewing techniques which reveal and attend to potentially pathogenic verbal and nonverbal communication patterns between parents and their very young preschool children.

A case in point from my own clinical experience is that of a *nine-month-old* infant boy brought by his young parents for evaluation of his persistent head-banging. It was of note that little Joey's head-banging occurred most often when his parents were involved with others, or each other. His mother and father felt that his self-destructive behavior was aimless and without goal direction. After the half-hour point in a family meeting, I suggested to them that Joey's head-banging seemed to be his way of telling them of his wish for noninterrupted parental attention, as well as his direct attempt to interrupt their involvement with each other and with me. They reluctantly and skeptically accepted my hypothesis, but broke out in laughter when I further suggested that they talk with Joey about it. They reminded me that their boy was only nine months old and could not comprehend any language, let alone any type of verbal prohibition. As Joey began to next bang his head on the floor, I turned to him, shook my finger, and with a firm and somewhat stern voice, said, "Now Joey, stop that! It's silly to bang your head because mommy and daddy are not talking or playing with you! Now, just play for a while and don't hurt your head!" Joey stared at me, looked surprised—but not puzzled—and suddenly sat up and occupied himself with some play objects. About five minutes later, as the parents and I were engaged in an intense discussion about what had happened, Joey put his head down next to the floor, while looking at me out of the corner of one eye. I merely raised my finger and said, "Joey, remember what I said!" whereupon Joey again sat up. In response to Joey's subsequent third challenge, I simply raised my finger; he did not follow through with his usual pattern of head-banging. One year later, Joey's parents reported that from that day, he never again indulged in head-banging.

In evaluating what had occurred, I do not feel that the winning of a power struggle was the primary factor which helped Joey and his parents avert the consequences of a dangerous symptom. Rather, I believe that the significant corrective force had to do with the parents genuinely learning about their child's capacity to relate to them, as well as their own capacity to relate to him with meaningful communication. Such opportunities to effectively demonstrate communication patterns are readily available in parent-teacher conferences, as well as in therapy guidance sessions, provided the interview includes both parents together with their child. In more traditional parent counseling, the professional thinks he is offering sound advice when frequently he is merely presenting only partly perceived recipes. This is in spite of the parents' nodding their heads and verbally agreeing during the presentation of such advice.

### Elective Mutism—A Symptom of Faulty Intrafamilial Communication

Children with varying degrees of elective mutism frustrate many teachers, in that they often completely "shut out" the adult, no matter how warm or friendly the teacher might be. In cases of very young children with elective mutism, I believe that analytic interpretive approaches which deal with psychodynamics, like mother-child autonomy—"anal"—struggles, generally fail when used as isolated techniques. Similarly, I believe operant-conditioning techniques, when used alone, are also doomed to fail. Either technique, or both, however, can be enhanced in the direction of success with the use of concomitant *family interviews*, which attend to those parental and sibling communications which reinforce and encourage the mutism.

A five-and-one-half-year-old girl, Susie, who had not spoken a word outside of her home for two and one-half years was seen with her mother, father, and three-year-old sister, Tammie. Susie was mute, only communicating with an occasional head nod or shoulder shrug. Tammie and mother had a pattern of automatically answering all questions directed toward Susie. In spite of the therapist's suggestion that they give Susie time to answer, little Tammie continued to jump in, in an apparent effort to display her own brightness and cooperative spirit. Neither mother nor father discouraged Tammie from this verbal taking-over. After Tammie left the room, the therapist asked Susie about her kindergarten teacher, who had referred her to the Clinic. Father quickly said, "I don't think she'll say anything!" After three family sessions in which the parents were repeatedly confronted with their unwitting methods of blocking Susie's verbal and social interactions with others, Susie spoke for the first time. Her sudden speech came after mother openly talked about her ambivalent feelings concerning her attachment to Susie. She told how, in spite of her wish to "get away" from Susie, she feared "dying" should the girl make a relationship with her kindergarten teacher or any other adult outside the family. The open expression of these feelings, which till then had been underground but potent, seemed to relieve the family's anxieties about saying "dangerous" things. What followed was a release of verbal expression and affect in all areas of communication. We have seen, in our Clinic, other similar dramatic results with brief family-interviewing approaches involving children with elective mutism, after just a few sessions of such observation and confrontation.

**Familial Communication and the Development of Autism**

Family-interviewing techniques are most useful in assessing and altering these familial communication distortions which foster autistic disturbances in preschool children. One can observe directly certain pathogenic parent-child communication patterns which confuse and overwhelm a young child, thus encouraging a retreat toward autistic isolation. For example, in a family session with Jerry, a four-year-old autistic child, mother says to him, "Good-bye, you can go now, it is time to leave the room," while she holds him close against her body and sheds tears. In a family interview, the therapist or teacher can confront her with this contradictory communication pattern, and encourage, with demonstration if necessary, an alternate, less confusing approach. The author has described elsewhere similar double-bind communication styles, as seen with mothers and their very young autistic children.[11] An example would be one in which a mother verbally says, "I love you," but physically and emotionally withdraws from her child. I should like, here, to note that the "double-bind" does not necessarily reflect *etiology* in cases of autism. The mother's ambivalence may be a secondary response of frustration to the autistic state in her child, and may be unrelated to the original etiologic factors.

With psychotic preschool children, family techniques can greatly enhance and complement those gains being made in the cognitive and social sphere in the therapeutic nursery school. By watching the teacher or therapist with their child, the parents can learn to relate to their youngster in ways which appropriately interrupt inordinate, omnipotent demands. The parents can learn—by observation and by quickly trying out what they see effectively working—how to insist upon word language and eye contact in return for gratifying their child's desires. A case is described by Williams[10] in which a three-year-old atypical child gained the use of meaningful language after several family meetings. During the first three family meetings, the boy persisted in climbing all over his parents, getting his way without the use of language. Whenever he attempted to get by the therapist's foot, the therapist insisted, "You must first say *move!*" The parents would laugh each time the therapist made this request of their mute child, insisting that he was not able to speak and that the therapist was wasting his time. In the fourth session, again following the therapist's firm insistence upon the use of language while the child was pushing and tugging at his knee, the boy loudly and clearly said, "Move!" This experience opened a new vista for the parents regarding their child's capacity to speak and their potential for helping him. The family therapy modality in this case offered not only important diagnostic data, but also permitted, in time, parental reinforcement of gains. Such reinforcement is less available in individual analytic, intensive anaclitic, or one-to-one operant-conditioning approaches, where the parents are not directly present. In studying autistic children with their families, we have been very impressed by the input of their fathers and siblings in fostering the omnipotent withdrawal, control, and isolation. Family interviews provide a vehicle for enlisting fathers and siblings as active allies in the total treatment approach to such very disturbed children.

## CONCLUSION

There is in our country today, particularly in education, a growing movement in the direction of keeping handicapped children, including those with severe emotional problems, within regular community settings, and outside of segregated special classes, special hospitals, and other special therapeutic institutions. One objective related to this movement aims toward maximizing modeling of behavior after healthier peers. Tied to this movement is a push toward maximum parent participation in preschool programs in an effort to strengthen parents' capacities to help their handicapped youngsters at home.*

I believe that direct family-intervention methods used with psychological problems and learning disorders of preschool children offer

*Handicapped Children's Early Education Act P.L. 90-538, Bureau of Education for the Handicapped, U.S. Office of Education.

some of the best modalities by which to insure a troubled youngster's maintenance in a regular community nursery school or day care center. It is most important that the teacher and therapist work together with the parents and the child, thus fostering a climate of mutual trust between school staff and parents. Traditionally, when parents were sent off to the social worker for a separate "therapy," mistrust and mutual anxieties often developed between teacher or therapist and parent. The teacher or therapist would often feel that the parents were "sabotaging" therapeutic gains at home; the parents would often resist the teacher or therapist who underlined their feelings of guilt and helplessness by succeeding where they had failed. Family approaches tend to avert such mutual suspicions and pulling-in-opposite-directions by the nature of the working-together atmosphere, which includes teacher, therapist, and parent. Such approaches, which increase parental strength and foster cooperation between parents and professional staff, have been described in pioneer programs with disturbed preschoolers at the Julia Ann Singer Early Prevention Unit of the Department of Child Psychiatry, Cedars-Sinai Medical Center.[12] Glimpses of potential successes with troubled preschool children by the family approach are not surprising. The child develops and feels most secure within his own family, no matter how psychopathogenic that family structure may be.

The teacher in a preschool setting can offer great stimulus toward growth in a child with restricted ego, cognitive, or perceptual-motor development. However, that stimulus needs maximum reinforcement, once the child leaves school each day. The effective working together of parents, therapist, and teacher allows for such reinforcement, as well as reciprocal growth and understanding in the child, in the parent, and in the teacher-therapist.

## REFERENCES

1. Bangs, Tina E.: *Language and Learning Disorders of the Preacademic Child: with Curriculum Guide.* New York, Appleton-Century-Crofts, 1968.

2. Bowen, M.: A family concept of schizophrenia. In Jackson, D.D. (Ed.): *The Etiology of Schizophrenia.* New York, Basic Books, 1960.

3. Brown, S.L.: Family therapy viewed in terms of resistance to change. American Psychiatric Association, *Psychiatric Research Report No. 20,* 1966.

4. Doernberg, N.; Rosen, B, and Walker, T.: A home training program for young mentally ill children. League School for Seriously Disturbed Children, Brooklyn, New York.
5. Haley, J.: *Strategies of Psychotherapy*. New York, Grune & Stratton, 1963.
6. Jackson, D.D.: The question of family homeostasis. *Psychiatr Q Suppl 31*, 1957.
7. Furman, R., and Katan, A.: *The Therapeutic Nursery School*. New York, International Universities Press, 1969.
8. Ruesch, J., and Bateson, G.: *Communication: The Social Matrix of Psychiatry*. New York, Norton, 1951.
9. Tasem, M.; Augenbraun, B, and Brown, S.L.: Family group interviewing with the preschool child and both parents. *J Am Acad Child Psychiatry, 4,* 1965.
10. Williams, F.S.: Family therapy with a severely atypical child. Paper presented at Regional American Association of Psychiatric Clinics for Children, Los Angeles, California, 1964.
11. Williams, F.S.: Family therapy. In Marmor, J. (Ed.): *Modern Psychoanalysis: New Directions and Perspectives*. New York, Basic Books, 1968.
12. Williams, F.S., and Jones, E.F.: The effectiveness of community mental health treatment and prevention programs for children—a critical issue for the 70's. Paper presented at the Annual Meeting of the American Orthopsychiatric Association, Washington, D.C., March 1971.

# Chapter VIII

# THE FAMILY APPROACH TO
# SCHOOL PROBLEMS IN AN AGENCY SETTING

### HARRY PANNOR

An INCREASING number of children with school problems are being seen today in social agencies. The situation appears overwhelming when one considers the large number of underachievers, failures, and school dropouts in need of help. In addition, the traditional methods of dealing with these children may not always be the most helpful, and a great need exists for agencies to be both flexible and innovative in selecting appropriate strategies when working with school difficulties. Social work literature currently reflects the pressures of school problems and describes attempts to alleviate them. For example, Walton[13] speaks about "crisis team intervention in school community unrest" situations; Mishne[7] describes group therapy for children with learning and behavior problems in elementary schools. Wadsworth[12] discusses social conditioning casework in a school setting, and Springer[11] emphasizes the importance of working in the area of parent-child relations in the early school years.

## AGENCY PRACTICE AND NEEDED CHANGE
### Intake Procedures

When an agency has reached out and developed a mutually trusting relationship with the school, why not attempt different methods of intake? In many instances, the traditional agency approach of requiring the parents to initiate service, meet the agency's eligibility requirements, and often live with the anxiety of a waiting period before they can be seen, may only be useful to highly motivated parents. If a child is in trouble at school and the teacher wishes to make a referral to an agency, why could not the teacher, with the parents' permission, invite a member of that agency's staff to the school to meet with her and the parents? The purpose of such a conference would be to discuss further the child's problem, hear what the agency has to offer in the way of help, and where indicated, facilitate an ongoing treatment program that has the support and backing of teacher, parents, and agency. Some pitfalls are avoided by beginning in this manner, such as the parents', teachers', and workers' projection of responsibility for the problem on each other. The fact that everyone gets to meet each other may, in many instances, be constructively innovative in itself. This team approach can initiate interest in cooperation between the agency and the school. Along these lines, it has been the author's experience that it is extremely helpful, when indicated, to invite a teacher to participate in a family interview at the agency. This experience can have value to the teacher, who may begin to conduct her "parent conferences" with a more family-centered approach. Although it is encouraging to see more interest and discussion in the area of school problems currently going on in regard to new approaches, there seems to be a great lag in putting some of these ideas into current practice.

## The Agency Role in School Problems

Since school is such a vital part of our culture, it is incumbent upon agencies to give more direct attention to problems that children have in school. Some therapists often assume that school problems will in effect take care of themselves if other treatment areas are dealt with satisfactorily. Often, school principals become impatient when children with serious behavior problems are referred to an agency and do not get treatment that is focused on the problem the child is having in school. It seems to me that the problems stated by these principals can be dealt with more effectively if agencies recognize that treatment of school problems by them involves not only the child and his family but other personnel and resources. Working with youngsters who have difficulty in school may entail contacts with school personnel, clarification of past testing, the need for new or additional educational or psychological testing, the possibility of tutoring (and its availability), contacts with vocational service, etc. It must be stressed that in order to have the necessary close working relationships with school personnel, agencies need to acquaint themselves with the enormously complex and changing school structure. How this can be achieved most effectively is a challenging question. Perhaps what might be useful are specially designed institutes where school and agency personnel can learn about each other. Periodic face-to-face contact, telephone contacts, and the sharing of reports which alert school and agency to shifts or changes that are occurring with the child are useful in maintaining good communication between school and agency. It is understandable that most parents with children who present problems at school would find it difficult and confusing to negotiate their way through today's school system. Thus, it seems crucial that agencies help parents become knowledgeable in how to mobilize whatever resources are available to help their children.

This chapter will describe what one social agency does in response to a child with school difficulties. Emphasis will be placed on ways of helping these children through the modality of family and peer interviewing. The author is Casework Director of Jewish Big Brothers Association in Los Angeles, California, a community supported private agency. Through its Parent-Child Guidance Service, Volunteer Big Brother Service, and a therapeutic camp program, the agency offers a wide range of services to boys and their families. The responsibility for treatment is carried by a staff of professionally educated social workers who, to a large degree, function independently. The agency provides an environment conducive to family-oriented treatment. Intake is decentralized so that each worker is responsible for a family case from intake to closing. This procedure offers continuity and cohesion to both worker and client, and it minimizes the confusion and distortion often inherent in splitting cases and services.

Over the years, the agency has found that problems in school top the list of reasons for which families come for help. In fact, for school-age children, almost all other presenting problems are generally found to affect the child's school performance. It is rare, for example, to find delinquent youngsters referred by the courts who are not having school problems. Because children spend a large portion of their waking hours in school, it is understandable how vital the need for alleviation of these difficulties is for them.

Since there is a somewhat authoritarian nature to referrals made by the school, many parents come to agencies with resistance, defensiveness, and a degree of suspicion. This can lead to very intense ambivalence about getting involved in treatment; therefore, agencies need to deal with these families promptly by organizing themselves to render immediate service. Red tape should be cut to a minimum, intake procedures need to be streamlined, and channels of communication with school personnel, as indicated previously, must be available and utilized.

## Need for Immediate Service

The need for immediate service is underscored by the fact that a learning problem may become entrenched and the student may therefore fall further behind academically. Continued failure in school can lead to the emergence of new problems. This in turn can affect family equilibrium, thus creating a circular pattern of cause and effect, which may be very difficult to disengage. A child with academic problems of long duration can be discouraging to the family as well as to the social worker.

In this kind of situation the child may well be on his way to developing entrenched mechanisms of dealing with stress, which result in faulty study patterns, poor concentration ability, and an inability to organize himself adequately for learning. Families at this point can often respond well to conjoint family therapy.

## The Social Worker's Personal Involvement

To illustrate the potential value of the worker's personal involvement as well as the impact of school problems, let me cite the example of Mr. and Mrs. J:

Mr. and Mrs. J were referred by the school because their eleven-year-old son in the sixth grade was failing most of his subjects. When the parents called requesting help they were told that both of them would be required to come in for the intake interview and that a worker would be contacting them for an appointment.

In evaluating their request for service, the worker responsible for the case telephoned the parents and requested that their son come with them for the intake interview. When the worker began the session by asking what it felt like to be here, Mrs. J responded by saying that they had been negligent by not seeking help sooner. She went on to say she had noticed problems with her son since he was in the first grade. Although this had been brought to their attention, mother remarked that she felt that John was slow and therefore doing the best he could. Mother said she felt hopeless and wondered if perhaps it wouldn't be a good idea to retain John this semester. Worker remarked that he could hear Mrs. J's hopelessness and then turned to Mr. J and wondered what he thought about his wife's remarks. Mr. J, in a somewhat passive, detached manner, calmly remarked that his son was not "too sharp," and that perhaps the boy ought to be thinking about an apprentice-type job. He recalled that this is what he had done while attending high school in a small town where he had lived and as a result had became a very skilled toolmaker. The worker at this point wondered whether Mr. J had ever shared these feelings with his son, and he replied that he had not. Worker asked if he could do this now. Mr. J tried to look at his son but it was apparent that this was difficult to do, as both seemed anxious and uncomfortable. Mr. J began by saying, "I always felt that John wasn't cut out for academic——," at which point the worker interrupted and gently stated, "Talk to John, not about him." Mr. J went on, "John, I——," and at that moment John began to cry. Father became uncomfortable and remarked that John had nothing to cry about. Worker commented that it was all right for all of us to cry, although some people may think it isn't manly. After a minute or so John dried his tears and father went on talking to his son, indicating that perhaps he was best cut out for a trade, since he knew how difficult it was for him to be struggling in school. Mother nodded her head in agreement. Worker turned to John and wondered what he was feeling. To the parents' surprise John remarked that he felt he was dumb and was ashamed of himself. He said that he could not do the work in class, but he had never said anything about it in school. Continuing, he remarked that he had always felt this way and he just couldn't make it, as he always fell behind and therefore found it difficult to ask questions in class.

As the interview continued, the parents began communicating more with each other and listening to John. At this point, father wondered whether the worker had experienced any school problems in his own growing up, to which the worker responded by sharing episodes from his own early school background which tended to show that it was difficult for him to decide on his own vocational goals. These goals were not really crystallized for the worker until he returned from service in the Army. As the hour drew to a close, the family had begun to focus on exploring possibilities for John's education.

For six years this family accepted the labeling of John as almost a failure in his functioning in all phases of life. Having labeled him in a certain manner, they responded accordingly, had minimal expectations of him, did not take him seriously, and generally dismissed his thoughts and feelings. The above-described family interview mobilized the parents to request a meeting with the school, to give consideration to tutoring for John, and to continue in ongoing treatment with the agency.

The willingness of the worker to share some of his past is important in family interviewing because it indicates that the worker is human and not omnipotent as many clients believe their therapists to be. When the therapist is able to comfortably share something of his past, the family members are often free to recognize that their own abilities and ways of coping can have value. This often helps to mobilize self-esteem in clients who have felt that their ways of functioning were inadequate and inferior.

## WORKING WITH THE ADOLESCENT AND HIS FRIEND
### Peer Pressures

In working with families where their presenting problem is school functioning, it is significant to note what the impact of peer pressure is on the child, particularly on teen-agers. To hear parents say, "He [or she] is running around with the wrong crowd and he pays no attention to his homework" is quite common. To place responsibility for problems outside the family and away from the child is not un-usual, particularly if there is a great deal of family stress. To some extent, blaming others is anticipated as part of the adolescent-parent emancipation struggle. However, the struggle often becomes over-whelming to parents or child, and one sometimes witnesses an extreme overreaction by the parents, in which the brunt of their anger and frustration is placed on the child and his peer group.

Brantley[2], in discussing the importance of peers stated, "For some teen-agers, group associations, even when not sanctioned by adults, serve as an important source of support."

In writing about drug use among the young, as teen-agers see it, Elizabeth Herzok[5] reported:

> The importance teen-agers attach to peer groups is evident in these reports, especially in the strong emphasis put on status and confor-mity as reasons for drug use, and on peer influence and lack of peer pressure as reasons for nonuse. The general assumption seems to be that if either family or the peer group exercises a very strong force, it can prevail over the other.

In today's world, where values and institutions are being challenged, the school also is under serious attack; school philosophy, programs, methods, and techniques are being questioned. One frequently hears,

"School is irrelevant." Such questioning must have an effect on the student who is having difficulties in school. For this student the attitude of his peer group as well as his immediate family can affect efforts to help him.

## Family and Peer-Group Interviewing

The Marcus case illustrates the use of different modalities; that is, the value of family interviewing as well as a peer-group interview in dealing with the family's concern around school difficulties.

In the family interview Mr. and Mrs. Marcus, their seventeen-year-old son, Joseph, and two younger siblings were present. What immediately evolved was a somewhat intellectual discussion about the way Joe's school was being run. Parents, both of whom are college graduates, were very critical of the teachers. They said classes were dull and uninteresting and based their view of the problem on the thesis that most of the school subjects their son was taking were not relevant to current times. In the interaction that followed, the parents often disagreed on specific issues, the younger children seemed to tune out most of the discussion, and Joseph agreed with their remarks, commenting that his friends felt the same way that he did. When worker wondered what the parents felt could be done about it, mother remarked, "Not very much, the way things are at school." The father wondered about private schools. However, they concluded they could not afford a private school. They also didn't know whether Joseph would be accepted because he was doing so poorly at school. When worker asked how Joseph felt about the three classes he was failing he at first tended to deny any negative reactions. Generally he felt that he was a bright person (his parents agreed), and that if things were different he could do very well. However, he went on to say that although he understood all this, when he got his grades he had a feeling of shame and felt bad all day, not wanting to talk to anyone.

As the interview progressed, parents moved from their attack on the school system and on differing with each other to directing their anger at Joseph's friends. Although they appeared sympathetic to the problems of youth and their disenchantment with the Establishment, they seemed overly distressed at the fact that several of the son's friends were "school dropouts." In the interaction that followed, which was quite heated, Joe defended his friends, called his parents hypercritical, and complained that they did not really understand him, although in the past he had thought they did.

In this family interview the parents began to realize the lack of understanding they had about their son. This was a surprise to them in that they had assumed they were "tuning in" accurately to what was going on and thus felt they were supportive and understanding. In their intellectual approach to the school problem, which stemmed in part from their own disappointments with their own achievements and from beliefs they held, they assumed that an intellectual interpretation of the problem would satisfy their son. In not really "tuning in" to Joseph's feelings of inadequacy and his beginning feelings of failure, they failed to help him find alternative channels for the energies he had previously tried to expend in school. Joseph had rather quickly moved from falling behind in his work, to where, for all practical purposes, he had completely "given up on school." As a result, he abandoned previous good study habits and shifted his energies to peer-group activities which gave him emotional support but failed to help him find a direction for himself.

The social worker was seeing Joseph individually, in addition to the family sessions. For one of the individual sessions, Joe arrived with two friends and wondered if they could sit in on the interview. The worker agreed and soon the discussion focused on school: (One of the peer group had dropped out of school in the tenth grade and was currently attending continuation school one-half day a week. The other friend had returned from a correctional setting where he had spent nine months for car theft and was only recently back in the public school setting.) As Joseph began a criticism of his teachers and school in general, he was somewhat surprised that his friends did not appear to be as supportive as he thought they would be. The boy who was currently in continuation school, for example, remarked that after a semester of this he had been unable to find a satisfying job and although he has fun going out with the guys, he is hard-pressed for money. Apparently being out of school had thrust him into the adult labor market and the pressures and responsibilities for coping were more difficult than he had anticipated. School looked good to him at this point.

As the friend who was in continuation school commented that he planned to go back to a regular school next semester, Joseph looked downcast. The boy who had returned from the correctional school felt that he was so far behind that he didn't know whether he would be able to make it at school. His talk about leaving the community, without any specific plans, seemed to be upsetting to Joseph. For a while Joseph became excited about the possibility of getting an apartment. However, neither of them seemed to be able to figure out how they would be able to support such a plan since they knew their parents would not support them and jobs were hard to come by. When the hour ended it seemed that Joe was somewhat moody. His friends seemed at ease during the interview.

The interview with his friends had an impact on Joe. It became a turning point for him. He became more anxious about what was happening to him, and although he had failed three of his five subjects that semester, he resolved to graduate from high school and find a college where the school philosophy and atmosphere were more in tune with his thinking. Joe did graduate from high school, and following a summer of traveling around the United States, was accepted in a small college.

In reporting his ideas about peers as therapeutic agents, Bernard Guerney, Jr.[4] commented:

> It seems clear that the question the reader should ask himself is not whether it is appropriate to encourage peers to influence the behavior of others, since this is obviously occurring anyway, but whether ways can be found to structure the interpersonal environment so that this influence is beneficial rather than detrimental to the group and the individuals comprising it.

## Working with Significant Peers—Buddies, Girlfriends

The impact of peer-group influence where the members are known to one another is often not given enough recognition by agencies when working with school problems, particularly those of adolescents. In group therapy, the peer groups are usually composed of youngsters who do not know each other. Working with a teen-ager and his immediate circle of friends, on the other hand, can be both meaningful to the youngster and beneficial to his peers.

For the past fifteen years the author has been aware that teen-agers who come for interviews often bring friends with them to the agency. In the past, the agency's philosophy has been to have the friend remain in the waiting room. The teen-ager in the waiting room would often be a girlfriend, a close buddy, or a small group of two to four friends. In observing these youngsters in the waiting room, it generally was reported that they appeared anxious and fidgety, as if they had something they wished to contribute to their friend's counseling session. On the other hand, the youngster having the session would very often talk about his friends in the waiting room. Periodically, some adolescent client would ask his worker if his friend could sit in on the session with them. In observing and studying this phenomenon, staff members wondered if this indicated resistance on the teen-ager's part to "looking at himself," an attempt to get needed help for a friend or other possible motivations. This issue was decided five years ago with the consensus that in most situations adolescents who bring a friend had a legitimate need to do so. The adolescent may be saying to the worker, "I need my friend to be with me to have support," "I need to find out if I'm all right," "I need an ally," "My friend could help me clarify things for myself," "I need to give you a better picture of my friends," or "I want you to see the kind of problem I am having with peers so you can help me in this area." As a result of these observations we now accept the adolescent's request for friends to sit in during the interview. In situations where the adolescent does not request this, the worker will ask the hesitant youngster if he would like to have his friends sit in on the session. There are also times when a worker, following the youngster's continued discussion about a girlfriend, or friend, will ask if the adolescent client would like to bring this person to the interview. Many professionals and parents fail to recognize the positive aspects of peer relationships perhaps because so much emphasis is placed on the negative aspects of peer groups. Many parents see peer groups as a threat to their parenting role. In this regard, Won,[14] in writing about the importance and impact parents and peers can have on each other, maintained:

> The differentiation of parents and peers as agents involved in the socialization and control of the young in the State of Hawaii does not result in pervasive conflict and strains between the adolescent and his parents. Moreover, the control and influence exercised by the peers tend to be congruent with parental expectations. Deviant behavior is more the exception than the rule. Such behavior also is more likely where the adolescent is not likely to consult either parent or peer over the typical adolescent concerns.

In relation to peers, it seems to me that agencies should give more deliberate, conscious thought in working with the youthful client and his immediate peer relationships.

## FAMILY LOSS AND SCHOOL FUNCTIONING
### Grieving: Impact on Educational Goals

A problem not often recognized when working with families who have children with school problems is that of the parent who is harboring pain over his own unfulfilled educational goals. Workers generally are aware that loss needs to be faced directly in order that grieving may take place. Grayson[3] concluded:

Patients frequently need to mourn intangible as well as tangible losses that have occurred in their lives. In psychotherapy or psychoanalysis the patient confronts the necessity to abandon as hopeless earlier unfulfilled wishes or hopes.

Parents often talk about the way things were when they went to school and one sees them "living their lives through their children." This frequently takes the form of talking about past hardships, how they dealt with them, and comparing their own past with what is happening currently with their children. Parents look back at their educational experiences with a feeling of loss, a feeling they very often continue to cling to. The case of the Brown family illustrates this point:

Mr. and Mrs. Brown requested help for their fifteen-year-old son because "he was a superior child and until recently had been doing outstanding work." The boy's grades had slipped to B's and C's, and this change was very upsetting to the father. In the family interview all of them seemed rather sad and somewhat unhappy, particularly the father. In this session the discussion centered around their son's school, with the father expressing feelings about how easy things were these days for his son. During the interview he tended to interrupt whenever his son became defensive, and at times became very angry and almost belligerent toward him. As he spoke, it was very apparent that he could not listen to his son's remarks or comments. Although Mrs. Brown tended to support her husband, she seemed puzzled as to why he was so intense about his son's schooling. This emotionality had been talked about previously, since father would become agitated and at times depressed whenever his son would bring home poor grades or did not seem to have the kind of interest in school that the father thought he should have. At times, parents would have differences about what was going on. However, mother was upset because they seemed to get nowhere, particularly when she tried being supportive and identifying with father's point of view. As this session progressed and worker wondered what Mr. Brown's school experience had been, Mr. Brown became rather sad. Mr. Brown is a postal worker who has been going to night school for the past four years, taking courses to enable him to become an accountant. As Mr. Brown talked about his early childhood, he recalled how, during the depression, he left high school in the eleventh grade because his father had been injured at work, and he was needed to support the family. As he spoke about what a blow this was for him, tears came to his eyes and he began to cry quietly. Mrs. Brown was empathetic, and their son was rather quiet as Mr. Brown continued. Although he had wanted to resume his education, he later married and went into the service and somehow was unable to finish his schooling.

Several subsequent family interviews continued along the same theme, with worker seeing Mr. Brown twice during this period for individual interviews. Although this father had in recent years been attending night school, he was plodding and suffering through his courses. His main concern and focus was his son's academic achievement. It was almost as if Mr. Brown had totally given up on himself and was now relying on his son's "making it" for him. Had Mr. Brown not repressed this area of loss for so many years, he might have been more effective in guiding his son. As it was, he seemed to come through with exaggerated anger and rage at times, with little ability to make room for his son's feelings. In helping Mr. Brown to identify and experience the lost hope he had about achieving an education, it was necessary to get across to him that the worker felt his loss to be very real and crucial to him. As Mr. Brown was able to express his feelings of grief, he could then talk about fantasies he had in regard to what he wished he could have done. As a result of bringing these feelings to awareness he was able to let go of them. Working this area through enabled Mr. Brown to develop a better understanding of his son's problems with school. Family interviews resulted in closer understanding and greater intimacy among the family members.

## Traumatic Events

Often traumatic events occur in a family such as separation, divorce, a death, or job loss. These events can precipitate a family crisis. As is known by most practitioners, parents tend to overlook the impact that the traumatic event may have on the child. Rabichow[10] asserted:

> It is, of course, obvious that a child can be so disturbed by traumatic occurrences at home as to be unable to concentrate. The child attempting to understand the anguished relationship between himself and his parents expends his energy in coping with emotions aroused by tragic home situations and has no motivation for study.

An effective modality to use in dealing with unresolved feelings and tensions during a crisis is the family interview. In writing about crises situations, Bassin[1] stated:

> The impact of any one family member's severe emotional distress adversely affects all members of the household. Parad and Caplan, in their delineation of a crisis explain: "During a crisis a person is faced by a problem which, on the one hand, is of basic importance to him because it is linked with his fundamental instinctual needs, and on the

other, cannot be solved quickly by means of his normal range of problem-solving mechanisms." When a crisis is centered around the behavior of one child, the "person" (referred to above) becomes—at the very least—the child, both his parents, and his immediate family. Individually and as a group the family is in disequilibrium. In varying degree past methods of meeting problems have failed; defenses are in disorder. During a state of crisis, persons within it are much more susceptible to outside therapeutic influences.

## The Single-Parent Family

In agencies that deal with predominantly single-parent families, where the father is absent due to either separation, desertion, divorce, or death, mothers generally come in with concern over the fact that their son is fatherless, and that this loss is the cause of their problems. In the counseling that follows, other problems emerge, the most frequent one being problems in school functioning. Although some mothers seem to have made a connection between the absence or loss of the father and the child's school difficulty, many of them have been unable to see the effect on school functioning. The case of Mrs. B is an example of this factor:

When Mrs. B spoke about her son's need for a Big Brother, she remarked that her husband had passed away four years ago when her son was seven years old. In the joint interview where her son was present, Mrs. B quickly suppressed tears that came to her eyes as she spoke about her main concern, which was the son's poor school functioning. At this point in the interview the son became fidgety and complained about his mother's nagging him about homework and the grades he got on papers. As a result of the nagging, he had stopped bringing his papers home. In the interaction that followed, mother angrily complained about how hard she worked on her job, and how difficult life generally was for her. She had hoped that her children would do well at school, even though they were not too helpful around the house. The younger child was performing adequately at school. However, an older sister was also of great concern to her mother in terms of school work. At this point worker intervened and commented that it appeared the mother had a great deal of feeling about her husband and wondered if she would mind talking about it. Mother looked at her son, giving the worker the feeling that she was wondering whether it would be all right to speak in front of him. With worker's assurance, mother began talking about her husband's death. Father apparently had had a coronary condition which caused his sudden death seven months after he became aware of his illness. As mother spoke about it the son asked questions in regard to what had happened, as if he had not heard this before. The boy had been told the details of his father's death, but he was only now beginning to be able to integrate what had happened. At this point the boy asked a great many questions about heart conditions and wondered whether this might happen to him. Mother seemingly was suddenly aware that her son may have been worrying about this for some time. She attempted to reassure him and remarked that she wasn't too knowledgeable about the father's condition, but that they could discuss this at the clinic where they go for medical care. Before this interview concluded, worker spoke about the need for mourning in the presence of the children and the appropriateness of doing this whenever one needed to.

Although the mother in this situation initially came in for a Big Brother, the primary concern appeared to be in the school performance of the children. Enabling this mother to release her feelings of loss around her husband and to perceive more clearly what this meant to her children helped the family to become more unified in their common grief. The child, too, was released by this experience so that he could begin to function better in school, and soon began to show evidence of improvement.

Jones[6] discussed the loss of a husband and father in these terms:

> To the extent that this feeling has been buried and repudiated, however, it continues to exert a hidden force upon your life, making you more easily exasperated with imperfection, making you more insistent on attaining other ideals. It may even lead to extravagant mourning and longlasting depression. In either case, it increases the likelihood that you will face other frustrations in your life, and so ultimately it tends to increase your overall load of anger.

The impact of separation, divorce, or death of a parent on a child is often recognized by the parent. However, action to alleviate the resultant stress on the youngster is often not taken. This omission is understandable when one recognizes that the stress of the parent, in divorce for example, consumes a great deal of emotional energy. Parents reacting to the impact of separation, desertion, or divorce, can often become engrossed in their own bewilderment, sadness, anger, hostility, or depression. This expenditure of emotional energy can leave little opportunity for the mother to respond to what the child is experiencing at this time.

Family breakup has increased in recent times to the point where in some classrooms it is not unusual to find one third of all children having experienced separation or divorce in their families. It is alarming to note that at the recent White House Conference[9], the fact emerged

> . . . that seven million children under the age of fourteen are being raised in families in which the father is absent. Each year, because of divorces, hundreds of thousands of children are added to those living in one-parent families. In addition, uncounted numbers of boys and girls live in homes broken by separation other than divorce.

In speaking of the impact of divorce on children, Pannor[8] observed:

> Today there appears to be a minimal use of professional help with divorcements, possibly because we are coming to view divorce as being achieved with relative emotional ease. Perhaps this attitude is prevalent because of the large numbers of divorces and the seeming cultural acceptance of divorce as an adequate problem-solving device.

In view of the above facts, it is extremely important for school and agency personnel, as well as significant adults in a child's life, to be very sensitive to any clues that might indicate the child's adverse reaction to a separation or loss of a parent. Often significant clues in relation to school can be found, such as the child's refusal to attend school, daydreaming or withdrawal in the classroom, a drop in academic performance, shifts in class participation, not completing homework assignments, or acting-out behavior. An early scheduled family interview can be very effective in determining quickly the severity of problems of this nature and in arranging an appropriate treatment program.

## CONCLUSIONS

Although the number of children with school problems is increasing steadily, traditional modalities of treatment have not yet given way to more innovative approaches to any significant degree. Today, when our values and institutions are being challenged, the school is coming under serious scrutiny. The transition period we are going through is difficult for everyone, including schools, families, and agencies. There is a need for more careful examination of the philosophy and techniques of reaching out to children with school problems. Agencies need to question whether old methods are still applicable today. It seems to me there is danger that traditional ways of dealing with school problems may be becoming institutionalized, so that agencies may be reaching only a small segment of our population; that is, the so-called "highly motivated family."

Family interviewing, and when appropriate, peer interviewing are two valuable modalities that can hasten the diagnosis of school problems and help more quickly to decide on the best course of treatment for that youngster. Since school problems are not the single province of the therapist, family interviewing should include, where possible, other "significant people" in the child's school life, such as teacher, counselor, or school nurse. The agency needs to explore the advantages in meeting the youngster and his family in the school setting. In this way, one gets away from the so-called "sick model" that seems to persist in the way children and families tend to view the agency. The realistic problems of traveling to an agency, missing classes, and overcoming some aspects of resistance can often be greatly diminished when the family is able to meet on the school premises. This approach also tends to focus the problem more sharply in the school area. Help can be facilitated by working closely with the school personnel who are crucial factors in the overall treatment of school problems. In so doing, agency personnel may no longer need to feel the full responsibility of resolving the youngster's school difficulties.

As our educational process becomes more advanced, it tends to be further removed from parental understanding. Until the schools can work out a way of helping parents move through this maze, I feel it is appropriate for agencies to undertake this task. Agencies need to help parents understand and learn how to negotiate the proper channels necessary to help their children who may be experiencing difficulties in school.

School problems are almost always a concomitant of any presenting problem brought to agencies. Thus, immediate attention becomes vital in order to avoid compounding the problem for the youngster. When the problem at school becomes entrenched, it can persist for many years, and often these children find themselves labeled by parents or teachers as "educationally handicapped." If problems persist, these children can later require educational programs which are extremely costly in terms of money, resources, and personnel.

Family interviewing lends itself to breaking down the barrier between the therapist and client. As the worker allows more of himself to evolve in the family sessions the family can begin to see him as a person, rather than as an omnipotent professional that clients may be threatened by and tend to avoid. If we are to be effective and reach large numbers of people, we need to employ more approaches that add to a family's adequacy so that they can feel more secure and confident in doing their own problem-solving and continue to develop on their own.

Bringing peers into the treatment of school problems is beginning to be seen as a very valuable adjunct over and above the inclusion of the family. Immediate peers, like buddies or girlfriends, can be a positive source of understanding and help to the adolescent child. Serious consideration should be given to including these peers in interviews with the adolescent, as well as including them in the adolescent's family sessions. More study is indicated to see what adolescents may be re-enacting in their immediate peer relationships that stems from their own family background.

An important dynamic underlying the frequent difficulties parents have in seeing school problems in their children objectively, is their own unfinished business in related areas, such as father's unfulfilled educational goals. Losses of this kind, or direct losses, such as death or separation, need to be brought to acknowledgment by the significant adults in a child's life when they are experiencing them. Connections need to be made between the traumatic events in family history and the impact these events have on the family as a whole, and how this relates to school in particular. The single-parent family is an intense unit which can create for the parent special problems that in turn have an imapct on the child.

In working with school problems, family interviews are effective in early discovery and treatment and can be used in varying degrees by most agencies as well as school personnel. Conjoint sessions are useful in clarifying distortions and misunderstandings within families as well as between parents, children, teachers, and other school personnel. Thus, family interviews can be useful in dealing with crises such as transfer or expulsion from school. Other situations in which family sessions are productive include proposed retention or skipping a grade, preparation for psychological testing, severe learning difficulty, vocational choice, and parent conferences.

## REFERENCES

1. Bassin, Ellen, Pannor, Harry, and Shinoff, Bernice: Family interviewing as practiced in a parent-child guidance agency. *Child Welfare,* 45, 1966.

2. Brantley, Dale: Family stress and academic failure. *Social Casework,* 50, 1969.

3. Grayson, Henry, Ph.D.: Grief reactions to the relinquishing of unfulfilled wishes. *Am J Psychother,* 1970.

4. Guerney, Bernard G., Jr.: *Psychotherapeutic Agents, New Roles for Nonprofessional, Parents, and Teachers.* New York, Holt, Rinehart & Winston, 1969.

5. Herzok, Elizabeth, Sudia, Ceceilia E., and Harwood, Jane: Drug use among the young—as teenagers see it. *Children,* 17.

6. Jones, Eve: *Raising Your Child in a Fatherless Home.* Free Press of Glencoe, Collier-Macmillan Ltd., London.

7. Mishne, Judith: Group therapy in an elementary school. *Social Casework,* 52, 1971.

8. Pannor, Harry, and Schild, Sylvia: Impact of divorce on children. *Child Welfare,* 39, 1960.

9. *Profiles of Children.* 1970 White House Conference on Children, Washington, D.C. U. S. Government Printing Office, 1970.

10. Rabichow, Helen: Casework treatment of adolescents with learning inhibitions. *J Soc Work,* 8, 1963.

11. Springer, Lorraine, A.: Parent-child relations in the early school years. *Social Work,* 9, 1954.

12. Wadsworth, H.S.: Social conditioning casework in a school setting. *Social Casework,* 52, 1971.

13. Walton, Maxine, Reeves, Gloria D., and Shannon, Robert F.: Crisis team intervention in school community unrest. *Social Casework,* 52, 1971.

14. Won, George Y.N., Yamanura, Douglas S., and Ikeda, Kiyoshi: The correlation of communications with parents and peers to deviate behavior of youth. *J Marriage Family,* 31, 1969.

*Chapter IX*

# FAMILY ASPECTS OF DRUG TREATMENT OF SCHOOL RELATED PROBLEMS

EDWARD L. GREEN

F AMILY attitudes toward drug treatment of school related problems are influenced by many factors including the history of a particular family, its medical experiences, cultural background, and other factors related to the locale in which one lives. Society at large and specialists in the field of mental health condition family attitudes, and we therefore need to briefly explore current trends in American attitudes toward the use of medication for mental health as well as the attitudes which the mental health professionals themselves hold.

## SOCIETAL AND PROFESSIONAL ATTITUDES CONCERNING THE USE OF MEDICATION FOR MENTAL HEALTH

When asked to include among his philanthrophies a child guidance clinic, an eminent industrialist responded, "I don't believe in tampering with children's minds." The industrialist's succinct comments bring out a problem that is being increasingly recognized in the field of mental health and it has to do with the position of psychiatrists and other mental health specialists as agents of government or societal control. The whole community mental health movement has been called "a quasi-political movement supported by state-sanctioned power and money."[15] Most mental health workers reject this categorical assignment and see themselves as free agents who are helping others to achieve their freedom—freedom in many areas—a personal sense of identity, a freedom to utilize potential, political freedom, etc.

It is undoubtedly true that we exercise another function that does run counter to individual freedom. Such function is exercised when

195

the freedom of the larger society is at stake. We aid in the process which marks a small percentage of our citizens as dangerous and therefore in need of confinement. To enlarge the freedom of society, we restrict the freedom of the minority. Though critics may see us as conformists who are largely acting out of our intolerance of deviance, the issue is much more complex.

When we work with children, these issues are present in a very complicated way. The child may be satisfied with his behavior or achievement but his parents or his school or his neighborhood may see him as in need of "treatment." The concept of "treatment" may range from the more traditional concepts of treatment by a physician to exclusion from his home. Treatment that seems appropriate from the educator's viewpoint may be totally unacceptable to the parents or the child. Sometimes the mental health worker is used as a judge or a pawn who can be convinced of the justice of one's position or as subject to manipulation in a complex of power plays. These issues are seldom explicitly stated when a child's needs are being evaluated, but they greatly influence what can be done for him. This is especially true when the use of medication is being considered for problems related to school maladjustment which is expressed in behavior or learning disorders.

Some authorities, notably Glasser,[6] have focused on what changes can be brought about in the school system. Other chapters in this book have recommended a full involvement of the family with the school. The focus in this chapter will be more on the child and his family and the basic assumption will be that school reports are essentially accurate.

We are said to be a drug-orientated culture and there is justifiable alarm at the increase in drug abuse problems heightened by recent statistics showing that narcotic abusage kills more teen-agers in New York City than any other cause. In part, our drug preoccupation may relate to our insistence that for every problem there is a solution—hopefully an instant solution. As a culture then, we expect and demand a cure for ills and all too often the physician has himself been caught up in this appealing simple philosophy or has been pressured into measures about which he may have scientific reservation, for example, compliance in administering penicillin for the common cold.

Conflicting emotions influence the ease with which a physician prescribes medication for a child and the responsiveness with which the child and family accept his prescription. To complicate matters more, the medications used in the mental health field are not known to be curative and must therefore be taken until bodily functions assume control (again not an unusual medical situation, in fact more common than not).

Some of our reluctance to use medication has to do with the qualities of the agents themselves. Some of the principal agents used have euphoriant, energizing, or mood-elevating qualities when used *by adults*. They therefore become subject to abuse *by adults*, though instances of abuse *by a child* for whom these medications have been prescribed are rare. This potential problem has never been reported as a deterrent in various trials of medication effectiveness.

A regimen of medication cannot be universally applied to learning disorders. The cause of learning difficulties are complex and can seldom be ascribed to a single determinant. Even if one assumes that most of a particular child's problems are due to a specific deficit such as a problem in coordinating vision and muscle movement, this deficit has other ramifications such as subjecting him to ridicule of peers or parents because of his clumsiness. What begins as a relatively demarcated problem tends to spread and lead to psychological malfunctioning. The investigator must search for the many possibilities coexistent in any one child that lead to his disorder.

Few professionals prior to this generation saw any relationship between school problems and medication aside from the possible treatment of an obvious affliction which consumed the energies of the ill child and therefore indirectly limited his abilities. Today there is still little basic understanding of the mechanisms by which medications may help in learning disorders. This is not an unusual situation when we remember the employment of quinine and digitalis for many decades preceding a rational explanation of the way in which they helped.

For years the mental health field has been polarized into "organicists" and those who advocated a psychodynamic approach. The "eclectic" who attempted to pragmatically adapt whatever he found useful has, in the past, been derogated to the "jack of all trades" category but a more recent trend, perhaps spurred by the demands of community psychiatry, is elevating the eclectic position to respectability. In spite of this development a minority of professionals vigorously oppose the use of medication for a variety of reasons. These reasons are expressed in generalizations that cannot be validated consistently. Some fear that the medication is a "short cut" to control the child rather than correct the underlying problems leading to his difficulty. When a child makes obvious improvement the success is attributed to a "transference cure," suggestion, attempts to please the physician, the need of the patient to experience success, and other factors which exist in any therapeutic work.

There are now many studies indicating that medication is helpful in treating learning and behavioral disorders.[2, 3, 7, 12, 13, 17] Earlier reports tended to be overly optimistic and the studies were often uncontrolled for various variables such as social class, diagnostic category, and age dosage level. DiMascio[5] has pointed out many of the deficiencies of such studies and has made suggestions for avoiding the errors of the past. Though recent evaluations are still deficient, there is an unmistakable trend in demonstrating the usefulness of judiciously prescribed medication. Why then has the use of medication had such a mixed reaction among professionals who pride themselves in applying scientific method? Aside from the reasons already referred to and the logical desire to avoid the introduction into the body of any foreign substances with potential toxicity, there are psychodynamic considerations.

Owing to the polarization previously mentioned, some therapists view the prescription of medication as a depreciation of one's talents in understanding human psychology—an admission of failure, almost a surrender or an act of betrayal of one's convictions, a second-class form of treatment. As any psychotherapist, administrator, or observing parent can verify, change itself is sometimes stubbornly resisted.

Therapists of parents often perceive two conflicting tendencies in parents. On the one hand there is a strong desire to protect the child from the suffering that the parent may have experienced as a child and to give to the child the advantages the parent did not have. Less easily recognized is a countertendency which has various dynamic roots. For example, a wealthy parent may force his child to experience deprivation on the basis that it will "build his character." A more important factor may be that the parent experiences a competitive threat from his child akin to that he previously experienced as a sibling. In such an instance he covers his psychic threat by such thoughts or statements as "It was good enough for me and it should be good enough for you."

Therapists, too, as surrogate parents must guard against their unconscious needs to keep the patient impotent. The obsessional complaining of some educators and therapists about "spoon feeding" is a closely related phenomenon. An investment of years of psychotherapeutic work (and thousands of dollars) in achieving his own psychic well-being does not predispose the therapist to the acceptance of easy solutions.

Unawareness is also a potent factor. Our understanding of behavioral and learning disorders has advanced considerably in recent years. Those who have had earlier training or those whose training has been tradition-bound have simply missed the later developments. This omission seems overdetermined, since ordinarily we are eager to learn new developments.

Over the years since psychotherapy has been a mode of treatment, therapists have observed that patients may benefit regardless of whether the therapist is Freudian, Jungian, Sullivanian, or of another "school." Sometimes this has led to adoption of a maxim that "anything will work as long as an interested therapist spends time with his patient." This is a greatly oversimplified statement and leaves out many important technical features that are common to various approaches of psychotherapy. The risk involved in such a generalization is that one may conclude that all remedial efforts, education, and therapy can be reduced to a single modality. The fallacy of this generalization is more readily understood if one attempts to apply it to the psychosomatic illness.

It is well known that certain conditions such as asthma have psychic as well as other environmental precipitants. When working with an asthmatic, there is ideally a multiple approach. Medication for asthmatic attacks continues to be used to control the condition as long as necessary even though psychotherapy has been initiated. In some cases the medication usage may taper and eventually be dispensed with as the asthmatic is able to integrate and achieve control over psychic determinants.

A similar analogy could be made for other conditions such as epilepsy, but the wise psychotherapist knows that there are limitations imposed by the particular illness or the stage of the illness. It would be foolish to attempt to substitute psychotherapy for an anticonvulsive medication without having investigated the condition.

Similarly, a child who does not perceive images properly cannot always be expected to change his perception because he is given psychotherapy. Four hours per week of psychotherapy will not improve his perception more than one hour of psychotherapy if his basic need is for perceptual training. In other words, psychotherapy cannot be exchanged for remedial training anymore than it can be substituted for basic educational measures.

Drug "oversell" has affected professional and lay judgment concerning medications. We have become inured to drug advertisements whose claims far outstrip later performance. Consequently we have come to distrust claims for all new drugs and even new uses for established medications.

Recently there has been a revival of interest in natural food products as part of the ecology movement and in response to a growing concern about the safety of food additives. This understandable concern is subject to the distortion of rejection of all manufactured food products and aggravates the worries regarding medication usage. It is certainly preferable to be able to sleep without taking sleeping pills, to limit one's weight without anorectics, and to avoid analgesics for minor pains. But what about the instances of natural deficiencies such as a lack of insulin in diabetes? The *natural* solution is death or severe disability in some deficiencies. Nature's remedy is not always acceptable. The choice one makes is the degree of disability he is willing to exchange for lack of treatment.

The image of the medicine man in a primitive society calls forth many images associated with magical acts. The magical aspects of medicines persist in modern societies. At times we are in awe of their curative powers but we also fear such agents. This topic is elaborated upon by Wahl,[19] who decries the excessive use of medication and heightens our awareness of the psychological aspects of the prescription of drugs.

The word "drug," incidentally, is representative of the contamination of our thinking about medication. "To drug" has acquired the meaning "to sedate," and to avoid this connotation it is probably best to substitute "medicate" for "drug." Recent publicity implies that the purpose of medications used for learning and behavioral disorders is to achieve a sedative effect. Actually, precise measurements show that the reverse is true. The quality of activity changes, but there is no decrease in total activity.[4] In this connection one of our commonly used adjectives, "hyperkinetic," used to describe a certain group of children, is not a literally precise term.

## FAMILY EXPERIENCES AS A DETERMINANT IN AFFECTING ATTITUDES TOWARD MEDICATION

Derek's family was one of "high visibility" when they appeared in our waiting room because their dress and mannerisms reflected complete acceptance of the hippie subculture. Derek was a "hyperactive" child with learning problems, severe and prolonged tantrums, and free use of obscene language. His parents considered the charge of obscenity to be unfair, as the words were "natural—just used with improper timing or in improper places." Derek had been given LSD by a family friend with very bad results. Parental concern about the recommended use of a psychostimulant was completely understandable, and extra care was spent in explaining the expected actions and side reactions of the medication. They were able to use the information and Derek responded well.

A mother who had survived the terrors of a concentration camp was faced with the added injustice of losing a child who had a fatal illness. The illness was progressive and affected the child's behavior and learning ability well in advance of affecting the child's outward evidence of the illness. This mother became extremely suspicious when medication was suggested. She felt it was potentially very toxic and badgered the psychiatrist into listing every possible side effect. When he would mention one side effect, she accused him of attempting to harm her child by choosing a drug that would have this effect. It is unlikely that she accepted the advice of the consulting psychiatrist.

Another mother seemed to be making slow progress in psychotherapeutic work at a guidance clinic. She had shown little interest when medication was suggested as an adjunctive form of treatment to her child. During one interview she revealed that her mother had died in a state mental hospital. In her mind she had connected this death with insanity and indirectly with drugs. To have accepted drug therapy was to acknowledge insanity in her child. When this illogical chain of thought processes was opened to discussion, she was able to accept a medication trial for her child's behavioral and learning disturbances.

Thousands of children have had positive experiences with medication that has helped their school adjustment. These experiences have greatly influenced many families and therapists and have markedly altered clinical procedures in child guidance and private practice settings.

### Two Cases Examples in Which Medication Played an Important Part in Dramatic Improvement—A Pragmatic Approach to Changing Attitudes

Psychotherapeutic work is often slow because the therapist deals with his patients' attitudes, well-engrained personality characteristics, and fixed methods of interpersonal interactions. The clinician's training may encourage him to expect slow changes or even to be wary of rapid improvement. Imagine the delight then to the family and clinician when genuine progress is quickly made. Consider the following account* of marked improvement:

**Example (Case 1)**                                                    **Age 6**

4th Session Review: Eleanor's functioning has improved greatly with the use of medication. Her school performance has been miraculous, with her grades that previously ranged from C and F now consisting of A's and B's. As we have been able to manage the child's minimal brain dysfunction medically, we now see more clearly that some emotional factors may also be involved in Eleanor's total functioning. For instance, there is now an indication that her headaches are emotionally based. Mother is responsive to our efforts to understand this further and to suggestions for dealing with the child somewhat differently. Follow-up will continue on an every-other-week basis. L.G., M.A.

The above report was written by a therapist who had been dubious about the use of medication. The teacher of this child was

*All names and other identifying information have been changed for purposes of confidentiality.

equally impressed and jokingly asked if she could send the rest of her class to the clinic.

Eleanor's case is a reminder of another controversy which relates to the use of medication. Some clinicians oppose measures which give symptomatic relief on the basis that the patient will not then have the motivation to continue treatment aimed at a more basic understanding of the psychodynamic factors involved. Such a contention, though possibly valid, is an extremely difficult point to prove. Repeated studies show little evidence that long-term therapy has longer lasting effects than short-term therapy.

Eleanor's parents withdrew from therapy within a few weeks of starting and the therapist wrote a quarterly progress note from which the following excerpt was taken:

> Although Mrs. I had a strong motivation for treatment when she made the initial contact with this clinic, the circumstances have been altered by the effective use of Ritalin®. Her school performance has improved considerably and her behavior at home has been more manageable. The psychological aspects of the problem that have been presented have been adequately dealt with by mother so that there is no apparent need for ongoing treatment at the present time. This case will remain on active status for the next three months to continue medical supervision.

Sometimes patients also achieve symptomatic relief from short-term psychotherapy and "prematurely" withdraw. Perhaps we should consider that the patient's goals have been met though the therapists see other needs.

Another example of dramatic change is illustrated by Robert, who resembled a profoundly retarded child on admission.

**Example (Case 2)**            **Age 5**

Mrs. B brought her five-year-old son Robert to the clinic due to her concern about his infantile behavior.

He was hyperactive, ignored directions, soiled, drooled, laughed inappropriately, was inarticulate, and spoke in monosyllables. Recent information revealed mother's rejection and father's complete detachment in relating to the boy.

With Dr. F, educational psychologist, as consultant, six sessions were devoted to mother's instruction in rage-reduction technique. These sessions ran from three hours to thirty minutes before mother was able to revise her inappropriate affect and convey her control of the situation. Medication was used for probable minimal brain dysfunction (abbreviated MBD) and the mother was seen alone and with child for support of her revisions in her role with child as well as in relation to her own dependency needs.

By the ninth session, it was clear Robert was intellectually average and above. By the twentieth session, the child was adjusting well in nursery school, able to follow directions, talking in sentences, had given up soiling and drooling, and was seen by the school as functioning above the four-year level. Contacts continue with focus on mother's own needs and role with the child as well as Robert's functioning relative to entry into school in September. A.E.P., A.C.S.W.

In Robert's case a multiple approach was used. We cannot be certain that the same results would have occurred if the treatment program had omitted medication. What we do know is that children like Robert seldom respond so completely and so quickly when we limit ourselves to nonmedical approaches.

Case samples are notoriously inadequate when taken in isolation, but there are studies, previously cited, which deal with the statistical aspects. One aspect not conveyed by numerical approach, however, is the immense relief of human suffering. Though we have the tools to measure changes in attitude, individuals such as the patient's neighbors, grandparents, and playmates are seldom asked their opinions concerning the improvement or worsening condition of a child in treatment. If it is true that at the base of many neuroses there is a lack of self-esteem, we need to give more adequate weight to the tremendous difference in social acceptance of such a child as Eleanor. How much less rejection did she encounter? What did her progress mean in terms of her self-perception?

Since we have no way of predicting with certainty which patients will respond as remarkably as Eleanor did, what is the value of a medication trial if we experience this result once in four trials, once in ten, or once in twenty, assuming the majority of others will also obtain some benefit and that none will be significantly harmed?

### Summary

Family attitudes toward the use of medication in school-related problems are influenced by many forces within the family and in the external environment. The family often raises seemingly simple questions such as the following:

1. How long does the medication have to be taken?

2. Does it need to be taken every day?
3. Is it addictive?
4. Does the medication have harmful side effects?

However, these questions really reflect underlying larger concerns which vary with the sophistication of the family, their personal experiences, and many other factors influencing educators, mental health professionals, and our larger society. Our mixed attitudes toward the employment of medication will hopefully shift toward more consensus as we gain knowledge concerning the specific indications for the type of medication, the quantity to be employed, results to be expected, and more fundamental knowledge of the conditions causing school-related problems.

## THE ADJUNCTIVE USE OF MEDICATION IN TREATING SCHOOL-RELATED PROBLEMS

### Identifying the Problems

We sometimes simplify our terminology by referring to "learning disorders" or "behavior problems" but these are not valid diagnostic categories in the sense of having a specific etiology, a predictable course, definite identifying symptoms, and features usually associated with an illness. Rather we have a cluster of traits, symptoms, and descriptive observations. A similar concept applies to such "diagnostic" labels as "congestive failure." A child may have a learning disorder secondary to a neurosis, a familial crisis, a developmental deficit, or a psychosis. Obviously, the treatment of the disorder cannot be approached in a uniform manner.

The medication chosen by the physician is an attempt to treat the underlying condition responsible for the learning disorder or behavior disorder. His approach is to evaluate the child and, to some degree, the milieu in which the child functions. He establishes a diagnosis and on the basis of this diagnosis develops a treatment plan. In a narrow sense, a diagnosis is a label applied to the child, such as "anxiety reaction." This narrow labeling is, in itself, insufficient because it does not provide a description of those forces previously or presently operative in the child's life which caused or maintained his malfunction. Broader consideration of etiological factors is usually included in a dynamic diagnosis.

We shall not attempt to discuss the entire topic of chemotherapy for psychological problems of children. Instead, we shall use one condition as a representative example of a clinical approach to drug treatment of school related problems. The entity to be considered, minimal brain dysfunction, illustrates the relatedness of such matters as academic skill, improper bodily function, behavior, learning difficulties, and family dynamics. The previously cited case examples of Eleanor I. and Robert B. are examples of children diagnosed as having MBD. Let us turn our attention to this syndrome from a descriptive standpoint.

## Minimal Brain Dysfunction: An Example of One Syndrome Involved In School-Related Problems

In the past decade our awareness of this syndrome has been heightened by hundreds of journal articles, drug company advertisements, and more recently, the lay press and television. A congressional committee has become involved in the polemic. Parents of MBD children have been accused of being unable to tolerate the normal exuberance of active, healthy males. School systems stand accused of prescribing medication and enforcing a brain-washing technique upon minority member children.[14] Simultaneously, some physicians whose successful methods have been described in popular news weeklies, have been inundated by the requests for help by harassed parents. Another polarity has developed.

That there exists such a syndrome as MBD is itself a matter of controversy.[1, 8] A term formerly used, "minimal brain damage," has caused much of the disagreement because there is no evidence that children with a history of minor head trauma, prolonged high fevers, periods of anoxia, or other cerebral insults uniformly develop a subsequent brain syndrome. On the other hand, there are studies, for example Pasamanick's,[18] that show "there are positive and probably etiological relationships between low socioeconomic status and prenatal and paranatal abnormalities which may in turn serve as precursors to retarded behavioral development, and to certain neuropsychiatric disorders in childhood such as cerebral palsy, epilepsy, mental deficiency, and behavior disorders."

There are conceptual and clinical advantages in considering MBD to be a developmental lag involving central nervous system function. This lag may be the result of trauma, metabolic defect, genetic predisposition, or other factors as yet unknown. The lag may turn out to be a permanent arrest in development, but prediction of this is difficult. When the term "damage" rather than "lag" is used, parents naturally raise the question regarding *by whom* and *in what manner* was the child damaged. The therapist is seldom in a position to answer with any degree of certainty.

Unfortunately, there has been much changing and borrowing of terms so that researchers may agree that the syndrome MBD exists but disagree on its name. Others choose certain frequently occurring aspects of the syndrome such as dyslexia (inability to read with understanding) or hyperactivity, and in describing a spectrum of children, include a wide assortment of diagnostic entities under one symptom.

Zrull and associates[20] postuate that MBD is sometimes a condition comparable to the adult state of agitated depression. Some children with hyperactivity are undoubtedly depressed, but this is not a consistent finding in our evaluation or psychological testing. Antidepressant medications (other than amphetamines and methylphenidate) are seldom effective. Nevertheless one sometimes finds that when the hyperactivity is reduced by medication, the child temporarily becomes "moody," usually meaning depressed.

The delineation of a symptom complex, most facets of which are present in any one child, offers more promise. The following description is taken from *The Encyclopedia of Human Behavior: Psychology, Psychiatry, and Mental Health*:[7]

> Perceptual Disturbances—(a) the child cannot integrate what he sees and hears, perceives only parts rather than wholes, such as letters but not words, isolated sounds instead of sentences, one part of an act like lacing shoes instead of the entire act—therefore has trouble in drawing, reading, talking, singing, buttoning clothes; (b) cannot place own body in space and therefore judges distance, size, and direction poorly; frequently trips, and bumps into things, and is slow in mastering running, skipping, throwing, catching; (c) confuses background with foreground, and cannot see or draw things in perspective; (d) perseveration: writes one letter over and over, covers entire page with one crayon color, talks about one subject incessantly for days or weeks; (e) cannot "filter out" or "tune out" unimportant details such as trivial sights and sounds like the ticking of a clock or a view outside the window, and therefore has a short attention span and is constantly sidetracked and distracted; (f) has a faulty body

image, since he is not sure where the parts of his body are at a given time, and therefore has trouble initiating simple movements or postures or in putting together a jigsaw of a human figure correctly; (g) has difficulty in spatial relationships; may be unable to find the corner or center of a square, or see the difference between a vertical and horizontal line, or between a straight and curved line; shows poor, crabbed, irregular handwriting and frequent reversals in reading, writing, putting on shoes, and other clothing.

Conceptual Disturbances—(a) has difficulty in forming associations, discriminating differences, summoning of images; (b) cannot adequately use words as symbols for meaning, and therefore shows impairment in thinking and communication; (c) has difficulty in thinking abstractly, due to inability to see similarities and to generalize from the specific instances, and therefore thinks concretely and literally and does poorly in most academic work; (d) some brain-injured children are extremely talkative but fail to communicate meaningfully—they engage in repetitive chatter echoed from television or other people's conversation, often dominated by words and phrases chanted over and over.

Behavior Disturbances—(a) general emotional immaturity; talks, acts, and reacts like a much younger child, and shows great emotional lability (laughs one moment, cries the next); (b) general lack of control (sometimes termed hyperkinetic impulse disorder); hyperactive, impulsive, irritable, and disinhibited, with a tendency to run, scream, cry without restraint, and be talkative, restless, and volatile; (c) destructive—generally untidy with books, papers, and clothing, breaks toys and other belongings; (d) aggressive — especially when he is shunned or ridiculed by others; may hurt himself as well as others, and is defensively hostile toward adults, including teachers; (e) animistic—often invests inanimate objects with life such as making two pencils fight each other, or two books run a race; (f) often appears bewildered, anxious, frustrated, due to awareness of his inadequacy and failure in coping with reality; (g) in general, behavior is disorganized, unpredictable, and bizarre, and the child often appears to be clowning though this may merely be a cover for poor performance or poor understanding.

It is important to emphasize that the above description is a *symptom complex*. Each child will present his individual assortment of symptomatology, but the cluster will include most of the above components.

We need to consider the natural course of the kind of condition described above. Menkes, Rowe, and Menkes[16] did a retrospective study (mean follow-up period of 24 years) of eighteen patients whose presenting symptoms were hyperactivity and short attention span. At the time of the follow-up, four were institutionalized as psychotic; two were retarded, and although eight were self-supporting, four of these eight had spent time in institutions. These children probably represent a more seriously affected group than we are now labeling as having a minimal cerebral dysfunction, but their mostly unfortunate fates are sobering in that none had been diagnosed as psychotic and all had IQ levels of at least 70. None of these children had the advantage of current remedial and treatment methods. Our hope is that with modern treatment the severity of the disability these children experienced will be markedly reduced.

## A Procedure

In a guidance center where I am a consultant,* almost all of the therapy is done by nonmedical personnel, a situation typical of most guidance clinics. Each therapist has been trained to recognize the cardinal symptoms of the syndrome and to administer a simple screening test (the Rutgers Drawing Test†) for "organicity." The child who scores poorly on this test is usually given additional testing by a psychologist to refine the analysis of the deficit. Concurrently, psychotherapeutic work continues with the child and his family.

When the clinician suspects a diagnosis of minimal brain dysfunction, the family is referred to the child psychiatrist, but in most instances the interview is conducted with the mother and child only. If the nonmedical clinician is present, he usually gives a condensed history in the presence of the family. Occasionally, a parent objects and wonders about the wisdom of being this direct in the confrontation of the child with his problems. Such objections are usually dealt with by a statement to the effect that the child needs to know what we are concerned about so he can know how he is being perceived and what changes are expected of him. While this is going on, the child's response is observed. Some children, described as hyperactive, are able to maintain control and remain seated even when not provided with toys or drawing materials. Usually the mother will comment on this and indicate that the behavior is unusual and that she has sometimes had difficulty persuading other physicians that this behavior is not rep-

*Kaiser Parent Child Guidance Center, Los Angeles, California.
†The Rutgers Drawing Test, Anna Spiesman Starr, Highland Park, New Jersey, 1952.

resentative. Her statements can be verified by lengthening the interview or by scheduling subsequent appointments, but this is not necessary because the therapist can readily obtain confirmatory information from the school or other outside sources. In the instances when the child is quiet and controlled, he nevertheless appears tense and highly constricted as if exerting maximal effort to stay still. Most children who are afflicted with this syndrome are not readily contained and will begin exploring the room and frequently will attempt to open cabinets or drawers or show other inappropriate behavior. One needs to remember that in judging behavior, age must be taken into consideration. Nursery school children frequently behave in a manner that would be labeled hyperactive or inappropriate in a child of elementary-school age.

If the child is given crayons and paper or other age-appropriate materials, his use of materials helps to establish his perceptual acuity, muscle coordination, willingness to cooperate, and other abilities. An excellent description of a similar diagnostic approach is given by Kernberg.[11]

The term "minimal brain dysfunction" is used to differentiate children with this syndrome from those who have a more obvious brain syndrome such as cerebral palsy. If a specific neurological disorder is suspected, the child is referred to a neurologist for a more complete evaluation.

Some children also need referral for services of ophthalmologists or other specialists when there is doubt about such functions as visual acuity, hearing ability, or other related physical conditions. Many children have had pediatric evaluations before they have been seen in a guidance clinic setting.

If an electroencephalographic (EEG) interpretation is sought, this is usually done in conjunction with a referral to a neurologist. Authorities generally feel that the EEG is not a particularly sensitive and specific aid in the detection of MBD. Hughes[10] has developed some data on the patterns frequently found. Because of the non-specificity of the EEG, most psychiatrists resent the request of school personnel to have this particular test ordered because it sets up an expectation in the minds of parents that this procedure will provide the diagnostic answer. It is sometimes interpreted to be the cure!

Most authorities feel that psychological testing, particularly visual perceptual testing, is the single most important technical diagnostic aid. Auditory perception is also important but most clinics still rely more heavily on visual-motor tests of coordination and perception. The Wepman* test of auditory discrimination is a practical measure that can be readily adopted.

Studies on medications used as an aid in the therapy of behavioral and learning disorders usually indicate that the physician starts with one medication, and if this one gives troublesome side reactions or is ineffective, he shifts to another. The two principal medications used have been d-amphetamine (various trade names such as Dexedrine®) and methylphenidate (Ritalin®). Sometimes other amphetamine products are recommended. Methylphenidate is prescribed in doses that are twice those of d-amphetamine though it is not clear on what basis this dose ratio determination has developed.

When the child's condition fits the diagnostic criteria for MBD, parents are asked if medications have previously been used and what the effects were. Aside from learning the specific drug effects, by asking this and related questions one is frequently able to discern parental attitudes toward the administration of medication. For example, a parent may immediately state that he does not believe in tranquilizers or express disappointment that a physician was unable to help previously.

Parents are advised to give the medication a three- or four-day trial and to report back at that time unless obvious side effects appear. The medication trial is often initiated on a Saturday so that parents can observe the child more closely. Also, in the event of an adverse reaction there is less likelihood of causing additional anxieties about school performance. When the return call is made, there may be an adjustment of dosage. At the time the family reports to the nonmedical therapist, he also takes note of medication effects and advises the psychiatrist or arranges a follow-up appointment with him. In short-term treatment an additional phone contact or two may complete the involvement of the psychiatrist. When the family is no longer in active therapy, the psychiatrist may continue to prescribe for a few months on the basis of telephone contacts, but generally we feel it wise to involve the family physician or pediatrician at this point

*Wepman Auditory Discrimination Test, Joseph M. Wepman, Chicago, 1958.

so that there is continuing supervision of the medication. As the child gets older he may require an increase in dosage but at adolescence he often loses some of the behavioral symptoms such as "hyperactivity." Follow-up studies of adolescents indicate continued maladjustment, however.[9] Whether or not medication should be continued beyond adolescence is a question as yet unanswered. Most of the children who have been in such studies have not received medication earlier, so we do not know if the early use of medication prevents the severity of symptoms in postadolescent MBD youngsters. This also is an area requiring additional research.

## PARENTAL REACTIONS TO DRUG THERAPY—SOME REPRESENTATIVE CASE EXAMPLES

### A Mother Wants Medication Prescribed but Cannot Recognize the Emotional Factors Involved in the Child's Problem

**Konrad I (Case 3)**                            **Age 6**

*Closing Progress Note* after approximately twenty-seven visits.

Konrad, mother, and Mr. E (mother's fiance) seen together. Boy was quiet but could respond. Seems very repressed. Both adults seem determined he is brain damaged seriously and want to make much of this. I again went over the testing results. Later conference with Dr. G indicated take boy off Dexedrine® and see how he reacts to this. Call to school (2nd grade teacher—Mrs. E) reveals him as strange, hungry for male attention, disruptive and fidgety, unable to sit. Academics are poor but boy in the best reading group. Teacher stated clinic had told her when she came here before that "there was nothing wrong with the boy." Mother seems unable to grasp idea of an emotional problem.

Dr. L changed boy's medication. In spite of second meeting with mother in which emotional component stressed, the mother again brought Dr. L clippings from magazine on organicity.

Mother phones in today to state because of financial problems she would not want more appointments here. New medication seemed to help boy and I referred her then to family pediatrician to have it re-evaluated in six months unless it seemed indicated sooner. Told her clinic had offered her all it could and referred her to Glenwood Child Guidance.

Mrs. I seemed determined to validate her concept that Konrad was an organically damaged child. The fee charged her was modest and in keeping with standard community practice of establishing a fee appropriate to income. Mr. E was an art collector and connoisseur of antiques which were displayed in the home and were a constant source of friction because of Konrad's consequent restricted activity. We were never able to successfully intervene to have Mrs. I appreciate the inappropriateness of these demands. In this instance the pediatrician assumed control of medication, which was helpful to Konrad, but the boy could not be expected to reach optimal benefit from the drug because of his mother's inability to deal with the emotional factors involved.

## Mother Has Difficulty Accepting Use of Medication
**Raymond F. (Case 4)** Age 10½

Raymond F had a severe emotional problem with evidence of organic impairment. The following material was taken verbatim from a progress note which his therapist, a psychologist, had made after repeating a battery of psychological tests.

Raymond was originally seen first at this clinic as a fat, anxious seven year old, whose thought processes were disorganized and his affect inappropriate. It was obvious that he had been stressed by his father's recent death. Psychological testing showed good intelligence, but suggested that he was functioning as a borderline psychotic child, his oral demands were extremely intense and engulfing. The nature of his functioning suggested that there had been considerable regression from a somewhat better level of personality integration. Raymond and his mother were seen in treatment from October of 1964 on a weekly basis. Mr. R saw Raymond until the fall of 1966, when he was transferred to me because of Mr. R's leaving the clinic.

When I began seeing Raymond, I was appalled by his extremely uncontrolled behavior, and impressed by evidence of neurological impairment; for example, it is impossible for Raymond to wink only one eye, he slurs his words, shows jerky verbalization and extremely poor coordination. I therefore decided to retest Raymond. His IQ was exactly the same as before but the evidence of organic impairment was much clearer now that he is showing less of the gross disorganization more characteristic of psychotic disturbance. His WISC Verbal IQ is 121 while Performance IQ is only 97. Although evidence of fantasy dominated, inappropriate thought and feeling reaction were much reduced, he remains emotionally infantile and impulse-dominated, and his self-perception is damaged and deformed, as strong as before.

At the time I began seeing Raymond the external situation was in bad shape, because it seemed we could not find a public school or a Catholic school that would take Raymond, and the mother became quite disturbed in reaction to this threat. However, this was worked out, and Raymond's school situation has been much more favorable for him than it has been previously. His experience of some acceptance and success in school was definitely a positive contribution to his progress. I began strenuously objecting to Raymond's wild, silly, destructive behavior and his attacks upon me, attacked his defense that he did not care about anything or anybody, and pointed out that his real problem was that he had such a low opinion of himself that he thought there was no point in trying to be acceptable to other people. I was able to point out some of his positive gains, suggested that he was overcoming a lot of his problems, and that things could take an upward trend. However, I was not going to try to change him until he agreed that he wanted to change, but that when he himself wanted to do better, I would try to help him. I suggested that he needed some help from medication, Dr. G prescribed Dexedrine®. There was an immediate and dramatic improvement, with Raymond pointing out that all of a sudden he enjoyed reading, was able to read eight chapters of history straight through, and was not losing his temper in games. The mother, apparently impressed, reported that for the first time in his life Raymond had been able to put a model together. However, the mother has conflicts about the medication, and the first evening that Raymond was irritable and difficult with her, she blamed the medication and took him off of it. She was at the same time trying to work out her process of separation from Mrs. T (a co-therapist), so that this was a difficult time to deal with her problems around the medication, and temporarily we had to accept her resistance.

Although Raymond has gradually been developing a much more positive relationship with me, when he was off the medication there was immediately much more disruptive behavior. It was very difficult to do any "therapy" with Raymond when he was behaving in an uncontrolled manner, but some gains have remained. The experience, relatively brief though it was, of functioning better gave Raymond more confidence in himself, I believe. However I am anxious to get Raymond back on medication, and with this help I would have some hope that we might make enough progress to terminate within the year. VA., Ph.D.

Mrs. F had been depressed and at times almost immobilized. It was not enough for her to intellectually understand the logical need of medication for Raymond. Even when he exhibited dramatic improvement she continued to resist its use. She closely identified with Raymond and could not accept his need for continuing daily medication until Raymond's behavior reached such intolerable levels that the family was evicted from their apartment. To accept her son's need for medication was tantamount to admitting that he was "crazy," and because she saw him as an extension of herself, this would be labeling *her* as crazy, too. Ultimately, Mrs. F accepted Raymond's need and he improved sufficiently to be maintained in a public school in the new location. Part of her difficulty in accepting medication was related to her personal experience in a family which had severe reactions to medications. After months of psychotherapeutic work with Mrs. F, she revealed that her mother had almost died of a drug reaction and another relative had also had a bad experience. When this information became available and subject to further investigation and explanation by the clinician, Mrs. F was able to drop her objections to the use of medication by Raymond.

Raymond's case is a reminder that behavior in school is generally typical of behavior elsewhere. We usually find that when a child makes improvement as measured by standards of his therapist, his behavior in school shows a corresponding change.

Occasionally there are exceptions. One exception that is encountered is the child with MBD who can function well at home and at play in relatively unstructured activities but cannot tolerate the restrictions imposed by the school setting, such as the necessity to sit quietly.

Another exception is the overly quiet and isolated child, who during the course of therapy, becomes more expressive of his previously guarded thoughts. The child may even become too vocal in the process of arriving at a better balance. This new development can be disconcerting to his parents and teachers.

## Multiple Problems in the Family Limit Effectiveness of Drug Treatment

### Caroline K. (Case 5)           Age 7

Caroline is an adopted child whose adoption probably represented an attempt to fill the void of chronically unhappy parents. The following summary was written to the adoption agency which had placed her, when the adoptive mother requested placement in another home. Dear Mrs. C:

The family has been known to this center on and off since July 1968. At first their complaints centered around Caroline's hyperactivity, impulsive behavior, poor school adjustment. It was also apparent to us that Caroline outwardly did what adults told her to do; she used charm, evasion, "played dumb," any manipulation to avoid compliance. Caroline usually seemed unaware of her own feelings, quite often smiling when she was obviously anxious.

We offered the family all of the diagnostic and treatment modalities available at this clinic. They were seen as a family, as a couple, and individually. Caroline was offered treatment and specialized tutoring to overcome her perceptual difficulties. Three therapists worked with them and a fourth, Dr. F, our educational psychology consultant, tested Caroline twice, in August 1968 and November 1969.

As you can see from Dr. F's report it was our impression that Caroline was an emotionally disturbed youngster who, in addition, had minimal brain dysfunction, a mild organic condition most frequently characterized by hyperactivity, impulsiveness, short attention span and perceptual difficulties. It was not possible to arrive at a valid intellectual assessment because of the degree of emotional disturbance which affected Caroline's score on testing. However, as the second report shows, Caroline made considerable progress while her parents were working with us and she was functioning in a regular first grade public school class without benefit of medication.

We have prescribed a variety of medicines for Caroline. Valium®, a tranquilizer, and Dilantin®, tried because of the EEG report, had no effect on behavior, and Caroline had a negative physical reaction to Dilantin.® Dextroamphetamine, 5 mg in A.M., was prescribed after Dr. F's second report in hopes it would help Caroline's school performance. Mrs. K reported the dextroamphetamine seemed effective. Dosage was increased at Mrs. K's request in June 1970 to 10 mg each A.M.

In general, I would say that the difficulties we encountered in working with this family were due to the severity of the parents' problems. Mrs. K is a chronically depressed woman who periodically becomes suicidal. Whenever she felt better about herself and her marriage and Caroline she would simply forget her appointments here and would drop out of treatment until internal pressures or external difficulties brought her back. The parents seemed to use up all of their energy on their personal, financial, and marital conflicts and to have little left over for Caroline. My co-therapist and I had decided by the end of May to confront them with their apparent inability to give sustained effort toward effecting changes in the family interaction and to ask that they commit themselves to this task. We also offered to resume individual tutoring therapy sessions for Caroline (interrupted when Mrs. K found temporary employment), but the K's did not request further appointments either for themselves or Caroline. Mrs. K returned only once—without an appointment—asking for new or increased medication because of school complaints. She was still seeking an outside solution—pills—rather than recognizing the child's need for a feeling of security within the family.

Therefore, it is our impression that unless the K's can begin to participate in making meaningful changes in their family relationships, it might be wise to consider placing Caroline in a foster home. Whether they decide to work toward a more secure home or toward placement, this agency would be available to help them accomplish their goal.

I am enclosing copies of Dr. F's two reports and the EEG. Children frequently have slightly abnormal EEGs without overt organic symptoms and often a second EEG will be interpreted as normal. The K's never complained about Caroline's physical health but early in the year Mrs. K tended more and more to speak of Caroline as retarded because of her poor school performance and uncooperativeness at home. Certainly Caroline's school behavior deteriorated sharply after Dr. F's last report. I would attribute this negative change to two major factors: (a) her parents' marital and personal difficulties during this period—they separated once for two weeks and Mrs. K made one known suicide attempt and (b) Caroline was transferred without warning from her first grade class in St. Michael's School to an EMR (Educable Mentally Retarded) class in Lotus Avenue School. She seemed to feel hurt and rejected by this transfer which took place so suddenly not in response to the teacher's request but because a vacancy occurred at Lotus Avenue and Caroline's name was next on the list. We urged the family to request a conference before agreeing to transfer for Caroline. It is quite possible that this EMR class is the most appropriate available public school resource for Caroline but from the beginning it was apparent that Caroline felt the transfer was a punishment. Adequate preparation for the change might have secured her cooperation rather than a resumption of acting-out.

In summary then, we saw Caroline as an emotionally disturbed child with a mild organic dysfunction. She demonstrated an ability to respond favorably to positive changes in the family but when her parents were caught up in personal and marital conflicts and Caroline was suddenly transferred to a new school, the child reverted to former patterns of destructive behavior. We would recommend placement in a foster home unless the parents are strongly motivated to work toward helping Caroline and themselves in regularly scheduled therapeutic sessions.

Sincerely,

P.S., M.S.W.

Caroline's case was particularly disappointing to the clinic personnel because Caroline had been able to show marked improvement when her parents were able to work together with clinic therapists.

This case also indicates that medication may aid in achieving good results but cannot be considered the cure-all. In Caroline's case the reports of the effectiveness of the medication were variable. When the parents absented themselves from the clinic, medication was seen by them as a solution, even though this solution resulted in less than optimal benefit. The K family was pressured by the school to obtain medication and this prompted Mrs. K's last visit.

There is always the possibility that Mrs. K narrowed and distorted the recommendation of the school for therapy to a request for drug treatment. In ongoing treatment the clinic solicits the observations of the teachers and tries to establish a working relationship with them to reduce the opportunity for distortion and to exchange helpful information, provided that such an exchange does not breach the ethics of confidentiality.

## Parent Expresses Concern About Medication but Resolves Doubts

**Trevor (Case 6)**                                                    **Age 7**

Trevor's family was eager for help and readily followed suggestions offered to them. Trevor's mother expressed appropriate concern about his need to take medication, but when she accepted the need, worked well with the staff.

*Psychological Examination—Retest*

Trevor was brought to this clinic when he was five years of age, because of his hyperactivity, low frustration tolerance, attention-demanding behavior, poor relationship with other children, and defiance of authority. Diagnostic studies suggested organic instability and an emotional problem, originating primarily from his identification with the recently deceased, domineering, senile grandfather who had terrorized the mother and father. The parents participated in a parent group, and Trevor was placed on medication and seen in individual therapy for seventeen sessions. This combined treatment program resulted in dramatic and consistent improvement in Trevor. The parents have remained in contact with the clinic for supervision of medication and occasional consultation. Recently the mother called, stating that there is some resurgence of the former hyperactivity, though to nowhere near the same degree as before, in home and at school. She was interested in having a reevaluation of Trevor when Dr. G had suggested this.

*Summary*

According to this examination Trevor would be classified as of superior intelligence. His ability to function on intelligence tests has improved so remarkably that the IQ has advanced 24 points. There also is a remarkable change in his behavior from the excitable, hyperactive, impulsive child who was darting here and there, responding with warmth and friendliness, but at the same time behaving in a deliberately challenging, defiant, and disobedient manner. His behavior is now very well controlled, he is conscientious and conforming and perhaps somewhat overly serious, so that there was some feeling of strain. He appears to be a sensitive child, and still experiences some feelings of inner distress, but his attitudes in interpersonal relationships are quite positive, and the aggressive, omnipotent identification which he previously displayed has certainly been modified. V.A., Ph.D.

Trevor was fortunate in that he attended a parochial school where classes are smaller than the public schools in his area and his teachers were helpful in supplementing the reports of his parents. When he was first seen he was not yet in grade school, so the demands upon him were less exacting than those required of him later.

Children like Trevor often are not in great conflict until the school situation demands more in terms of sustained attention, ability to sit through a lesson or demonstration, limits on physical activity, and the ability to screen out the stimuli provided by other children. The behavior of children with MBD is often tolerated in kindergarten but as the expectations for academic achievement rise the child has increasing difficulties with the increasingly confining rules of the school. Consequently many such children are referred to clinics during their first and second years of grade school. Trevor's referral was made at age five when the clinic staff could work with him before his condition led to more serious psychological consequences of rejection by peers and feelings of gross incompetence.

## SUMMARY

In this chapter we have taken an overview of the family aspects of drug treatment of school-related problems from the vantage point of a child psychiatrist. Drug treatment is one modality employed and is rarely considered definitive treatment which can be used without other supportive services such as psychotherapy or remedial training. The emphasis on the kind(s) of service provided depends on an evaluation of the child, family, school, and community with regard to needs and resources.

Attitudes toward medication for the treatment of school-related problems vary widely with families which are in turn influenced by mental health professionals, school systems, communities, and cultural factors. Recently the controversial aspects have been heightened by sensationalized publicity.

There is a need for better controlled studies which could provide us with the kind of data we need to intelligently apply the skills we now have. Individual children to whom medication has been given have made sudden and remarkable, positive changes which have undoubtedly spared them from subsequent psychological maladjustment. More rational societal attitudes would encourage the opportunity to further refine our skills in selecting those children who achieve significant benefit from those who do not.

Some parents readily grasp the concept of a constitutional inadequacy and seize upon it as the total basis for the child's learning and/or behavioral difficulties. This rationalization is used to relieve the family of responsibility for and contribution to the problems of the child. Other parents, at the opposite end of the spectrum, totally reject the idea of an inherent deficit and prefer an environmental explanation that places responsibility with external agents such as a school system. Such parents may place total blame on the school for inadequately educating or coping with the child. Less frequently, parents assume that the child's difficulty is a result of their defective parenting. Fortunately, the majority of parents are able to recognize that many factors in a child's life mold him into the unique individual he has become.

## REFERENCES

1. Abrams, Alfred L.: Delayed and irregular maturation versus minimal brain injury, recommendations for a change in current nomenclature. *Clin Pediatr (Phil)* 7, 1968.
2. Benton, Paul C., and McGavock, Wanda: Medication in child psychiatry. *South Med J, 61,* 1968.
3. Conners, C. Keith: A teacher rating scale for use in drug studies with children. *Am J Psychiatry, 126,* 1969.
4. Conners, C. Keith: Speech at American Medical Association clinical convention, as reported in *Medical Tribune and Medical News,* January 6, 1971.
5. DiMascio, Alberto: Psychopharmacology in children. *Massachusetts Journal of Mental Health, 1,* 1970.
6. Glasser, William: *Schools Without Failure.* New York, Harper & Row, 1969.
7. Goldenson, Robert M. (Ed.): *The Encyclopedia of Human Behavior,*

*Psychology, Psychiatry and Mental Health.* Garden City, Doubleday, 1970, Vol. II.

8. Gomez, Manuel R.: Minimal cerebral dysfunction, (maximal neurological confusion). *Clin Pediatr, 6,* 1967.

9. Greene, Stephanie: Life styles in adolescents with brain dysfunction. Paper presented at the 47th annual meeting, American Orthopsychiatry Association, 1970.

10. Hughes, John R.: Electroencephalography and learning. In Myklebust, Helmer R. (Ed.): *Progress in Learning Disabilities.* New York, Grune & Stratton, 1968.

11. Kernberg, Paulina F.: The problem of organicity in the child. *J Am Acad Child Psychiatry, 8,* 1969.

12. Knights, Robert M., and Hinton, George G.: The effect of methylphenidate on the motor skills and behavior of children with learning problems. *J Nerv Ment Dis, 148,* 1969.

13. Knobel, Mauricio: Psychopharmacology for the hyperkinetic child. *Arch Gen Psychiatry, 6,* 1962.

14. Ladd, Edward T.: Pills for classroom peace? *Saturday Review,* November 21, 1970.

15. Leifer, Ronald: The medical model as ideology. *Int J Psychiatry, 9,* 1970-1971.

16. Menkes, Miriam; Rowe, Jane, and Menkes, John: A twenty-five year follow-up study on the hyperkinetic child with minimal cerebral dysfunction. *Pediatrics, 39,* 1967.

17. Millichap, J. Gordon, and Fowler, Glenn W.: Treatment of "minimal brain dysfunction" syndromes. *Pediatr Clin North Am, 14,* 1967.

18. Pasamanick, Benjamin; Knoblock, Hilda, and Lilienfield, Abraham M.: Socioeconomic status and some precursors of neuropsychiatric disorder. *Am J Orthopsychiatry, 26,* 1956.

19. Wahl, Charles W.: Diagnosis and treatment of status medicamentosis. *Dis Nerv Syst, 28,* 1967.

20. Zrull, Joel P; McDermott, John F., and Poznanski, Elva: Hyperkinetic syndrome: the role of depression. *Child Psychiatry and Human Development, 1,* 1970.

# PART FOUR

# INTERVENTION: SCHOOL GUIDANCE

*Chapter X*

# WORKING WITH PARENTS OF PRESCHOOL CHILDREN

Rose M. Bromwich

THE focus of this chapter is on the nature of a productive helping relationship between the families of preschool children and preschool personnel. Within the context of this relationship, there will be emphasis on the prevention of children's difficulties, the amelioration of normal developmental problems, and the identification of problems of a more serious nature. Young children's difficulties are seldom limited to the child himself but are involved in the interactions and relationships between the child and others, first his mother, and then other "significant persons" in his life-space. Potential problems in early childhood are discussed in terms of the background of familial and cultural values, behaviors, and practices. Some distinctions are drawn as they exist in actual life between working with middle-class families and with families in poverty communities.

## BASIC TENETS

Every professional who works with young children and their parents operates within a particular theoretical frame of reference, whether he is aware of it or not. Some of the basic tenets of the philosophy which underlies this chapter are stated below.

1. Education of the young child is the joint responsibility of home and school (preschool); therefore, it is essential that teachers and parents share their observations and perceptions and work together for the benefit of the child.

2. The child develops as a result of his interaction with his ever-expanding world. The nature of his environment affects the child's development, but the child also affects the nature of his

225

environment, especially its human component, as he acts upon it.

3. The younger the child, the more prominent is the role of his mother or mother surrogate* in his life. As he grows beyond the infancy stage others in his home (father, siblings, extended family) gradually assume an increasingly important role. Significant persons outside his home begin to have an impact on the child as they become part of his psychological environment.

4. In the interaction between the child and others, first and foremost in his relationship with his mother, each is affected by the other. The mother (except in atypical relationships) cannot and does not behave toward the child in an objective and detached manner. She is emotionally involved and, in the process of interacting with her child, she grows, changes, as the child grows and changes.

5. The everyday encounters between mother and child have an impact on mother's overall functioning as well as, more specifically, on her relationship with that child.

6. When this mutuality in the parent-child relationship is given serious consideration by the professional worker, he is likely to be more accepting of the parent, which makes their working relationship more productive.

7. The mother cannot be dealt with only, or even primarily, as "the parent of that child," but first of all as a human being with her own personality structure, value system, attitudes, life experience, and problems.

8. A feeling of self-worth, a sense of adequacy, a feeling of competence, these are basic and necessary aspects of a person's psychological well-being. This is true for the child as well as for the parent.

9. The parent is ego-involved with the child—the child is an extension of the parent's ego, and therefore how the parent feels about his (or her) child plays a major part in the parent's self-concept. In western society the image a woman has of herself in the role of mother is a criterion of primary importance in her evaluation of herself as a person.

*Whenever the word "mother" is used from here on, it will signify the person who functions in the role of mother to the child, be it grandmother, father, foster mother, etc.

10. The younger the child, the more crucial is the woman's perception of herself as mother to her overall self-image.

11. An essential requirement in any kind of contact between a professional worker and parents of young children is that the worker must be aware of some of the above-mentioned principles. The worker considers the parent first as a human being; second as the parent of a particular child, with her own strengths and weaknesses, areas of sensitivity, and vulnerability, her own feelings of adequacy and inadequacy; someone who, in the role of parent, experiences something between a relative sense of success and a despairing feeling of failure in that role.

12. The child and the parent, each for himself, must move in the direction of maximizing a feeling of self-worth and a sense of competence. A mutual trust between parent and child is dependent on each one feeling adequate as an individual and secure in his relationship with the other.

Medinnus and Curtis[17] have found parental self-acceptance to be an important antecedent to child acceptance (by parent) which, in turn, is essential to the child's self-acceptance.

## GENERAL GUIDELINES FOR WORKING WITH PARENTS OF YOUNG CHILDREN

It must be kept in mind in this section that even though some generalizations are made in the interest of promoting desirable practices in working with parents, the teacher or worker should never lose his awareness of the importance of individual differences when dealing with individual parents and children. The overclassification of cases, the rigid pigeonholing of individuals into tight categories, clinical or other (a practice that is fairly common among clinicians and teachers), can have very destructive effects on work with parents and with children. These oversimplifications overshadow any belief in individual differences and thereby prevent the worker from perceiving the parent (or the child) as a unique person, making it very difficult to interact effectively with the parent on a person-to-person basis. The fact that certain children as well as certain parents appear to have some problems in common does not make the persons who have these problems identical. It is with the whole person who has the problems that the worker must deal, not with the problems themselves in isolation. This commitment to the whole person and to the uniqueness of each person, child or adult has important implications for work with parents.

In counseling parents individually or in groups, it is best to avoid making statements or answering questions in terms of "the right method" of dealing with *the child* in general or with *children* in particular situations. This practice would belie the belief that children as individuals differ, parents as individuals differ, parent-child interactional patterns vary, and that every situation is unique in terms of the meanings it has for those involved in it.

In working with groups of parents or with parents on an individual basis, it is important to create an atmosphere in which parents can honestly explore, individually, their feelings and thoughts as well as their own responses to their children and their children's reactions to their actions. If the parents can feel safe; if they do not feel they are being blamed or accused of being responsible for the child's problem; if they are encouraged to gain new perceptions of recurring problems and undesirable patterns of interaction; if they can get support in reconstructing situations in new ways, in finding new and more effective methods of dealing with the child; then the parents will have gained much, including greater confidence in themselves.

Sometimes it is desirable to provide parents with knowledge of some principles of child development. This knowledge is most helpful when the parent himself can relate it to his problem with his child. In the end, it is the parent who must be the problem-solver of his own situation with whatever help he or she can get that will shed light on his as well as the child's problem.

Following are statements of some important objectives and guidelines for reaching these objectives oriented to professionals who work with parents of young children. The objectives are stated in terms of behavioral outcomes; behavior as conceptualized here includes *acting, feeling,* and *thinking.*

> *Objective 1:* The parent feels more adequate as a parent and receives new hope toward being able to effectively handle everyday situations involving the child.
> *Guideline:* The teacher (or other personnel) should be empathetic, encouraging, and she should try to help the parent build on her positive attitudes and feelings toward the child.
>
> *Objective 2:* The parent understands the nature of the problem(s)

a little better and, if it is a common problem of children in a particular stage of development, the parent becomes aware of this fact. This helps to alleviate her tension and possible guilt.

*Guideline*: Encouraging parents to share their problems with each other in a group situation will give relief to those parents who may feel that their particular problem is unique. The burden of a child's emotional problem for which the parent feels somewhat responsible gives the parent a painful experience of aloneness. The awareness that others have similar situations to live with or possibly worse ones can be extremely reassuring to parents.

*Objective 3:* The parent realizes that the preschool years are not considered to be easy ones either for the children or their parents, and that the range of normal behavior in preschool children is wide.

*Guideline*: Some discussions should take place, preferably in a group, about the kinds of crises that many children go through during this often-difficult developmental period. The sharing of feelings by parents about the difficulties they experience, as well as empathy and understanding from the teacher are helpful.

*Objective 4:* Parents begin to accept and understand the nature of constitutional differences between children and the nature of the interactional process between the child and others that affect both the child and the significant other in their behavior toward each other.

*Guideline:* It is important to show evidence of the above whenever possible in the course of informal contacts or more formal discussion until the parent gradually begins to accept these realities. As a result, the mother feels more able to cope with the child as an individual separate from herself rather than an extension of herself—a being for whose every action she feels solely responsible.

*Objective 5:* The mother becomes aware of her right to see herself and to be seen by others as a person who has needs of her own; one of those needs usually is to spend some time away from the child or children, doing something that gives her satisfaction and is self-enhancing.

*Guideline*: The worker or teacher must be aware of the stress that a mother is under when she is constantly with her child or children. This is especially true if the child has emotional problems, is going through a difficult period, or simply, if the mother *finds* it strenuous and difficult to take care of the child. It is important to recognize the parent's right as an individual to pursue some interest of her own outside the home, and sometimes to give her the reassurance that it may be better for the child if the mother feels more fulfilled as a person and not resentful of having to stay home constantly. The time the mother spends with the child, even though it may be less, is likely to be more productive in improving the parent-child relationship if she feels that she is able to satisfy some of her own personal needs and do some things she *wants* to do. In some homes in poverty communities where mothers often do not have opportunity to leave the home for a variety of reasons, the mother can feel "imprisoned" in her own home if she is having a difficult time with her children. When mothers get together, it is sometimes possible to arrange car pools and mutual baby-sitting arrangements to allow some mothers to "get away" occasionally.

*Objective 6:* Fathers and mothers support each other in their dealings with the child. This does not imply that both have to behave in an identical manner toward him. There is often the danger that if the mother goes to parent education groups or classes, she will then come home, use what she has "learned" to justify *her* way of dealing with the child as being the *right* way and the father's, the wrong way. Everything possible has to be done to prevent this emotional rift from developing between the parents.

*Guideline:* The parents should be encouraged to attend sessions together. This is not always possible. It should be made clear that there is no need for both parents to deal with a child exactly in the same manner. A child soon learns that every individual is different from every other, beginning with his own two parents. He also learns that certain behaviors are acceptable in the presence of one but not in the presence of the other, and vice versa. The myth, however, that both parents always have to deal with the child in the same manner is often a clout that one parent uses over the other when there are already some disagreements or problems between them. Fathers should be invited to attend parent sessions whenever they can, and in some situations, it is desirable to have a "father's session" occasionally.

*Objective 7:* Parents become more resourceful and try new ways of dealing with particular situations. They should be aware that there is *no one right way;* a particular way is a good one for a particular parent with a particular child only if the parent feels comfortable with it.

*Guideline:* The worker should communicate a feeling of trust in parents' ability to find adequate ways of dealing with their children in various situations. Whatever the worker can do to *value* the parent as a *person* and a *problem-solver* will help that parent *be* more adequate (because she will feel more adequate) with her child. The worst possible way for a parent to feel, especially one with a child who already has a problem, is helpless, dependent on someone else's directions, and totally inadequate with the child. A feeling of utter helplessness with a child is an extremely anxiety-producing, painful, and stressful experience. There are situations, however, for example when a parent mistreats her child severely and seems unaware of the effect this has on the child, in which the parent must be helped to become aware of what she is doing even if this entails producing a certain degree of anxiety which, with help, might encourage behavior change.

*Objective 8:* Parents learn to enjoy their children and develop a feeling of mutual trust in their relationship with them.

*Guideline:* This sense of trust is more likely to develop when the parent feels competent as a parent, appreciates and likes the child, and perceives him as an individual separate from herself. With children with more serious problems, this feeling is more difficult to accomplish, but the same principle is valid. The more adequate the mother feels in her relationship with her child who has problems, the more positively she will feel toward that child; this, in turn, makes it much easier for her to cope with him.

There are times when parents and children need more help than the preschool personnel can provide. Therefore, it is important for personnel connected with preschool settings to be knowledgeable regarding places for possible clinical referrals; that is, community clinics, agencies, private clinics, and other services that provide various types of help.

When does it become necessary to consider clinical referral? How serious is the problem observed in the preschool setting? There are various clues that teachers need to watch for in helping them make decisions of whether or when to refer families for clinical help. Following are some ways in which parents of children indicate that the problems are serious enough to warrant consideration of referral:

1. The parent, or more specifically the mother, feels that the problem is one of major proportions; she cannot begin to deal with it. This in itself signifies that *she* needs help regardless of what the objective evaluation of the *child's problem* might be. If the parent *feels* totally inadequate in dealing with the child, a referral is necessary.

2. When a child has emotional problems of a relatively serious nature, these are usually demonstrated not just in one area of his behavior but in several. Therefore, teachers need to observe children in a variety of situations and contexts before drawing conclusions about manifest behavior in one situation.

3. Serious problems are likely to persist for a prolonged period and/or are exhibited at a very high level of intensity.

One very common characteristic of children with problems and of parents who react strongly to extremes of children's behavior is a low threshold of tolerance for frustration or stress. Mother and child may each have their own way of giving evidence of this low threshold. Some therapeutic help may be necessary in either case as such conditions may contribute to tension in the relationship between parent and child.

If it is clear that either the parent or the child or both need clinical help, referral should be made with tact and sensitivity, but without wasting too much of what may be valuable time. A case in point is one which I witnessed several years ago. A director of a private nursery school told me that a child attending her school was exhibiting very strange behavior. She proudly revealed that her entire staff was involved in a thorough case study of the child—this had been going on for over a year—and the director mentioned that it was very interesting to all her teachers who participated in this study. Upon hearing some of the behavior descriptions and after observing the child briefly, it was obvious to me that this little boy (5 years old) was severely autistic. No attempt had been made to refer the mother for help. In this case, valuable therapeutic time was lost.

## DIFFERENT CHILDREN, DIFFERENT PARENTS, DIFFERENT RELATIONSHIPS

Real differences between human beings, certainly between children, and very importantly among newborn infants, should be given as much credence in fact as in theory. Josselyn[18] in her classic work on the psychosocial development of children very succinctly states the case for individual differences at birth, in infancy, and in the early years:

> The observation of young children offers the clearest indication of the interrelationship between constitutional and environmental factors. Certain children appear to have a capacity to deal with even severely threatening situations, and to be able to master them instead of succumbing to them. Other children react with poor adaptation to seemingly minor situations. Some children show a basic sensitivity to such experiences as befall them, while others show an almost stolid indifference to the same events. . . . In the writer's opinion, there is no

convincing evidence that experiences following birth alone explain the total personality picture. Where life experience appears to have been destructive, the degree of destructiveness is partially dependent from the outset upon the constitutional pattern of the individual. This constitutional factor itself, however, must be considered in the broadest terms. . . . A constitutionally sensitive child may be deeply hurt or frightened and respond to hurt or fear by withdrawing. . . . On the other hand, a constitutionally sensitive child may find expression in artistic achievement. He may, responding still otherwise, deny his sensitivity and defend himself by building a shell of metallic indifference around himself. He may choose one of a multitude of other solutions to protect him from the pain to which his sensitivity exposes him.

Prenatal factors have been found to influence the physical as well as the psychological makeup of the newborn child. Awareness of the importance of constitutional differences, only some of which may be genetic, can be very useful to the teacher or clinician working with parents. Such awareness tends to prevent the worker from subconsciously placing blame on the parent for difficulties that children have, and consequently enables him genuinely to assure the parent that children are different constitutionally at birth. Children differ in sensitivity and vulnerability to forces in their environment, making it unreasonable for the mother, who is usually responsible for the initial care of the young child, to assume the entire burden of responsibility for the child as he is.

Furthermore, there is increasing research evidence for the belief that children are not passive beings that *re*act to stimuli in their environment and are entirely shaped by these forces, as rocks are by water flowing over them year after year, century after century. In fact, even rocks differ with respect to their "vulnerability," owing to the nature of their makeup, to the forces of weather and water current. Research by Piaget,[19] Hebb,[7] White,[27] and others, has shown that the child, or rather the human organism, is an *active* (not a passive) being who grows and develops by "acting upon" (Piaget) or interacting with his environment; in other words, the child is active by nature, exploratory, and goal seeking, rather than strictly *re*active to forces inside or outside of himself.

Constitutional factors, including disposition and temperament, not necessarily all genetic in nature, play an important role in how the child acts upon and interacts with his human and physical surroundings. Schaffer and Emerson[24] have shown that infants differ in their liking for physical contact or "cuddling" and therefore in their responsiveness to it. Obviously the infant who is very responsive to cuddling is going to receive more cuddling than the infant who does not respond as readily and therefore may develop a closer bond between himself and his mother than the noncuddler. Mussen, Conger, and Kagan[18] effectively use a metaphor to express the interactional process between parent and child:

> . . . the child's temperament makes as important a contribution to his own social development as the mother's behavior toward the child. The relationship between parent and child is a kind of ballet with each partner contributing his own personality and dispositions to the form of the behavior each shows toward the other.

Probably one of the factors most inhibiting of positive relationships between parents and children is the sense of guilt that the mother frequently feels about her child's problems. Such guilt tends to be more prevalent in middle-class mothers than in mothers from poverty communities. The mother's realization that she does not carry sole responsibility for the personality of her child can considerably alleviate the burden of this guilt. In fact, children with physical handicaps are generally easier for parents to accept than children with either emotional problems or mental retardation (unless there is diagnosed brain damage) because the parent can more readily accept that the causes of the former are physical-constitutional and therefore she is not to blame. Society has done little to help the parent feel a little less guilty for her children's mental or emotional difficulties.

The teacher or clinical worker and the parent must genuinely accept the notion that all relationships, including those with one's children, are interactional—that each individual affects the other and influences subsequent behavior toward the other. This acceptance allows the mother to develop feelings of adequacy and an openness leading to a combination of spontaneity and a thoughtful and rational approach to child-rearing required for healthy parent-child relationships.

While individual differences in children and in parents make for different relationships, certainly the nature of the cultural and social milieu has additional impact on these relationships. This issue will be discussed further on in the chapter.

## COMMON PROBLEMS OF PARENTS WITH
## YOUNG CHILDREN

The period of early childhood is not the happy, carefree time of life that adults often like to believe it is. Adults are often baffled by the child's behavior during that period. Why the angry outbursts, the temper tantrums, the fears, the short attention span, the aggressiveness, the unwillingness to follow directions, the ambivalence between wanting to do it himself and clinging to an adult or asking continuously for help, and so on? Fraiberg[6] explains that the adult's inability to understand or cope with the young child's behavior is due to the parent or teacher not remembering his own first five years of life. This period "is submerged like a buried city, and when we come back to these times with our children, we are strangers and we cannot easily find our way."

The purpose of this section of the chapter is to help the reader see the child's behavior in the preschool setting in the context of the totality of the child's human interactions and experiences. For the young child, his relationship first with his mother and then with other members of his family has major bearing on his development and on his overall behavior. The specific problem of separation from mother when the child first enters a preschool program is part of the broader dependency relationship between mother and child. Difficulties in the area of child discipline in the preschool setting are more clearly understood when they are viewed in the context of the total relationship between the child and his parents and the issue of authority and discipline in the home. Further on in the chapter, some specific behaviors identifiable in the preschool setting are discussed: hyperactivity, aggressive behavior, and withdrawal behavior. As much as possible the focus will be on the role of the teacher (or other professional) in relation to the parents of the child exhibiting these behaviors.

The subject of academic learning problems is not relevant to the preschool setting, or, at least, it should not be. In an appropriate school situation for young children between the ages of two and five, the child is offered many learning opportunities in various areas to promote all aspects of his growth—intellectual, psychosocial, and neuromotor. If the child develops negative responses, they are often attitudinal and may have to do primarily with the inappropriateness of the learning opportunities offered to that child, the way in which they are presented to him, or the psychological climate in which he finds himself. The building of a positive self-image, a feeling of self-worth, a sense of competence in dealing or coping effectively with his world, which includes the development of language, conceptual learning, and problem-solving of various kinds—these developmental tasks are basic in importance to the child and his healthy development. The child, however, does not need to be faced with the task of *formally* learning any specific and prescribed set of academic skills during the preschool years. Thus, there is minimal danger of his experiencing failure with academic-type learning tasks, failures that would only contribute to a negative self-concept and foster poor attitudes toward the later learning of needed academic skills.

Anxiety about early academic learning of children in middle-class America has become so pervasive that it has begun to infiltrate Head Start programs and children's centers for children of working parents (mostly one-parent families). The assumption that the early years constitute a "critical period" for cognitive learning has been seriously challenged by Kohlberg[12] in the light of Piaget's research and theory on intellectual development. Kohlberg cogently argues that "academic" learning in the preschool years may enhance intellectual development less than other types of activities to which the young child is more naturally drawn. Smilansky[25] stresses the importance of sociodramatic play in the intellectual development of young children, and Almy[1] explains how central all young children's play is in the development of intellectual processes.

Directors and teachers of preschool programs often succumb to the pressures of parents to force early academic learning onto children who do not naturally turn to that type of activity when it is offered. It is quite appropriate to make such learning opportunities available to children (such as activities related to reading) if this can be done in a relaxed, nonpressuring manner, without insisting that all children participate in the same type of learning activities. Educators and psychologists bear the responsibility for interpreting to the parent what the important learnings are for the young child. Unfortunately, formalized academic instruction at the preschool level takes place in some preschool settings in order to *please the parent*. This practice may instill negative attitudes toward learning and a sense of failure in many children, as well as a sense of despair in parents.

If the child continuously fails to deal successfully with his environment and the tasks he chooses to tackle in that environment, he should receive support and help from others. If the mother participates in the school or observes occasionally, the teacher can help her to understand the learnings that the school considers to be important for that particular child at his particular stage of development. If the mother cannot be in the school setting, discussion with the parent individually or in a group setting can communicate the educational objectives that are of primary importance during the early years.

## Dependence-Independence: A Critical Area in Mother-Child Relationship

The early childhood period has a potential for deep satisfaction as well as considerable tensions for parents. The satisfactions are those of witnessing the emerging personality, the development of a wide range of capabilities, traits, attributes, and the gratifications of the mother's nurturing her young — being able to provide the ingredients necessary for physical and psychological development. But there are also tensions that often arise during the early childhood years.

The problem of separation, a manifestation of the struggle between dependence and independence involving both the mother and the young child, has been given much attention, mostly in psychiatric literature. The emphasis in the discussion that follows is on the behavior of the child as he enters nursery school (or any initial school experience) related to separation from his mother, and the various reactions by mothers to this developmental milestone—sometimes crisis. An effort is made to show the connection between the child's and the mother's manifest behavior at the time of separation and the possible underlying crisis in the mother-child relationship.

### Beginnings of Dependence-Independence Ambivalence

The infant is in a state of complete dependency on the mother and her care of him. Unless the child is physically not well and consequently presents special problems, the mother can satisfy the physical as well as the emerging affective needs of the child. For many mothers, especially for those who do not have other concerns that overshadow their care of the child, the infant, in a sense, is perceived as part of mother—an extension of herself—therefore, meeting the infant's needs can be almost like meeting her own needs.

An early critical phase in the mother-child relationship is when the toddler begins to "feel his oats." He gradually perceives himself as a separate entity from his mother and both physically and psychologically attempts to demonstrate this separateness to himself and others. Erikson[5] calls this the stage of "autonomy versus shame and doubt," a stage when the child begins to say "no" or "me do it" which shows that he is beginning to be aware that he is a being separate from his mother, and that he therefore has certain powers, powers to control his body, what goes into it and what comes out of it, an important beginning toward independence. For some mothers, the child's emerging power to exercise control over his body and his environment is difficult to accept. All of a sudden the completely dependent infant becomes the child who wants to *do* things for himself, be on his own, at least in a physical sense, and assert himself and his newly discovered powers to those around him. Also, his needs grow more complex and are not as easily satisfied by the mother.

It is at this point that mothers who have the ability to *let the child BE*, to let him go forth toward increasing self-dependence, can be distinguished from those who suffer during this first stage of the child's asserting his separateness. Some mothers have great difficulty in accepting the child's striving for his own control of himself and of his surroundings—his movement *away from her* and toward greater independence. This difficulty probably occurs more frequently with the first or the only child.

In large families, especially in poverty areas, this assertive phase of development often means the transfer of the major responsibility for the baby's care from the mother to the older siblings. It is also the time when some mothers with little time interval between pregnancies begin to be preoccupied with their newborn infant. In one particular family, the mother of seven children in a public housing project, who was described as engaging in serious child neglect, did not stop giving adequate care to each child until he or she had reached the toddler stage. The care of the infant while totally dependent was quite adequate. As soon as the child began to fare for himself, even to a limited degree, the mother became almost aloof to the needs of that child, and the children in the fatherless family survived with the help they gave each other and by the good graces of neighbors (equally poor) who often fed the hungry children. This is certainly an extreme example, but it may serve to illustrate some type of shift in the mother's relationship to her child at that point in the child's development. If such a shift occurs, it is expressed differently by different women and in different subcultures. The period can be identified as that during which the child becomes more mobile with the beginning of locomotion and the initiation of verbal communication.

Most mothers whose basic needs are satisfied and who are psychologically reasonably mature rejoice in each step that the child takes toward greater self-care during this stage; they can enjoy with him every movement toward increased control of his environment. Such a mother is usually very supportive of the child as he attempts to cope successfully with his expanding world. In some families, however, this period marks the beginnings of certain types of difficulties. How mother and child resolve the inital phase of the child's striving for greater independence may (or may not) be reflected in the type of separation situation that occurs when the child enters some type of school-like setting.

It is important to help mother and child deal with the separation situation as smoothly as possible because the transition from home to school is a very important step in the child's development. If this transition is comfortable, the child will tend to have strengthened his self-concept by having gained trust in himself in dealing with potentially stressful situations. He will also strengthen his trust in the world around him which helped him through this transition from home to school. His own satisfactory resolution of this separation may constitute an important model for him to follow in meeting further critical periods in his life.

Mother and child are both psychologically involved in the separation situation; sometimes the mother actually experiences greater difficulty than the child and, in this type of case, the child's behavior in the nursery school may be, in major part, a reflection of the mother's problem. Some illustrations of actual cases will clarify the multifaceted problem of separation.

THE CLINGING MOTHER. An example of a mother's difficulty in separating from her child is given below.

A mother of three children, two girls and a younger boy, brought her son to a nursery school because she felt he needed to have contact with other children. The mother could not leave the child in care of the professionally trained staff. She explained that she had never been separated from her children until the older girl began elementary school, which was a painful experience for the mother. She also had never left the children with a baby-sitter. The serious separation problem was clearly the mother's much more than the child's. The mother was encouraged to leave the child in the school for periods increasing in length from five minutes to the entire morning. The mother went through a tremendous struggle even with the short separations. When she was finally asked to leave for the whole morning (she later told the staff), she could not bear to leave the school premises, and stayed for 3½ hours in her car in the parking lot. After an initial response in kind to the mother's anxiety about separation, the boy accepted his mother's departures as he began to enjoy the school and to feel safe there.

The mother's inability to separate from her child in the above situation was, of course, an extreme case, but many mothers share this difficulty, in kind if not in degree, of letting the child go—accepting the child's movement away from his mother, both physically and psychologically. When this problem of *dependence by the mother* on her nurturing relationship with a completely dependent being does exist, it is often apparent in some form at the beginning of the child's preschool career (or whatever the child's first school experience might be). The mother attempts to keep the child as dependent on her as possible, although she usually does not do this on a conscious level. It is important for the teacher-in-charge to recognize the mother's problem and to help her plan her gradual separation from the child, giving *her* much support as well as giving the necessary help to the child.

The professional in the situation must determine for whom the separation is a greater problem, for the child or for the mother. Children, of course, differ in their degree of sensitivity, attachment to the mother, vulnerability to changes in their environment, anxiety relative to new experiences, and the degree of intensity of reaction to the first real separation, which nursery school or kindergarten is for many children. The example above simply demonstrates that it may be the mother's problem more than the child's. The mother may be deeply involved in terms of her internal struggle between holding on to the child and letting him go. It is often an oversimplification to state that the separation problem is *either* the mother's *or* the child's. Obviously the mother is involved in some way in the child's problem, but the degree to which she is involved in terms of her own ambivalence varies greatly. There are certainly cases where the child, from infancy on, seems to be highly sensitive and tends to overreact to the smallest changes—new experiences, new situations.

THE CLINGING CHILD. There is another type of separation problem which appears, in terms of the mother's surface behavior, to be solely that of the child, but may involve the mother rather deeply in a different way. Some mothers actively *push* the child away from them physically and psychologically when the child shows the slightest tendency toward "hanging on," not wanting to let go of mother at first when entering the school setting—a new situation. This is quite normal behavior on the part of the child, but again, it is the *mother's* behavior which needs to be examined. In some cases, the mother's behavior of pushing the child from her may simply be the result of her feeling embarrassed when she sees her child cling. Socio-cultural pressure may be involved: the mother believes that the "ideal mother's" child is ready to leave her side when he starts any kind of school. It may, on the other hand, be the outward evidence of some feelings of rejection on the mother's part which, when sensed by the child, makes the child's separating from mother that much more difficult. An illustration follows:

> The mother brings the child to school. The child holds on to mother for dear life. The mother either strips the child physically off her and leaves, or if asked by the teacher to stay, she stays but tries to rid herself of the child by taking him to various activity centers, attempting to get him involved either with other children or with playthings. She often seems very surprised when the child will not let go of her and goes right back with her to her chair or to the door.

At times, of course, when the mother has to go to work, she must leave the child right away. In those cases, if the child has some difficulty letting the mother go, the mother can be helped to understand this. Various procedures can ease the separation, such as one or two visits before the mother starts her job, or bringing the child a little earlier in the morning so that the mother can stay with him for at least a little while.

IMMEDIATE ADJUSTMENT? Another not uncommon occurrence is that of the child's apparent immediate acceptance of the separation only to regress a few days later to expressions of extreme need for mother. This is not really a regression but only appears to be. The initial apparent adjustment to the situation probably is due to the child's excitement with his new and stimulating environment and his involvement with new playthings and children; but a few days later, when the initial quality of adventure and exploration of the new has worn off, there comes the sudden realization that mother is not around. The child has really not been able to work through the separation, being mostly unaware of it. The child suddenly feels lost and alone in this relatively unfamiliar situation. Sometimes this "second thought" separation anxiety lasts longer and is more intense than anxiety experienced in a more gradual adjustment of the child to the new setting.

THE QUICK GETAWAY. Some mothers and teachers seem to believe that children are better off if the mother "disappears" immediately. Some mothers cannot bear to see their children cry at times of separation, and so they leave quickly to prevent a scene. Teachers occasionally encourage mothers to leave immediately because they feel they can handle the child more easily than they can deal with mother and child together. However, greater convenience for the teacher should not take precedence over what is best for the child. If at all possible, the child should get the necessary support from his mother to help him work through his separation from her.

THE LIE. The extreme case of the mother not wanting to see her child cry, in order to avoid feeling guilty for leaving him, is occasionally seen in hospitals. The rationale that when the mother does not see the child cry the child is better off, is, of course, not valid. A case in point is a mother saying to her child before she takes leave of him in the hospital, "I'm going downstairs to buy you some candy, I'll be right back," however, she does not return that day. This happened so often at a particular hospital that the writer felt it necessary to write a leaflet to be handed out to parents in that hospital's pediatric clinic, previous to a child's hospitalization, to assist the mother in helping the child make an adequate adjustment to hospitalization rather than making the hospital experience unnecessarily traumatic for the child.

OVERDOING THE GOOD-BYES. Although the mother's letting the

child know when she is leaving is of primary importance, this can be overdone. Occasionally a mother will act in a manner that seems to indicate that her overt behavior covers up her real feelings. This mother overwhelms her child with very physical and lengthy and elaborate goodbyes. This is done in the name of "being honest with your child and telling him when you are leaving." She takes leave of her child very dramatically, interrupting him in his play several times to tell him that she will be going soon, or uses other attention-getting devices. The observer suspects that the separation is more difficult for the mother than for the child, that the mother may be a little hurt because the child seems to fare so well by himself. She may want to make the child very much aware of her leaving. She may subconsciously want the child to miss her and therefore she does what she can to assure this result.

### Some Dependency Behavior Is Normal

Direct assistance can be given by the preschool staff to the mother and child to prevent or minimize problems for both the child and the mother in this inital separation situation. The teacher should take the responsibility for explaining to the mother that children between the ages of two and five, when entering an unknown setting, often show some reluctance to separate themselves from their mothers. When the mother is prepared to encounter this behavior and can trust it to be normal and expected, she will be more relaxed should some dependency behavior occur. The pressure in terms of cultural image of the "good" mother's child is thus alleviated. It may be helpful to take this opportunity to talk to the parents about individual differences in degree of help and support that different children need in the separation situation. This type of orientation can, of course, be given to parents in a group as well as individually, and may be an excellent opportunity for the professional person to introduce the idea of differences between children in general sensitivity and in reactions to new situations. Such a discussion may also help the parent to be more open and sensitive to her own child in other circumstances.

### A Supportive Mother

An actual case will illustrate how a mother who could accept some dependent behavior connected with separation effectively handled the situation.

Diane was entering a summer session in a college laboratory nursery school. She clung to mother who sat inside the playroom on a chair against the wall near the entrance. Mother had a magazine on her lap and smiled occasionally at the child. During the first fifteen minutes, Diane was in physical contact with her mother. First, she put her hand in her mother's lap, then held on to her skirt while looking about, visually examining the new setting. Then she left mother's side for a moment, went to a shelf nearby where other children were playing, picked up a toy fire engine, brought it to mother's side and sat down at mother's feet and played with it there. She showed it to her mother who looked at it with interest and smiled. Mother did not, however, actively involve herself in play with Diane. Occasionally Diane looked around to see what was going on in the playroom. After a while she took the engine back and brought a puzzle close to her mother. Diane gradually progressed from this stage to leaving her mother and involving herself in an activity in another part of the room for a few minutes. Mother looked toward her occasionally as she was reading her magazine. Whenever Diane came back to her mother's side, mother would acknowledge Diane's presence with a smile or some physical expression of support. On this first day, Diane made no approaches to other children or the teacher (although the teacher came over to her several times without attempting to take her away from her mother); neither the mother nor the teacher showed the slightest concern regarding the child's behavior.

The second day began in a similar manner, except that the periods away from mother became longer. Diane had juice with the children, although she took mother by the hand and brought her along to the table. On the third day, Diane returned more infrequently to her mother, but glanced toward her occasionally during the beginning of the morning. She managed to have juice with the children away from her mother. She became engaged in conversation with another child. After juice, Diane played in the doll corner with two other children for about ten minutes. At the end of this ten minute period, she ran to mother with a smile and said, "Mummy, you can go now, I don't need you any more!" The mother got up, gave Diane a friendly hug and a pat and walked out of the room. Diane watched her close the door behind her and then went back to her play.

The above episode indicates that a relationship of mutual trust existed between the mother and her young daughter. The mother showed acceptance of her child's dependent behavior in a new environment, was patient with her, and showed faith and trust in the child's ability to work her feelings through by being quietly supportive but not overbearing.

## When Is the Child Ready?

Children mature at different rates and although a child may be of a chronological age when most children are ready to leave mother and go to nursery school, a particular child may be better left at home a little longer. For some children, two or three times a week may be a better arrangement than everyday, if this is feasible. For other children, a good initiation into a preschool experience may be a once-a-week playgroup, such as those sponsored by adult education programs, where mother and child go together, and mother simply goes into another room part of the time.

Any of the following behaviors or a combination of them, especially if they last beyond the first or second day, should be cause for reconsidering whether the child should remain in the school: (a) if the child is totally unable to accept *needed* mothering from an adult in the school setting, (b) if he does not involve himself in any activity (including the watching of other children) with some degree of satisfaction or enjoyment, (c) if he engages in recurrent crying or intermittent sobbing throughout the day, and (d) if he moves from crying or obvious unhappiness (without crying) to withdrawal behavior. If the mother works and the child must remain in school, every effort should be made to permit a gentle and supportive transition from home to school. The child may be helped by holding on to something that he is fond of from home or something that belongs to his mother. Much mothering by someone in the preschool setting may be needed at first.

## Preparing the Parent

Just as the child needs to be prepared for certain events in his life, such as the new baby, going to school, being hospitalized, or forced separations from his family, the parents also need help in understanding certain reactions on the part of the child, especially if these are not easy to anticipate. The most dramatic instances of unexpected behavior may be exhibited by the child after a period of forced or sudden separation such as sudden illness and hospitalization of the mother or of the child himself. The more traumatic the actual separation was for the child, the more it is likely that the child will react in a hostile, rejecting manner toward the mother when she returns to the child. The mother needs to be prepared for this possibility and must understand that regardless of how much verbal explanation there might have been given to the child, he still may have emotionally *experienced* a feeling of having been deserted when the mother left him at the time of the forced separation. The mother's understanding of the child's behavior will help her to help the child and herself through this sometimes difficult period for both.

## Beginnings of Concern with Authority and Discipline

The area of authority and discipline is a major one in which problems often develop in the early years of the child's life; therefore, it is essential to have an understanding of the context in which difficulties may be observed. The first part of this section deals with that context.

### Parental Authority and Expected Child Behavior

Parents often have conflicts, each within himself, and between father and mother, on the issue of discipline. In the "mainstream" or middle-class culture, the father is often the one who tends to be somewhat more authoritarian, who feels that strict obedience by the child is paramount in child-rearing. The mother may see the child's assertion of his own powers as desirable initiative and movement toward greater independence.

Considerable conflict exists regarding expected behavior of boys. On the one hand, society says that boys, as all children, should respect their elders and obey, conform to the rules set by adults, be friendly, get along with others, and be unaggressive. On the other hand, boys, to be considered "masculine" (as expressed in western culture) must be aggressive, must be able to stand up for themselves, must not let other boys "walk all over them," must be assertive of their rights even if it means engaging in a physical fight (rather than running from a fight and thus be a "coward"). This conflict between two contradictory standards of behavior has, in the past, caused many problems for boys growing up in this culture; it also causes much stress within families. Often the father will encourage the boy to be assertive and aggressive, and when the boy behaves in this manner and gains acceptance from his father, he finds that mother is often very disapproving and believes him to be a bully and a trouble-some child.

There seems to be somewhat less conflict surrounding the expected behavior of girls, but when some girls exhibit assertive or aggressive behavior, it is often disapproved of by both parents. Of course, there are many exceptions. There is also a myriad of problems that arise in the family with regard to expected behavior and how to "train" the child or deal with him so that he will behave in a desired manner.

## Social-Class Differences in Child-Rearing Practices Related to Authority

Research has shown that differences exist in child-rearing practices and in the concept of parental authority between middle-class and lower-class families. Bronfenbrenner[3] made a thorough analysis of studies dealing with trends in child-rearing practices over a twenty-five-year period (1930 to 1955). He found that 1946 (end of Second World War) marked the climax of the view that "middle-class parents place their children under a stricter regimen with more frustration of their impulses than do lower-class parents." After the Second World War, another position emerged; middle-class parents were "more permissive" than parents in the lower class. Bronfenbrenner, using data from a large number of studies during that period, drew some interesting conclusions:[3]

1. The common assumptions about lower-class values in the home—expression of aggression, immediate gratification—in contrast to middle-class values of cleanliness, respect for property, sexual control, and educational achievement, are not upheld by evidence in terms of recent times although they do hold true for the period before World War II.

2. Although lower-class and middle-class mothers follow the same trends in child-rearing, the former lag somewhat behind the latter, very likely because lower-class parents are not in as close touch with written materials expressing current expert opinion. Between 1930 and 1946, lower-class mothers were more permissive in breast feeding, weaning, and toilet training, but after 1946, the trend was reversed; middle-class mothers became more permissive; the lower-class mother, less so. Middle-class mothers,

especially after 1946, have been consistently more permissive than lower-class mothers toward "children's expressed needs and wishes" and have had a more "acceptant, equalitarian relationship with their children."

Bronfenbrenner points out that whereas the lower-class parent employs punishment more often, middle-class parents often use "reasoning, isolation, appeals to guilt, and other methods involving the threat of loss of love. At least two independent lines of evidence suggest that the techniques preferred by middle-class parents are more likely to bring about the development of internalized values and controls."

A more recent study by Radin and Kamii[21] compared the child-rearing behavior of middle-class Anglo mothers and ghetto-dwelling black mothers of three-, four-, and five-year-olds living in a midwestern city.* The authors distinguished between standards of behavior which both groups shared and those that were more often in evidence in one group than in the other, as expressed by endorsement or rejection of a number of statements on the Parental Attitude Research Instrument. There was common agreement by both groups on the following statements:

> Children need discipline and firm rules. Children have certain rights as family members. Babies are helpless and need protection. Conflicts between a wife and a husband are to be expected. Motherhood is a nerve-wracking job.

The following attitudes were expressed much more frequently by lower-class Negro mothers than by middle-class Anglo mothers:

> Some children are just so bad that they must be taught to fear adults for their own good. Children must not be encouraged to talk about their own problems because the more they are allowed to complain, the more they will complain and pester mothers. Aggression in the form of boxing, wrestling, and hitting another child must be suppressed. It is desirable to get children out of the helpless stage of infancy as early as possible.

Seventy-five percent of the lower-class Negro mothers as against 14 percent of the middle-class Anglo mothers endorsed the following

---

*The Parental Attitude Research Instrument (PARI) was used with two samples, one year apart, of both types of populations; only those views that held up over both samples were recorded in the findings.

statement: Children should never learn things outside the home which make them doubt their parents' ideas.

The findings cited above are valuable background against which to view some of the issues related to discipline and authority that arise today in families of various types of communities and which are often reflected in preschool and school settings.

## The Educator's Concern with the Issue of Authority and Discipline

Most professionals working with parents of young children are concerned with discipline for two major reasons: first, because many teachers and directors of preschool programs are disturbed by parental discipline which they believe to be either too strict and authoritarian or too permissive and laissez-faire, and which they believe, results in a variety of problems in terms of child behavior in the preschool setting; second, because they find that discipline is the primary concern of most parents of young children with whom they come in contact. Whenever preschools have speakers or discussion groups for parents, discipline as a topic is frequently requested by parents or offered by the school because the director is aware of the widespread interest in this subject.

In order to deal realistically with this issue in parent groups or with parents individually, personnel working with parents need to be informed about the ideas and practices regarding discipline which are most prevalent in the immediate community as well as the concerns of particular parents. It is important to sort out which seemingly undesirable disciplinary practices are culturally accepted and common in the community subculture, and which practices result from parents' inadequacies, sometimes sheer frustrations.

## Cultural Differences in Family Structure

In the Mexican-American home, the father holds a strong position of authority. The implications for the child's, especially the boy's, attitude toward authority are important; in the preschool as well as in the later years in school, the Mexican-American boy may have difficulty in accepting the authority of a woman teacher. On the other hand, the young child, especially the little girl in the Mexican-American family, tends to be very close to and dependent on the mother, and is often overprotected. He or she may have difficulties with separation from the mother, although the little girl may manifest this with more passive behavior, such as shyness and a certain degree of withdrawal, than her Anglo middle-class counterpart. Boys often exhibit similar behavior.

In the black poverty community, a family structure somewhat different from the middle-class nuclear family unit* is quite common. The black family is usually described as an *extended family* (in contrast to the Anglo middle-class *nuclear* family), a structure in which grandparents, aunts and uncles, siblings, and cousins play an important role. All of these members of the extended family have their place in the authority structure of that family.

Even though the authority factor varies somewhat from one ethnic group to another, one phenomenon is common to the urban poor of all ethnic groups in this country—the high incidence of father-absence in the inner-city home. This situation probably is due most directly to the economic pressures on the poor as well as some welfare practices which tend to separate the father from the home. The resulting experience of many children of poor urban families (not as true of rural families where problems of poverty have a somewhat different effect on the family) is that of growing up without a father in the home. The hiring of male teachers, teacher assistants, and aides in Head Start programs has been encouraged and increasingly implemented because of the Head Start child's need for a male figure in his environment in the early years.

### The Male Image in the Preschool

Many educators and psychologists believe that it is vitally important to introduce more men into the lives of all young children. Some aspects of sex-role identification occur earlier in young children of poor families than in those of more affluent families in spite of the frequent absence of the father.[20] Young children, poor or affluent, even with fathers in the home, often do not have the kind of continuous contact with their fathers that would present a clear image of the male role in the family and in society. The problem that is created in terms of identification manifests itself frequently in dramatic play in the nursery school. The "father," in the child's dramatic play, is a

*"Nuclear family" signifies a structure that includes only mother, father, and children.

very uninteresting role to play—he leaves home and goes to the office (or to work), then returns home, but there isn't much to do for him at either place (the young middle-class boy rarely knows much of what his father does all day). Thus, the problem of psychologically sound sex-role identification exists for the boy who does not have a father living in the home, and also for the boy who rarely sees his father. Girls also have a need for early meaningful human relationships with men. Therefore, the presence of more male teachers in preschool settings is desirable.

In a study by Kagan,[11] boys in inner-city areas regarded materials and objects used in teaching and learning in the school, such as books, paper, pencil, pen, as having female identity. Dr. Kagan concluded that inner-city boys often reject school-type learning partly because it is perceived as activity identified with the female role. Another relevant factor may well be that children in kindergarten and the early grades usually have female teachers. A pilot study is under way in Akron, Ohio, which will examine the effect of black male teachers on the learning of black boys in the ghetto of that city.[11] One elementary school in Akron has been staffed entirely with black male teachers.

### Parental Discipline and Parents' Feelings of Adequacy

Most parents are quite sensitive to criticism of their way of dealing with their own children's behavior because the entire quality of parent-child relationship is deeply involved. The methods that parents use to "socialize" their children, to teach them to conform to certain behavior codes and boundaries that society at large or the immediate community have set, form an integral part of the mode of interaction and the psychological climate in the home.

When parents become aware that their children have some problems, one of the most likely reactions is to blame themselves for having been too strict or too lenient, for letting the child get away with too much or not allowing him enough freedom, for giving him too much responsibility or not giving him enough, for punishing him too severely or not severely enough, for being inconsistent, etc.* Teachers and clinical workers should be aware that these expressions of

*The reactions described are probably more typical of middle-class parents than of parents in communities in poverty areas.

self-criticism and doubt are often signs of much deeper feelings of inadequacy or even guilt. These feelings become more pronounced as the child's problems become more severe. The more guilty a parent feels or the more responsible she feels for the child's problem, the more inadequate she feels. Of course the mother's basic level of self-confidence as a person and as a parent certainly influences the degree of inadequacy that she experiences. Feelings of incompetence in the parental role usually cause resentments, overt or covert, toward the person or persons who are directly or indirectly responsible for these feelings. In this case, the result is likely to be that the parent begins to resent the child for causing him or her to feel inadequate; therefore, the parent is less able to cope with the child than before. Also, father and mother often become critical of each other in relation to problems that they see in their children because it is more comfortable to blame someone other than oneself. Such tensions between parents create additional stress for the child. These are some of the realities faced by those who work with parents of young children.

### School May Contribute to Problems of Discipline

Many problems related to discipline and authority in the school are brought about by the climate, routines, and adult attitudes toward and expectations of children in the school. The first order of business, when problems of discipline and authority arise in the school, is to try to discover what factors in the school environment might be contributing to the problem. Individual differences between children and differences in home environments must, of course, be taken into consideration too. The purpose of the preschool experience, hopefully, is not to fit children into a specific mold of behavior or even to teach them a particular way of responding to authority figures. The manner in which a child responds to teachers as figures of authority is the result of a multiplicity of complex factors interacting with each other. The child's authority relationship to his parents is only one of these factors. It is wise not to pass judgment on children or on their homes and families as a result of their behavior at school. Observing children's behavior in regard to authority or established standards or rules of behavior and distinguishing between a child's reactions to different adults help us learn more about the individual child.

## Teacher's Approaches to the Problem

When problems of discipline become extreme in the preschool setting and if the consensus of the school staff is that the problem is not largely caused by unreasonable expectations of teachers or the ignoring of the needs of the individual child, the child should be carefully observed in a variety of situations. Extreme problems in discipline are usually coexistent with other difficulties in areas such as the child's relationships with adults and children, his self-image, his play, and his feelings of competence.

If the child has problems of a serious nature, the *discipline problem* may be only a symptom. Therefore it would be shortsighted and inadvisable to deal with the discipline problem of a child with serious difficulties in isolation from the rest of his behavior by asking the mother to change her methods of discipline at home. All the different aspects of a child's difficulties should be dealt with in context of the whole child in his total environment at home and in school, and preoccupation with a particular behavioral manifestation should be avoided. On the other hand, if the teacher knows that the mother needs direct and immediate help in coping with the child to avoid further frustration, some specific suggestions might be in order. These should be given as *possible* ways of dealing with a particular situation, such as: "You might try to——, it is sometimes an effective way but it does not work with all children"; or "This works for me with Jamie, but it may not work for you—children react differently to their teachers and to their parents—but you might try it and see what happens." If the mother is approached in this manner, she can make choices and will not feel totally ineffective or guilty if the suggested practices are not helpful. Suggesting more than one possible way to deal with a situation is also a wise practice whenever possible. Direct suggestions should also be considered if what the mother or father does to the child is believed to be seriously harmful to the child. Suggestions, however, are not likely to be accepted or followed up unless good rapport has previously been established with the parents so that they have some trust in the teacher.

Teachers who are skilled in listening to parents can gain much from them. If the rapport between parent and teacher is good, the parent usually feels free to relate incidents involving the child's interactions with members of the family. As a result of newly gained insight about the child and his relationship in the home setting, the teacher may be able to deal with the child in school in a more rational and sensitive manner.

## Practices to Avoid

Teachers sometimes succumb to temptations that should be carefully resisted:

1. The temptation to tell the parents to deal with his child differently at home for the sole purpose of preventing a particular behavior at school that annoys the teacher. Why is this not a good idea? Children can adjust, in fact, should have the experience of adjusting to different expectations by different people in different situations. If the expectations are at all reasonable and not contrary to the child's needs, the child will have little problem in adjusting to different expectations in different environments involving different people. It is only when teachers find that the parental treatment of the child at home is unreasonable and seems in itself detrimental to both the parent-child relationship and to the child's well-being, that the teacher is justified in working toward modifications in parental practices.

2. The temptation to ask the parent to follow through with punishment at home for something objectionable that the child has done at school. This is a very unsound practice. The child must learn to deal effectively and comfortably with his environment at home and at school separately. The demands as well as the opportunities are different in the two settings. He must learn to deal with the consequences of his behavior at school, *in the school*, and at home, *in the home*. The reverse is just as inappropriate—a teacher should not follow through on punishment for something the child has done at home, no matter how much the parent insists. The parent has to be helped to understand the importance of keeping the consequences of behavior where the behavior occurs—the consequence should always be reasonable for that individual child, logical, and immediate and it should occur in the setting in which the rule was violated.

# SOME CONSIDERATIONS REGARDING CHILDREN IN HEAD START PROGRAMS

## Independence or Pseudoindependence

Some children in Head Start programs seem to indicate by their surface behavior that they are completely independent. This "independence" is expressed behaviorally by an apparent lack of need for adult help. This type of behavior may indicate an advanced level of actual independence that the particular child has achieved, and often, children of the poor learn self-reliance earlier than children from more protective, sometimes overprotective homes of middle-class families. At other times, children will reflect a home environment where adults have not been readily available to the child, to do things for him, to help him with everyday little tasks that may loom large to the child. In such cases, the child may not have been able to move from dependence to gradually increasing independence. The expectation of independence may have been rather abrupt and the child may not have been able to meet his dependency needs. Without the gradual development from dependence to independence, the sense of trust is not developed as readily between the child and the parent. This relative absence of the child's feeling of reliance upon the "significant adult" for support and help, when such help is needed, may well affect the child's relationship with and expectations from his teacher.

One way in which a pseudoindependent child may react to a Head Start program is to be aloof at first and rarely approach adults, even if he legitimately needs an adult's help. A case in point is that of a four and one-half-year-old Mexican-American girl who playfully stuck a part of a toy around her middle finger and could not free her finger from the toy. She sat by herself quietly, trying to loosen the toy but did not succeed. After several minutes of trying, she walked over to a drawer, picked up a dull knife, and proceeded to pry the toy off her finger. When, at that point, help was offered, the little girl did not reject it but rather passively accepted it. She had not been able to ask for the help that she certainly needed.

Sometimes the child who seems self-sufficient and independent at first will seek physical closeness (often called "clinging") and even excessive help from adults for a while. Thus, the child is seemingly regressing, but actually may be satisfying some of his unmet dependency needs. This type of experience with adults may help the child learn the very valuable behavior of utilizing adults as resources when approaching learning tasks. Using adults as resources will prevent a common behavior of many inner-city school children: that of passively sitting in the classroom when they do not understand assigned tasks, and gradually, when this experience repeats itself often, tune out and mentally drop out of school at a very early age.

Parents can be helped to understand that children relate to adults in a variety of ways, including occasionally expressing dependency needs. The importance of being responsive to the child's need for physical closeness or help can be pointed out. In child care centers, where children often spend long daytime hours, it is especially important for the teachers to be responsive to some children's strong needs for mothering. Parents may be helped to understand that meeting the dependency needs of the child at school and at home is not "spoiling" the child.

**The Child's Apprehensiveness in the New School Setting**

Families in poverty areas tend to operate within a somewhat more authoritarian structure than middle-class families.[3]

Mothers and fathers often put excessive emphasis on obedience to authority figures, be it the parent or the teacher. This is commonly true even in situations where parental control in the home is loose and discipline inconsistent. Punishment is usually physical and, at times, severe.

Hess and Shipman[8] found that mothers of black inner-city children tend to prepare their children for kindergarten by warning them that they had better obey the teacher, or else! Often little or nothing is said to the child about the opportunities he will have to learn all kinds of important and interesting things, or that he might even enjoy school. The facts are that most of these parents have themselves neither enjoyed school nor do they remember learning anything either interesting or useful. The same investigators also found that black children from middle-class families (parents with professional or managerial occupations) more often prepare their children for kindergarten by telling them how lucky they are to be able to go to school, how much they will enjoy it, and about some of the things they will learn to do.

Teachers in Head Start centers can do much to orient parents to see the importance of other things in the child's life besides obedient behavior. Sociologists and psychologists have frequently commented on this stress on obedience by the poor or the "underclass" in the following way: the parents may simply have grown up with the stark reality that obedience is the only path to self-preservation and survival. This holds true for all poor people, but especially for black people. Memory is only too vivid in the lives of those who have recently emigrated from the South. If the Negro in the South (and too often in the North) does not learn obedience or even obsequiousness, he is liable to live a short life, especially the black male. Mothers as well as black female teachers have been observed to be especially strict and punitive with the male child. Unfortunately, the conditions, even though they are gradually changing, are not so totally different now from those of a century ago in this respect. Black youth, however, has begun to change its attitude and its behavior and this change is gradually affecting the priorities with which black children are raised.

A good way to encourage change toward less authoritarian relationships in the home and the valuing of other behaviors equally or more than obedience is to have parents share in the Head Start experience. Parents participating in the ongoing program are exposed to a setting where obedience is not emphasized, but where the child is responsible for himself, is encouraged toward more mature behavior without the use of threat of punishment, where the child enjoys himself and learns at the same time. Preaching to the parent will create no changes but tends to produce resentment and anger in the parent ("Who is she to tell me how to treat my children?"); but parental exposure to a good preschool program can be extremely effective in getting the parent to reexamine her ways with her children, to gain new perceptions of the child as a human being functioning in all kinds of positive ways. In the casual contacts with the participating parent in the preschool setting, the teacher can call to the parent's attention the positive things about the child as he proceeds happily through the morning.

## Awareness of Particular Strengths of Children in the Head Start Program

Many children in poverty areas manifest, at an early age, some very desirable behaviors which should be valued as such by the teacher. If the teacher is aware of some of the strengths of her children, she can then encourage parents' awareness and valuing of these qualities and behaviors. Head Start children are often more caring, protective, and helpful toward each other than their more competitive middle-class peers. Natural cooperation and sharing often take the place of rivalry, both among siblings in the home and among children in Head Start and at school. This highly desirable human quality should be given recognition as well as be valued to the child directly and to his parent. This will help the parent be more appreciative and approving of the child and feel better about herself as a parent.

Head Start children often have highly developed large-muscle coordination and are usually able to accomplish physical feats that many of their middle-class counterparts are not able to do. Also, finger dexterity in manipulating objects is frequently more highly developed at an earlier age than in middle-class children. This may be due to the need for earlier self-reliance in dressing, tying shoes, and various other daily routines.

Some of these qualities and abilities are commonly ignored. Instead, great attention is called to the "deficits" of the "disadvantaged," even though it is generally considered good educational practice to build on the positive rather than stressing the negative in aiding the development of the young child. Parents can be helped immensely in feeling more adequate as parents when they hear genuine expressions of positive reactions to their children and some of their children's specific positive attributes.

## Who Takes Care of the Child at Home?

One important difference between the majority of middle-class homes and homes in poverty communities is the family structure, as explained previously. In the extended family it is not always the mother who takes the major responsibility for the care of the preschool child. It is certainly essential for the teacher at school to know who is closest to the child at home and who usually takes care of him. I once found myself conferring with a mother in her home about a five-year-old boy only to discover that it was the seven-year-old sister who took care of little Joey; in fact, as the conference proceeded, the seven-year-old girl began to respond much more relevantly than the mother, and the conference ended with the sister rather than with the mother. This serves to illustrate the importance of including members of the family who may have a closer relationship with the Head Start child than the mother and may be more helpful with the child as well as give more pertinent information about the child if the teacher should need such information.

## COMMON PROBLEMS OF CHILDREN IN THE PRESCHOOL SETTING

### Problem for Whom?

When examining problem behavior during the preschool years, a clear distinction needs to be made between that behavior which is indicative of a problem for the child in terms of his mental health or overall functioning and that which is only troublesome and inconvenient for the adult. When the teacher finds that the child's own behavior is detrimental or destructive to his own development, she needs to be aware of this and deal with the child in the most appropriate manner possible in the school situation.

How does the teacher distinguish between behavior that is a problem only to her (the teacher) or a problem also for the child? First of all, the teacher should avoid constructing a mental model of "what a three-year-old should be like" and then fitting all three-year-old children into that model, which becomes a mold of conformity. When a child then deviates from the pattern thus formulated, his behavior is considered deviant and the child is "a problem," and unfortunately is often perceived as "having a problem" with which he needs help. The antidote is for the teacher to be aware of each child as a separate human being with his own constitutional makeup, his own temperament,[26] and his own reservoir of life experience—all of which contribute to his own behavioral expression of his own personality at any particular time. Also, in the case of most children, the teacher should not focus on the problem behavior of a child but rather concentrate on discovering the child's strengths and help him build on these and gain a more positive self-image.

Second, the teacher needs to be conscious of the types of behaviors common among children that are especially annoying to her as an individual. Regardless of the reasons for the teacher's feelings of annoyance or even anxiety, reasons that often relate back to the teacher's own personal history,[9] the awareness of these feelings will help the teacher sort out when the child's behavior is hard for her to bear because of her "hang-ups" and when it is really indicative of a problem the child may have for himself. Also, it cannot be stated often enough that during the preschool years the range of normal behavior is very wide.

Third, there are many situations and circumstances in preschool settings, as well as teacher behaviors, which tend to cause particular reactions on the part of some children. When children exhibit certain behavioral reactions such as hostility, restlessness, lack of concentration, and withdrawal, there may be many contributing factors: too many directions, not enough variety of experiences, not enough opportunity for physical movement or rest, punitive adult behavior, and a host of other circumstances in their environment. It is a good idea, according to Redl,[22] for teachers or persons in a supervisory capacity periodically to "examine the plumbing"—find out what there might be in the school environment itself to cause a child to exhibit behavior that might or might not be signs of a child's problem. For example, young children need a daily rhythm of activity (physical) and rest—some need more rest; others, more activity. If groups of children are held too long in a state of relative inactivity, some will react with restless, "inappropriate" behavior.

## When the Problem Is the Child's

If the teacher, with the help of others in the situation, has decided, after considering all the above points, that the child exhibits behavior indicative of problems needing careful attention, involvement of the parent is usually necessary and beneficial to the child, the parent, and the teacher. Early contacts with all parents, in which the teacher shares with parents the child's strengths and positive qualities, will help greatly in cases where problems later arise. A genuine partnership between home and school can be realized when parent and teacher share with each other their impressions, observations, and experiences relative to the child. On the other hand, if the teacher waits to make personal contact with the parents until a problem arises (which unfortunately is a common practice in many schools), the parent tends to experience a threat to her self-image as parent, and senses tacit blame for the child's behavior which often results in parental defensiveness. This immediately creates a serious obstacle to communication with the parent. Whether or not the parent becomes defensive, she may feel anxious and helpless; these feelings create a barrier not only between the teacher and the parent, but also between the parent and the child, making the home atmosphere worse rather than better for the child.

## Differences in Behavior at School and at Home

The child's behaviors at school and at home are different expressions of who he is and what he is. When sharp differences in behavior are observed at home and at school, a variety of factors might be contributory:

1. Parent and teacher may have different norms relative to acceptable or unacceptable behavior—they may have divergent values which affect their standards for child behavior.

2. The child often behaves quite differently in two such completely different surroundings. Extreme differences may have to do with greater restrictiveness and exercise of adult control in one situation and greater freedom of choice and broader limits in the other. A child, for instance, who is raised in a rather strict home where much of his activity is closely directed and supervised may go to a nursery school where he finds less control and more freedom. His first reaction to the school may be mistrust, apprehension of this strange and open situation, but when he has learned to trust the new situation, when he begins to feel safe in it, he may become "wild" for a while and test the limits of his new freedom. On the other hand, the child who may have adjusted to the many limits and close direction in the home may remain somewhat frightened and overwhelmed by the new freedom, remain somewhat withdrawn, and may even have to be guided rather closely at first until he becomes more secure and sure of himself in the new situation. It is helpful if the teacher is acquainted with the nature of the home climate so that she can deal constructively with his reactions and aid the parents in coping with a child who may act somewhat differently at home after experiencing a new atmosphere in the school setting.

Some children will push the limits of freedom at home after an initial preschool experience. If several parents find themselves in the same situation, a few group meetings can be useful in helping parents interpret their children's new behavior and in reexamining the family's reactions to the child at home in the light of his new experience. By observing the child in school after he begins to settle down and is purposeful and constructive, the parent might see for herself that the child is quite capable of making certain choices, engaging in certain activities without being directed at every step. It should be made very clear to the parent, however, that home is not school, that the school setting is one specifically oriented to the needs of children of a particular age range, whereas home is a family setting where everyone's needs must be considered, where different members of the family, including children, have to make certain accommodations so that the family can live harmoniously together. Parents should not be encouraged to try to make their home a carbon copy of the school. A child may use the school to let out his pent-up energy and feelings when he comes from a very restrictive home. When the child is given a little more responsibility for himself and more freedom of choice at home, however, the child is likely to be less excitable and less difficult to deal with in the school.

The opposite may be as much or more of a problem, especially with children of some middle-class homes. Children from homes where few if any limits or routines are set may feel very strange at first in a situation where they find specific routines and certain limits imposed. It is difficult to predict how any one child will react to this type of change. He may be extremely rebellious and have difficulty accepting new limits, or even resentful and hostile toward the adults as well as toward the children in the new setting. On the other hand, a child who is used to excessive freedom or even license may, for the first time, feel secure within reasonable boundaries set for him; he may feel safe, and as a result, he may *experience* more actual freedom, be more productive and more socially outgoing than he may have been in his own home. In cases of extreme permissiveness in the home, the child might be reacting to an element of parental rejection. In either case, if the child seems to function well in the school situation, the parents might be encouraged to observe the child in school and be helped to think through how they might modify the life situation for the child at home to aid the child to be more comfortable and secure.

## High Activity Level or Hyperactivity?

Children's activity levels vary greatly from the placid infant and the mildly-active child to the extremely-active child. Sometimes it is very difficult to determine the fine line between high levels of activity resulting from the child's temperament and intensity, and hyperactivity in which there might be a slight or a more severe neurological involvement. Parents as well as teachers are frequently concerned about highly active behavior. Distinguishing between the normally active child and the neurologically-involved hyperactive child is an important challenge for both parents and teachers throughout the child's school career.

In the last few years there has been much discussion of the use of drugs in the treatment of hyperactive children. The overuse of drugs to control children's activity level has become an area of public concern and is currently under discussion in many quarters (*Los Angeles Times*, 1970).[16] In a recent article, Ladd[13] raises some of the issues and problems concerning the hyperactive child. According to Ladd, there is much confusion regarding the diagnosis as well as the drug remedies for what is generally called hyperkinesia, which involves the Central Nervous System (CNS). The hyperkinetic child is described as follows:

> ... compulsively responsive to stimuli from within or without, and hence compulsively hyperactive ... the instructions the child sends his CNS more or less deliberately are superseded or swamped by other messages coming in from elsewhere in his brain, his body, or his environment, and, as a Canadian researcher has put it, "The child tries to react to everything at once."

Ladd also refers to the recent news story that large numbers of school children in Omaha, Nebraska were given drugs. He suggests that in many cases the teacher in the elementary school becomes the main diagnostic agent on whose report the physician relies before prescribing medication. This puts a tremendous responsibility on the teacher in the preschool, and throughout the grades, not to draw conclusions prematurely about children with high levels of activity who, admittedly, may be more difficult to deal with in any school setting than the child with naturally lower levels of activity. When teachers actually identify as deviancy such behaviors as "a child dismantling his ballpoint pen, propping up his desk with his pencil, or stopping on the way back from the pencil sharpener to talk with someone or to look at things on the teacher's desk," as reported in Ladd's article, there is much cause for concern. The problem is that teachers will often perceive behavior that disturbs them and that seems to them to be different from what they like to expect from children, as deviant. The issue of whether a child is hyperkinetic or just highly active and maybe somewhat nonconformist is a serious one which should concern the teacher in the preschool also. The parents' impressions of the child's behavior at home should be carefully checked with the school personnel's impressions and observations of the child's behavior in the school setting before drawing any conclusions or suggesting to the mother that the child needs medical referral. A recommendation with even more serious implications would be that he might need medication.

Extreme care must be taken to safeguard the child against being *manipulated* with drugs into more conforming behavior and greater obedience, when there are no clear medical reasons for the administration of drugs. It must also be remembered that teachers, including those in preschool settings, often have considerable influence on mothers and their perceptions of their children, and as revealed more recently, they have possibly undue influence over some physicians. It is widely known that some physicians have minimum resistance to prescribing drugs, even to children, when the parent, possibly influenced by the teacher, so requests.

The very active child who is well within the normal range may also have difficulties in self-control. If the two coexist, he may have a greater need than the average child to feel the security of some limits and the reassurance of acceptance and love. Some assistance can be given to the parents in setting clear limits for the child and in helping him in a completely *nonpunitive manner* to stay within those limits. This tends to have a calming effect on the child; he is able to be in better control of himself, which, in itself, is reassuring and relaxing. Excessive freedom is often upsetting for such children. Also an abundance of expectations which the child cannot live up to because of his difficulty in self-control and sometimes in concentration span tends to cause additional stress and problems. This holds true for school and home alike.

If parents participate in the school program or observe occasionally, it will be easy to demonstrate to them how the highly active child with intense reactions might be helped to gain better control of himself. Following is an example of how a parent might be helped through a demonstration in the school setting:

> The child is engaged in outdoor play activity. He is prepared for an imminent transition or change in activity (transitions and changes can be experienced as stressful) by being told that it will be time to come into the playroom to have juice in a few minutes. Then, when it is time, instead of calling the child when the parent's or the teacher's previous experience with the child indicates that he will not come, or that he will have a temper tantrum, or that he will "go to pieces" in some other way, the adult goes to him, *takes him by the hand with a smile*, and says something like, "Harry, it's time to come in now. Let's go together."

This model could be demonstrated to the parent in a number of situations. For example the parent might have an opportunity to see the teacher helping a child put his blocks away rather than ordering him to do so alone. The *nonpunitive follow-through* with the child, the adult taking considerable responsibility for directly assisting the child in following through with the requested behavior, and the cooperative attitude on the part of the adult is usually very helpful and reduces tension and rebellious resistance to the adult by the child. With this kind of handling of the situation, neither the child nor the adult experiences a sense of failure. Such a cooperative attitude by the adult may be important as a model for the parent.

Parents, especially in middle-class communities, sometimes feel that the more freedom the child has, the better it is for him. This is especially not so in cases of highly active and very intense children who may have difficulty in staying within reasonable limits and exercising a reasonable degree of self-control. Being faced with too many choices can be very tension-producing for the child. As was stated rather dramatically by a psychologist-friend, some children who do not experience limits may feel that "with every step they take, they might fall off the edge of the world." In other words, absence of limits may sometimes actually restrict the child's psychological freedom. On the other hand, punitive parental measures also hinder the child in gaining self-control which is best learned in a calm, secure, and accepting climate.

## Aggressive and Hostile Behavior

Aggressive behavior has always troubled teachers and parents. Aggressive behavior which is self-assertive and signifies a kind of openness in the expression of feelings can be identified as a positive type of aggressiveness that should not cause concern. Many teachers, however, find it more difficult to deal with a child in the nursery school setting who is more assertive and outwardly expressive than with one who is less assertive and more quiet, calm, and sometimes even passive. Care must be taken not to confuse this assertive behavior with aggression that is *hostile against* children and adults. The child who is assertive in a positive sense is often also self-confident, exploratory (will try new things), unafraid of new situations, and purposeful in his activities, but will also dare to say "no" or refuse to do things that he either has no interest in doing or sees no sense in doing.

The hostile child tends to vacillate between aggressive-hostile behavior, fear, and sometimes extreme possessiveness. He often demonstrates an inability to tolerate other children's counteraggression by crying or becoming upset in some manner when children hit him back. He has a negative image of himself, is usually an anxious child, perceives others as being against him, is resentful of directions and admonishings, and will tend to rebel against limits set for him. His play is frequently not constructive or very purposeful, and he tends to be dissatisfied with what he produces. The sharp difference, then, between self-assertive, positive-aggressive behavior and hostile-aggressive behavior is that the former is usually that of a fairly happy child who thinks well of himself; the latter, of an unhappy child with a negative image of himself.

For the sake of differentiation, two extremes have been described here. Actually, most children who demonstrate any aggressive behavior may be somewhere between the two extremes, although children very much like the two described above are certainly found in preschool settings. Obviously these two children do not resemble each other psychologically, and teachers need to be aware of this difference when communicating with parents. If the teacher is having difficulties with the self-assertive child, it may be helpful to talk with the mother to discover how the child is perceived at home. He may become particularly difficult when he is bored. He may also need guidance in dealing with his peers if they react negatively to his so-called aggressive behavior.

The following dialogue illustrates some important aspects of conferring with a parent of such a child; in this case, a three and a-half-year-old boy who is assertive, intense, imaginative, but has some difficulties in his peer interactions:

TEACHER. How is Donnie doing at home, Mrs. Jones?

MOTHER. Well, I guess he's OK but he makes me pretty tired—he's so active, he gets into everything, and doesn't seem to have much consideration for others.

TEACHER. I guess children that young often are pretty preoccupied with themselves and don't have as much consideration for others as we would like them to. But does he seem to be happy?

MOTHER. Yes, I was just thinking about that last night. In spite of all the squabbles he gets into with his playmates and all our "no's," he really does seem to be a happy child.

TEACHER. Well, you are saying that he doesn't seem to be much of a problem to himself but he is difficult for you to handle because he is so very active and demanding.

MOTHER. Yes, but I think what really bothers me most is that he does not seem to get along very well with the children whom he plays with around home. In fact, I've been pretty rough with him lately and I'm afraid that he might begin to feel resentful, but he just wears me out. I have the baby to worry about and that's not always easy when Donnie is around. He'll go out to play and seems to be happy for a while, but pretty soon he'll come in and say, "Mommy, they won't play with me" and then he stays in the house and wants me to do things with him.

TEACHER. We see a very similar situation at school. He has lots of ideas when he plays but he tends to try to tell other children what to do; actually he wants them to accept his ideas and play his way but usually they do not like to be told what to do.

MOTHER. Oh, I don't want him to be a bully. I hope you stop that kind of behavior!

TEACHER. Well, we are aware of it, and it is really helpful for me to know that he has the same kind of problem at home. But we try to deal with Donnie so as not to undermine his self-confidence, his good ideas and good feelings about himself. You see, he is quite creative in his play but I think what he lacks at present is ways of communicating these ideas to other children without telling them what to do and how to do it. Some of the boys won't take this from him. They either push him or hit him, or, what disturbs Donnie most, they leave the situation. Donnie either hits back or stands there very puzzled about the whole thing.

MOTHER. You know, that's very much what happens in the neighborhood; only younger children will accept his directions, but the older ones won't and so he ends up playing either alone or with younger children, which I don't like very much—he'll get more and more bossy that way.

TEACHER. I guess what Donnie needs is to learn techniques of how to deal with other children in a more give-and-take way. You know, Donnie is quite bright and very verbal, and that's something we can use in helping him.

MOTHER. I don't know. I guess I haven't done a very good job of helping him. I have tried to. I have scolded him for being so bossy and now he is beginning to sulk and get rather unhappy with me. I'm afraid if I bawl him out much more about the way he plays with other children, he's going to start playing by himself and I really don't want that to happen. I'm glad that he seems to like other children and wants to play with them.

TEACHER. I guess what we have to try to do, both of us, is to help him take a look at what happens when he is not successful in play with others. Just yesterday Donnie was left alone with his block play although he obviously wanted the others to stay and play with him. So after Ted and Frankie had left, I went over to him; he looked rather unhappy and puzzled. I asked him what had happened, and he said, "They don't want to play with me." I asked him if he knew why. He said, "Maybe they don't like me."

MOTHER. Poor kid, that's not a very nice way to feel!

TEACHER. No, it isn't and I didn't want him to keep feeling that way; so I asked him if he thought he had done anything that might have caused them to go away. He really didn't know, so I sat down next to him and told him that sometimes I had noticed that he tends to tell Ted and Frankie what to do, and that maybe they didn't like that. He looked at me with those big brown eyes and didn't say a word. I asked him if he liked it when other children told him what to do. He said "no" rather indignantly. I asked him what he thought he could do to get other children to play with him. He said, "I'd better just shut up—and maybe they'll play."

MOTHER. Oh, I don't like that. I don't want him to get that way—and withdraw.

TEACHER. Don't worry, I doubt if he will. I was glad to tell him that I thought he had such good ideas and it would be a shame not to bring his ideas to his play. Wasn't there something else he could do? He just looked at me with great expectations. I asked him if he were joining a couple of other children in their play, and if someone else, say, Ted, had an idea of what to build, how would Ted get him, Donnie, to stay and play with him. Donnie said right away, "By letting me decide what I want to do." So I said, "You mean you would not want him to tell you exactly what to do and how to do it?" Donnie gave me a stare—then I was so pleased when Donnie said, "Maybe I should ask Ted and Frankie what they want to do, or maybe just let them do what they want." He gave me one more look and then ran over to join some of the children with rhythm instruments.

MOTHER. That was really great! But how could you be so calm about it all? I get so impatient with him when he does this sort of thing.

TEACHER. Well, if I had ten other things to worry about and a baby to take care of as you have, I think I'd have a pretty hard time with him too.

MOTHER. I'm really so pleased that he could think of a better way, with your help, and instead of making him feel unhappy, you made him think through the situation and kind of take stock of what he did to make such a mess. I think you're great!

TEACHER. Oh, I'm not so great with my own two children. I get very impatient with them. It's so much easier to be good with other people's children than with your own, especially when you have nothing else on your mind in school except the children, and when you know that you will spend only so many hours with them, and then, good-bye!—till the next day.

MOTHER. (*smiles*) Yes, I guess you have a point there. But I think that rather than blaming him for the mess he makes of things, I could try to get him to think about it and see if he can't find a better way. If only I can stop being so annoyed. Maybe I can now, because after listening to your story, I'm beginning to see Donnie again as a really great kid who just needs a little help to work things out for himself.

The mother was getting discouraged and was beginning to resent her child's bossiness and aggressive behavior with other children; she was expressing annoyance and anger to the child, but she was also feeling guilty for making him feel badly, which, without some kind of change, or, at least, opportunity to express this feeling, tends to increase the mother's resentment of the child. The teacher expressed empathy with how the mother felt, and instead of directing her how to deal with her child, she gave an example of what happened at school; she related an entire episode which made Donnie really look quite positive in the end. The teacher chose not to discuss some other episodes at school which might have been less useful here.

The mother saw what was involved but felt somewhat less capable of dealing with her child than the teacher. The teacher was sensitive to the mother's feeling of inadequacy and responded to it effectively toward the end of the dialogue. She was sincere and genuine all the way through the conference.

The mother was helped to discover a way of being supportive to the child and, at the same time, help *him* to solve a problem that he had created for himself. This preserves the dignity of the child and builds on his strength—that of being able to think through a problem and find a solution for it. The teacher, as demonstrated in this dialogue, should be careful not to widen the gap between the "professional" and the mother, but rather, communication should bring the two closer together, two people who play different roles in the child's life.

On the other hand, when dealing with a hostile, aggressive, fearful child who lacks self-assurance, one important principle is that the more serious the teacher thinks the child's problem is, the more careful *listening* the teacher should engage in when conferring with the mother. The more serious the problem, the more sensitive the mother is likely to be, as she usually has some awareness (perhaps not entirely at a conscious level) that there is something wrong with her child. Sometimes the teacher can get cues for handling the problem with the mother if she finds out how the mother feels toward the child. There is no law that says that the teacher has to tell the mother all the things that the child does at school which are disturbing to the teacher and which cause the teacher concern. Two important criterion questions for deciding what the teacher should communicate to the mother, should be (a) Is this likely to be helpful to the mother in being more effective and feeling more adequate with the child? and (b) Is it going to help the child in terms of how the mother feels and acts toward him?

Therefore, a teacher might proceed by saying, "I'm so glad you came, Mrs. Taylor, because I feel it would be so helpful to me to know Billy a little better by hearing you tell me a little about him at home."

If the mother, as she well might, becomes defensive and says, "Why, is there something wrong with Billy at school?", the teacher might answer, "Many children of this age go through crises and I think our talking together might help us both to understand what is going on inside Billy right now." The teacher continues to show her interest in Billy and what he might be experiencing, putting the focus on the way the child sees or interprets his world. This focus can be a constructive point of departure which tends to move the mother away from a defensive or self-blaming position. The conversation might take a turn toward a mutual agreement that Billy views his world rather negatively, reacts negatively to it, is fearful, and tends to strike out at people in his despair. The teacher might mention that some children are much more sensitive and vulnerable to everything they experience than others, tend to interpret their experiences more negatively, and end up having a low regard for themselves. If the mother, on her own, begins to relate how difficult it is for her to cope with Billy, and how she has arrived at a dead-end with him, the teacher might find a nonthreatening way to suggest that help for both child and mother is available.

For families who need clinical help for their children and for themselves, it is important not to rush into making a referral, but to approach it after having established a relationship of trust with the parents. This may take several conferences with the teacher before the parent is actually ready to accept the fact that she may need outside help.

Regardless of whether the child's behavior calls for outside help or not, the nursery school teacher can do much to help the mother deal with his hostility. The child's behavior may be a response to a particular stress that he is experiencing currently in his life; that is, a new baby, tension in the family, separation from mother, or any abrupt changes in the child's immediate environment. The teacher may show or suggest to the mother how she might recognize and accept the feelings the child is expressing but still not allow hostile-aggressive acts. For example, a mother observing or participating in a preschool may see a teacher deal with a situation in the school which suggests to her how she might deal with similar situations at home. The teacher has little Mary on her lap. Susie comes along and angrily tries to push Mary off her lap. The teacher says to Susie, "I know you are feeling angry because Mary is on my lap but I will not let you push her off." If mothers who have difficulties handling such behavior at home cannot observe at school, there can be discussion on how children's feelings can be accepted and sometimes reflected while still not allowing hostile-aggressive acts. This is only one of a variety of ways that parents can be helped to deal with children's hostile behavior.

A word needs to be said regarding the above illustrative conversations between mother and teacher. There is no intent here to be prescriptive. This would be going against the entire philosophy which is expressed throughout this chapter. Just as children are different from each other, so are parents and teachers, and each teacher has to find his own best way to deal with each situation. The above dialogue is intended to serve the purpose of illustrating some important principles in working with mothers of young children.

## Withdrawal Behavior

One of the behaviors which causes much concern is withdrawal by a child in the early years. "Withdrawal," however, is a label that is attached to a wide variety of complex behavior, the totality of which cannot be properly dealt with within the confines of this chapter. Suffice it to say here that withdrawal may be the particular pattern of behavior with which the child expresses his negative self-concept and his feelings of anxiety in dealing with his world and himself. Sensitive teachers can do much within the nursery school setting to help the child gain a feeling of self-worth and a sense of competence. This may initiate a change in the child's way of relating at home and at school and thus indirectly affect, positively, the parent-child relationship.

The mother can often be helped to see the child more clearly as he really is. The teacher can also help the mother become more sensitive and responsive to his needs. If the mother's own needs and problems interfere with her meeting the child's real needs, and if her manner of relating with the child seems to increase the child's withdrawal, the mother and the child probably need clinical help.

It is important to guard against labeling as withdrawn, a child who has a quiet, unaggressive temperament, a low activity level, one who "does his thing" without great intensity and without calling a great deal of attention to himself, who does not seek out others, adults or children, who likes to spend considerable time in activities by himself, but is constructive and happy in his solitary play. This child seems to have no fear of others, either children or adults. One might call him a "loner" but not necessarily withdrawn in an unhealthy sense. Sometimes a quiet child of this type may emulate his mother or father, or even an older sibling. If this is not the case, and if both parents are quite outgoing, they are more likely to show concern about this child who seems to be different. The parents, and often teachers too, may want to force the child into more social activities, push him into peer-group interactions when he does not choose this for himself. It is important for the teacher to be aware of the difference between a quiet independence, and a fearful withdrawal which tends to be indicative of emotional problems. Parents can be helped to recognize that their child is well within the normal range of behavior with a kind of temperament and interests that are inclined to keep him away from group play more often than not.

An excellent film, "Shyness,"[29] dealing with somewhat older children, illustrates the differences between three children, none of whom plays with other children. One, Robert, is the type described above —independent, creative, more interested in things and ideas than in people, at least temporarily, and about whom the film concludes, "Robert—there was nothing wrong with him in the first place!" Anna is a "shy" child who needs much support and encouragement to get her to do the things she really wants to do, which is to play with other children and be part of a group. Jimmy is desperately fearful of everything and everyone; he is very withdrawn, in fact, seriously emotionally disturbed. Jimmy and his mother need professional help—his fears and withdrawal from others have gone beyond the point where he can easily be helped by teacher and parent alone. Anna *can* be helped by teacher and parent, by more realistic expectations at home and much support and encouragement at home and in school to build up her self-confidence. In the case of Robert, the parents (and teachers) need to be reassured that he is an individual, different from others, that he has his own strengths, interests, and that he needs to be valued for what he is and for who he is. Pressure to try to change him, to try to make him conform and behave like others must be avoided. He needs to be allowed to be himself.[2, 4, 14, 15]

## TYPES OF CONTACTS WITH FAMILIES OF PRESCHOOL CHILDREN

When the preschool and the families of the children in the program work closely together, much is gained by both parties and ultimately, of course, by the child. The kinds of contacts and ways for home and school to work together are many. A few of these will be briefly discussed below.

### The Individual Conference

The individual conference is the traditional manner of maintaining contact with parents. The current trend has been in the direction of greater informality, bridging the gap between "professional and lay-man" in favor of a more personal and human relationship of sharing and mutual respect. Still, the teacher or other professional realistically sees himself as the "helping person" in a Rogerian sense,[23] a person who attempts to create a helping relationship in the context of which the other person (in this case, the parent) is better able to solve his problems and find the best answers to his questions for himself in his own life situation. This does not imply that the teacher, director, or other professional working with parents, does not at times make direct suggestions to the parent.

Individual conferences can be held in the school setting or in the home. It is best if the teacher or other responsible professional person decides where to hold the conference with each parent after weighing all the factors that might affect the choice of whether to have it at school or in the home. Much has been written on principles and procedures in parent-teacher conferences and will not, therefore, be repeated here.

### Informal Contacts with Parents

Informal unplanned contacts can easily be made on a day-by-day basis with the person who brings the child or picks him up from the preschool. Pick-up time affords a unique opportunity for the teacher to show that she cares about the parent as a person too, not only about the child. An example follows.

> TEACHER. You look tired today Mrs. L.; have you had a hard day?
> MOTHER. I sure have—my baby is sick and I had to drag her down-town to the clinic. Two whole hours I had to wait with a crying baby to see the doctor, and that's no picnic! I'll tell you that.

TEACHER. Oh, that sounds terrible. No wonder you look tired. How is the baby?

MOTHER. I think she is a little better. The doctor gave her a shot— I guess it was penicillin, she has some kind of infection.

TEACHER. I'm glad the baby is better. Why don't you sit down for a few minutes and have a cup of coffee; it's still hot.

MOTHER. I think I will. That'll hit the spot!

When dealing with families in poverty areas the contact may need to be with persons other than the mother (as mentioned earlier in the chapter), or others in addition to the mother—grandmother, older sister or brother, or other members of the family. The stress on obedience and authoritarian discipline, as already discussed, is very dominant in the poverty subculture. The family is often concerned with whether the child "did what he was told" at school—whether he obeyed the teacher. The mother who *participates* in the preschool program has the advantage of being able to discover that other things about children may be more important to the teachers and for the child than blind and prompt obedience. The mother from a poverty area who works and cannot participate or observe in the program can be helped to value other behaviors by the teacher's attitude reflected in conversation with the mother, for example:

MOTHER. Was Mary good today, did she mind you?

TEACHER. Mary was very happy today. She played with Rosa in the doll corner for a long time and she is really beginning to enjoy story time. I'm so pleased about that. We read a story about a dog and she told us about her dog, Trixie.

MOTHER. Don't let her talk while you are reading a story.

TEACHER. We encourage children to talk and tell us about themselves and their own experiences that fit with the stories they hear. That way we know they are really interested and involved.

MOTHER. You still haven't told me if she minds you.

TEACHER. She enjoys herself and is learning about a lot of things. Happy and busy children rarely make trouble. Mary is no trouble at all.

Without telling the mother that she should be less concerned with her child's obedience, the teacher has conveyed to the mother what is important to the teacher about Mary's behavior—her happy involvement in play and learning, which are one and the same in the child's preschool experience.

The teacher also needs to be aware of the kinds of concerns that usually dominate the lives of the poor—problems of day-to-day survival, enough money to buy food for the family, a roof over their heads, employment, keeping warm in the winter, having clothes and shoes to send the children to school, and other pressing concerns of everyday life.

Home visits can be a very comfortable way of relating to a family, or they can be unsatisfactory. The teacher needs to be sensitive to how the family feels about the teacher's coming to the home and to the kind of rapport that has been established with the family. If the teacher is nonjudgmental, accepting, and fully appreciative of the hospitality extended to her, no matter how poor the home, her visit to the child's home and with the family can be very helpful in building important bridges. Some teachers feel that they cannot go to any home unless specifically invited. This again depends on the relationships established, the sensitivity of the teacher, and the relative degree of relaxed, easy-going, and friendly manner of the mother and others in the family. In some situations, there is no harm in casually saying to a mother of a child, "I'm going to be in your neighborhood this afternoon, do you mind if I drop in and say hello and meet some of the rest of your family?"

## Working with Parents in Groups

The opportunity provided by a group for its participants to share with each other experiences, concerns, and problems is of major value to many parents of young children. Parents of children with emotional problems or handicaps of one sort or another usually make excellent use of a group situation with a skilled leader when the climate is accepting and supportive. A parent sometimes experiences a tremendous sense of relief when she finds out that she may not be such a bad mother, that others have similar problems, that her child may not be the most difficult one in the world, and that others have empathy with her and understand her feelings and concerns. The opportunity to talk freely in such a group may be very therapeutic for the parent.

One mother dramatically expressed to the writer how the experience of being in a parent group had helped her. The youngest of four children in this family was born with a serious physical handicap. After the parents had been participants for a few months in a group of parents of children with the same type of handicap, the mother said with considerable feeling that having had the child with the handicap had probably been a blessing in disguise—participation by the father and mother in this parent group had helped the entire family. She said to the leader, in this case a psychologist, that with her help and that of the group she had been able to reexamine herself in her role as mother of all four children, as a wife, and as an individual, and through this experience she had been able to gain a sense of inner peace and confidence in herself; the resulting changes in her had helped everyone in the family. Her husband concurred.

## Parent Groups in Poverty Communities

It is often difficult to reach those parents who seem to be most in need of help. It is even more unlikely that such parents will participate in a group organized for the expressed purpose of helping them to deal more effectively with their young children. Parents with pressing everyday problems regarding physical survival do not readily focus on "emotional" problems, either their own or their young children's. When families do worry about children, the major concern is often about their teen-agers rather than their preschool children.

The kind of problem orientation that some mothers may have is illustrated by the following incident. In a special program for young children in a federal housing project, the parents were invited to come to a group arranged for the purpose of helping them with problems they had with their children. An experienced clinical psychologist, familiar with the children and aware of the many problems in parent-child relationships in these families, donated her time to lead this group. The project staff working with the children informed the parents of the unique opportunity that was offered them. The fact that the leader was to be a psychologist was not specifically mentioned. It was difficult to communicate to the parents the purpose of this type of session and how it might help them. Very few mothers took advantage of the group even though baby-sitting was provided. From a group of approximately thirty-five families, the attendance was between one or two to four or five parents (including an occasional father). On a particular occasion one mother came in at the designated time dragging her preteen-age daughters with her. She took them to where the psychologist was sitting and said, "Here, I brought them both, they fight all the time and they're driving me crazy. See what you can do with them!" This was her way of getting help in dealing with her problem with her two quarrelsome daughters.

Additional contacts with families beyond the mothers attending groups were made with two older siblings, one, a twelve-year-old brother, and the other, a ten-year-old sister who usually picked up the young ones and inquired about them. The ten-year-old girl often stopped in for a little while and talked about some of her daily experiences, many of which were unhappy ones. She cared for the younger child at home and had the need to unburden herself, talk to people who seemed to be friendly and warm and cared about her younger sister. Why would they not care for her too and listen to her problems?

In short, the preschool center, the Head Start center in the poverty community, has possibilities of becoming an important place for all members of the family—a place where people are welcomed, are accepted, and listened to. The more formal parent group may or may not materialize, but the concept of a center where family members are welcome should be given high priority. The family center may be more important in terms of the needs and problems of the families, and may or may not lead to a parent group.

In one particular situation, a mother of eleven children who felt warmly toward and close to the personnel of a program similar to Head Start would come around when her welfare check did not arrive on time and ask for some fruit or canned food to help tide her family over until the check came. Often this is the most urgent help that mothers feel they need, which certainly seems justified in terms of the welfare of the family.

In some children's centers, informal coffee sessions to which parents are invited and urged to stay as long as they want have been effective in getting parents acquainted with each other and with the teaching staff. A two-to-three hour period is set aside once or twice a week; parents are invited to sit down, chat informally, and drink a cup of coffee before they take their children home for the day. Since different parents (mostly one-parent families in California children's centers) get through work at different hours, the period needs to be an extended one and becomes a kind of "open house." Potluck suppers have also been successful in children's centers and they, of course, have the advantage of including the entire family.

## Parent Participation—the Parents' Part in the Program

Parent participation in the preschool setting has been a highly successful way of helping mothers (and sometimes fathers) in getting new perspectives on children, how they develop, and the nature of their needs. It has given many a parent a fresh look at and sometimes a new approach to her own child or children. In the 1940's the cooperative nursery school movement was based on the idea that parent participation should be a very important part of the preschool program; in fact, the parents of most cooperatives not only worked in the educational program from day to day, but they organized the school and hired its teachers.

Experience with parent-participation programs suggests that mothers or those who care for the young preschool child in the home should work with children in the actual program when circumstances permit. In cases where mothers have younger children that require care, some programs (Head Start and cooperatives) have demonstrated that baby-sitting pools initiated by parents can permit such participation, as well as foster a very desirable spirit of cooperation and community.

Parent participation gives teachers who are skilled in working with parents a unique opportunity to help them become more effective with their own children. First, a participating parent has an opportunity to see her child interacting with other children. The teacher helps her function adequately as teacher's aide with all the children. The parent thus gains confidence in dealing with children. She also has the opportunity to see how her child acts with other children and with other adults in the school setting. The school is a unique place where the mother can get a more objective view of her child. She may be able to see him more clearly as a human being with needs and difficulties, but also with strengths, joys, and satisfactions. Often the mother, on her own, begins to see the child in new ways.

The teacher also functions as model as she deals with children. Mothers who are present absorb some of what goes on between teacher and children. The teacher has many opportunities to call the mother's attention to certain incidents, moments during the school day which may help the mother see her child more positively or more realistically. Brief talks with the parent right after an incident involving the child in the preschool setting can help clarify a great deal for the mother. Following is an example of a conversation between a teacher and a rather overprotective mother:

> TEACHER. Mrs. R, did you notice how frustrated John gets when an adult tries to do something for him? He wants so much to do it for himself, and the nice thing is that he really can do so much for himself and by himself.
> MOTHER. Yes, that's true. I've noticed that in school. Maybe I try to do too much for him at home, but it sure goes a lot faster when I do it. Maybe I should let him do more when I have the time.

Fathers also should be invited to participate whenever possible. A man's role in the preschool can be an important one. The usual enthusiasm with which children will welcome a man and relate to him in the preschool setting will make any man feel good about himself and often better about his own child.

Teachers should include in the school program parents who cannot actually work with children in the preschool by asking for their needed help and contribution in some other form. This may mean making doll clothes, participation in a Saturday workshop to repair or make equipment for the school, or helping to organize a rummage sale or a cake sale to raise money for materials and equipment for the school. When parents feel that they have a contribution to make that is important, they view the school in a different, more positive way, and they feel that they are part of the school.

Parent participation in the preschool program has other values—directly for the parent, indirectly for the child. As the parent feels that she is making an important contribution to the program she gains a greater sense of self-respect and feeling of importance and status in her community. This may have special value in poverty communities. The parent who participates in the school program becomes an important part of the school, and if teachers can genuinely feel that the parents are making an invaluable contribution, and express this sincerely, it becomes a very vital and self-enhancing life experience for the parent.

When teachers can genuinely feel that they have much to learn from parents—parents from all walks of life—as well as from children, an atmosphere of cooperation and mutuality can be established in which everyone feels himself to be an essential part of the program. When parents begin to feel that they are an important part of the program, the preschool center can develop into a vital community center. In poverty communities especially, social gatherings, parties, Bingo games, potluck suppers, workshops etc., are activities that frequently have been successful in creating an atmosphere in which everyone has a sense of belongingness. This new feeling of community can help give parents strength to face their everyday problems a little more effectively. When parents are needed, when they can make choices as to how they may want to contribute, they gain a sense of adequacy as human beings. This good feeling permeates their overall attitudes and behaviors, which also expresses itself in their relationships with their children. A sense of importance and adequacy as a human being and as a parent has been stressed throughout this chapter as being essential for a healthy relationship between parent and child.

Dr. Edward Ziegler, director of the newly-created Office of Child Development and Chief of the Children's Bureau, clearly recognizes that one of the purposes of Head Start is to involve parents actively in the Head Start centers for the benefit of the children.[28] Recently, he commented on the "oversights" of the much-criticized Westinghouse Learning Institute evaluation of Head Start:

> To my mind . . . the major fault of the Westinghouse study was its failure to recognize the multiple purposes encompassed in Head Start's view of the whole child in the context of his family: to introduce children to continuing comprehensive health services, to improve their nutrition, to raise their self-esteem, and to involve their parents in plans to improve the quality of their children's experiences.

## SUMMARY

When the child first leaves home to go to school, whether preschool or kindergarten, he extends himself into a new environment and vastly expands his experiences. It is an important time for the child's healthy growth and development. Contact between home and school, the two important aspects of the child's world, is essential. This implies the necessity for open communication and meaningful relationships between teachers and parents.

When problems occur, it is easiest to approach the parents when a cordial and trusting relationship between the two parties has already been established. Openness in this person-to-person relationship is essential for effective communication. This openness can be achieved in a variety of ways in different types of communities. There are many possible points of contact between teacher and parent, and there are many cultural and psychological factors and problems that the teacher should be cognizant of in order to be helpful and effective with the family of the child.

Throughout this chapter there has been emphasis on the importance of recognizing the complexity of human relationships and interactions, understanding individual differences between children as well as between parents, and accepting parents first and foremost as human beings with their own personalities, anxieties, and idiosyncracies.

## REFERENCES

1. Almy, Millie: Spontaneous play: An avenue for intellectual development. *Bull Inst Child Study, 28,* 1966.
2. Bailard, Virginia, and Strang, Ruth: *Parent-Teacher Conferences.* New York, McGraw-Hill, 1964.
3. Bronfenbrenner, Urie: Socialization and social class through time and space. In Maccoby, E.E.; Newcomb, T.M., and Hartley, E.L. (Eds.): *Readings in Social Psychology.* New York, Holt, 1958.
4. D'Evelyn, Katherine: *Individual Parent-Teacher Conferences.* New York, Bureau of Publications, Teachers College, Columbia University, 1963.
5. Erikson, Erik H.: *Childhood and Society.* New York, W. W. Norton, 1950.
6. Fraiberg, Selma H.: *The Magic Years.* New York, Scribner, 1959.
7. Hebb, Donald O.: *Organization of Behavior.* New York, John Wiley & Sons, 1949.
8. Hess, Robert D., and Shipman, Virginia C.: Maternal attitude toward the school and the role of pupil: some social class comparisons. Paper given at the Fifth Work Conference on Curriculum and Teaching in Depressed Urban Areas, New York, 1966.
9. Jersild, Arthur T.: *When Teachers Face Themselves.* New York, Teachers College, Columbia, University, 1955.
10. Josselyn, Irene M.: *The Psychosocial Development of Children.* New York, Family Service Association of America, 1948.
11. Kagan, Jerome: *Female Identification of School-Related Objects by Young Black Males.* Lecture given at UCLA, Los Angeles, 1969.
12. Kohlberg, Lawrence: Early education: Cognitive-developmental view. *Child Dev, 39,* 1968.

13. Ladd, Edward T.: Pills for classroom peace? *Saturday Review,* November 21, 1970.
14. Langdon, Grace, and Stout, Irving W.: *Teacher-Parent Interviews.* Englewood Cliffs, New Jersey, Prentice-Hall, 1954.
15. Leonard, Edith M., Van Deman, Dorothy D., and Miles, Lillian E.: *Counseling With Parents In Early Childhood Education.* New York, Macmillan, 1954.
16. *Los Angeles Times:* Drugs used to "manage" pupils, senators told. November 24, 1970.
17. Medinnus, Gene R., and Curtis, Floyd J.: The relationship between maternal self-acceptance and child acceptance. *J Consult Psychol,* 27, 1963
18. Mussen, Paul H.; Conger, J.J., and Kagan, J.: *Readings in Child Development and Personality.* New York, Harper & Row, 1970.
19. Piaget, Jean: *The Origins of Intelligence in Children.* New York, W.W. Norton, 1963.
20. Rabban, M.: Sex-role identification in young children in two diverse social groups. *Genet Psychol Monogr, 42,* 1950.
21. Radin, Norman, and Kamii, Constance K.: The child rearing attitudes of disadvantaged Negro mothers and some educational implications. *J Negro Educ 3,* 1965.
22. Redl, Fritz: *When We Deal With Children.* New York, Free Press, 1966.
23. Rogers, Carl R.: *On Becoming a Person.* Boston, Houghton Mifflin, 1961.
24. Schaffer, H.R., and Emerson, P.E.: Patterns of response to physical contact in early human development. *J Child Psychol Psychiatry, 5,* 1964.
25. Smilansky, Sara: *The Effects of Sociodramatic Play on Disadvantaged Preschool Children.* New York, John Wiley & Sons, 1968.
26. Thomas, A.; Chess, S., and Birch, H.G.: *Temperament and Behavior Disorders in Children.* New York, NYU Press, 1968.
27. White, R.W.: Motivation reconsidered: the concept of competence. *Psychol Rev, 66,* 1959.
28. Ziegler, Edward F.: A national priority: raising the quality of children's lives. *Children, 17,* 1970.
29. Film—"Shyness." Black and white, 23 minutes, McGraw-Hill, 1953.

*Chapter XI*

# SCHOOL GUIDANCE WITH PARENTS

ALFRED H. FOSTER AND WILLIAM W. CULP

IN THIS chapter we shall first look at guidance work with parents as it relates to the total school curriculum. Next, guidelines that promote effective school guidance with parents of pupils with learning and behavior problems will be presented. This section will emphasize general principles which facilitate effective communication and constructive intervention. The following section will describe types of guidance interventions. Four specific approaches to current school guidance work will then be discussed. The chapter will conclude with recommendations for improving school guidance work with parents.

## PARENT GUIDANCE AND THE CURRICULUM

The term "curriculum" refers to the totality of activities and experiences of children while under the guidance and authority of the school. It includes all those activities, both standard and supplementary, that affect the growth and development of pupils. The structuring of the curriculum involves the concept of fitting the function of the school to the needs of the individual child and to the needs of society. A dual approach to curriculum planning is again reflected in a concern for the immediate needs of the child as well as for his more diverse future needs. The curriculum should be thought of as a sequence of desirable life experiences, rather than blocks of subject matter to be learned. A school curriculum would be incomplete and lacking in relevance if it failed to take into account the tremendous influence of the home and its potential for complementing and supplementing the work of the school. Thus, to promote the maximum educational growth and personal adjustment of students, schools must actively solicit the support and involvement of parents in curriculum planning. This point of view has been implemented by the Los Angeles City Unified School District, which has mandated community advisory councils for each of its schools. A primary function of the council is to gain input from a broad representation of the families in the community on curriculum and other aspects of the school.

Guidance is an integral part of the curriculum and, as such, should also involve the parents. The aim of pupil guidance—the development of competent, self-actualizing individuals—is also a goal of parenting. If parent guidance is limited to a crisis-intervention model, the potential for a working partnership between home and school is limited. Guidance work with parents of children with learning and behavior problems should be viewed from the broader perspective of mutual cooperation in the total educational program. With this viewpoint in mind, we turn now to some basic principles.

## GENERAL CONCEPTS IN SCHOOL GUIDANCE WITH PARENTS

### Establishing and Maintaining Communication— A First Priority

Unless effective communication can be established and maintained between home and school, any effort to work cooperatively together for the benefit of the child will be destined to failure. There are two basic prerequisites to consider in the establishment of truly effective communication. First, school personnel must constantly strive to understand the feelings, attitudes, biases, and problems that parents bring with them to their encounters with the school. The word "understand" is used in this regard in view of the fact that it may be difficult or even impossible for school personnel to *accept* parental values that are alien to their own. The concept of understanding includes the quality of respecting the right of the parent to whatever value system he chooses. Second, school personnel must also achieve an understanding of how their own value systems and biases affect their relationships with parents. This is especially important when school personnel counsel with parents from an ethnic or cultural background different from their own. Failure to recognize their own biases often results in school personnel adding to the problem rather than contributing to a solution.

There are many factors that affect a parent's attitude toward the school. In the following paragraphs we shall examine four important factors that influence the communication (or lack of it), between parent and school.

The first factor deals with parental attitudes resulting from chronic problem situations that their children have experienced in school. These parents are accustomed to being called to school frequently to discuss difficulties. As a result, they may come to view the failures of their children as implying a failure in their parenting. Consequently, such parents often become defensive and develop a negative attitude toward a school which is continually presenting them with an unpleasant experience. Parents have every right to, and indeed should, be personally and emotionally involved on their children's behalf. They have a legal and moral duty to be aggressively concerned when they feel the best interests of their children are not being properly served. It is the task of the school guidance worker to channel this parental concern into cooperative efforts with the school to help the child's situation.

A second factor influencing parental attitudes toward their children's school lies in the parent's own background of school experiences. If a parent has had an unsatisfactory school experience and had encountered problems with teachers and other school personnel, he may view schools as authoritarian, unbending institutions. It is likely that he will have problems in developing rapport with his children's school, and may be defensive in attitude and inclined to blame the school for his child's problems. Such a parent might also respond by avoiding contacts with the school or by abdicating to the school all responsibility for the educational or personal development of the child.

The third variable that exerts much influence on parental attitudes is the orientation and attitude of the community in relation to the school. This factor can be of great importance in a minority group or low-socioeconomic-status community where the school establishment is viewed as middle class or dominant-culture oriented. The community, and in turn the parent, is inclined to view the school with suspicion and distrust. This negative attitude may have some factual basis, if school personnel have demonstrated a patronizing attitude toward parents or have not actively sought their involvement in educational planning. Consequently, it becomes the responsibility of the school administrator to see that all teachers and staff members dealing with parents and community members are adequately prepared to relate positively to the needs and concerns of the community. Staff development activities must include a plan for continuous assessment of the functional human relationships skills of staff members in their dealings with parents and community.

A fourth factor, involving the communication process itself, is found when there is a language barrier between the school and community. This may occur when the community uses a foreign language or a nonstandard English, such as ghetto argot. The foreign-language-oriented community provides a more dramatic illustration, with many parents feeling hopelessly handicapped in their ability to understand what is being said to them by the school and feeling even more at a loss when they are asked to comprehend the educational program. However, when English-speaking parents have limitations in their ability to utilize and comprehend the middle-class vocabulary typically used by school personnel, a similar "language barrier" may exist.

All parents, regardless of their language background, may become alienated if school personnel use an educational jargon that has little or no meaning to the community. Nothing can turn parents off more than terms like "well-rounded development" or "peer-group pressures." This is not to suggest that educators must talk in the language of the community, whether foreign language or nonstandard English. Rather, school personnel should use language that is easily understandable by the community. The parent whose primary language is other than English will more likely want to come to school for a conference if he knows that an interpreter will be available.

The factors we have presented, occuring either singly or in combination, may have a powerful influence on the relationships between parent and school. School personnel must recognize that parents are frequently faced with difficult situations and are often coping with them to the best of their ability. The school must not condemn these parents if they manifest an inability to cope adequately, systematically, or even logically with the problems of their children. Parents need to be guided toward improved insights into problem situations as well as needs of children. They need help designed to increase their ability to make more realistic responses to the needs and home-school problems of children. This is an educational role that demands much patient understanding and long-term support by school personnel.

When parents are hostile toward the school establishment, opportunities should be provided for them to express their feelings in school conferences. If these feelings are repressed, it is more difficult to involve parents in cooperative planning for the child. School personnel may feel defensive when angry feelings are expressed, and by their attitudes may make the parent feel increasingly hostile. When parents are critical, school personnel often feel that unless they defend the school's position the parent will think they agree with the criticism. However, it is possible to recognize the parent's feeling without accepting their position with a simple statement like "I can see you are very angry about the failure notice that John received. You think his teacher was very unfair."

Parents may operate at an affective level rather than a cognitive level in a conference. In this case, the parents need to perceive that their feelings have been recognized before they will be able to move to a problem-solving approach. A first conference may end with both parent and school being more aware of each other's feelings but with no real planning accomplished. This points up the need for scheduling a series of conferences rather than relying on a "one shot" contact.

As mentioned above, school personnel must recognize the part that their own attitudes and biases play in their communication and relationships with parents. A school person who comes from a white, middle-class background may be inclined to have built-in biases against low socioeconomic and/or minority groups. As another example, the minority-group faculty member who has succeeded in establishing himself as a professional person may have little empathy for the problems and values of members of his own minority group who are at a lower socioeconomic level.

In order to build self-understanding on the part of school personnel, a comprehensive staff-development program is needed. Such a program might utilize encounter-group experiences that will enable staff members to explore their attitudes and value systems, both conscious and unconscious. This enhanced self-understanding can lead the guidance worker to greater objectivity and openness in dealing with parents whose values are different from his own.

## Sharing Information Between Parent and School

Before any child's problem can be successfully dealt with, there must be an accurate definition of the problem and a sharing of all pertinent information between the home and the school. The school and the parent may view a child's problem quite differently, based on their own observations. For example, the school may interpret a child's lack of progress as a result of his slow learning ability, while the parent may see the problem as the child's lack of interest in the school program. An exchange of information between parent and school may verify that both of these factors are operating and that the chief cause of the child's lack of interest lies in his inability to perform at the level of his classmates.

A fundamental requirement for constructive information-sharing is objectivity. School personnel as well as parents, however, may become subjective and judgmental in their observations. When this occurs, information becomes slanted with opinion and the evaluation of the nature of the child's problem becomes more difficult. Objectivity reduces the possibility that school or parents will blame the other for the child's problem. Blame-placing can undermine the possibility of joint planning for constructive intervention.

Another benefit of objective information-sharing is that it helps to prevent the child from manipulating the parents or school, or both. It is not unusual for children to deliberately or unconsciously misrepresent a situation in order to meet their own needs or to avoid consequences of an unpleasant nature.

A striking example of this was reported by a school psychologist who was counseling an emotionally disturbed boy. On the way to the counseling office, the psychologist and child had passed through an outer office where two plumbers in white coveralls were working. The psychologist later learned from the boy's foster mother that he had told her he had been interrogated by an FBI agent and that all the time he was with the "agent," two uniformed guards had stood by outside the door. The "guards," of course, had been the two plumbers!

Objectivity also makes the sharing of information easier between parent and school. When objectivity is lost, difficult and emotionally laden situations frequently develop between participants in a parent-school conference. This tenseness can be avoided if an agreement is made that observations will be presented descriptively without value judgments being expressed. As an example, a teacher and a mother seemed to be in direct opposition with their statements regarding a pupil's reading ability. The teacher says, "Mary reads fairly well!" while mother insists, "Mary reads very poorly!" The teacher might serve as a model of objectivity by expanding her statement to say, "Mary reads well at the second grade level when presented with interesting material and when no oral reading is involved." Correspondingly, the parent might be helped to state, "Mary refuses to read aloud at home in the presence of her high-achieving brother." In this example, although the value judgments regarding the child's reading ability conflict, the more objective observations fit together to help explain the nature of Mary's reading problem.

In the behavioral area, a teacher might state more accurately, "John is often reported by teachers and children for fighting on the playground," rather than "John doesn't have the ability to get along well with his peers." In similar fashion, the parent's thinking might be more objectively channeled into the statement, "John often tells me that his teacher doesn't like him," rather than "John's teacher doesn't like him."

A major advantage of objective information-sharing is that it provides a child a basis for establishing specific behavioral objectives based on his current functioning. It is necessary to see clearly where a child *is*, before we can point him toward where we think he should be.

### Parental Expectations—Help or Hindrance?

As the teacher or guidance worker confers with the parent an assessment of the parent's expectations of the child should be made. Parents may not have a realistic concept of their child's abilities and thus may not know what would be reasonable to expect from him. This is true of both the academic and behavioral areas, but perhaps is more frequently apparent in the former.

When parental expectations are high and the child feels that he cannot possibly meet them, he often will withdraw from competing with classmates. Such children need to have expectation pressure reduced through parental acceptance of what they are producing. The parent should be encouraged to give the child praise and recognition whenever it is deserved.

It is also possible that parents may not be expecting enough of a child. Such parents should be made aware of their child's talents and potential so they can give him increased encouragement to utilize his ability. Guidance workers, however, should make clear to these parents the difference between encouragement and pressure.

The problem of parental expectations is often intertwined with that of sibling rivalry. The child who is competing with a more capable sibling may feel that he will lose parental affection and approval if he cannot compete successfully. This problem may be felt more severely when the more capable sibling is younger. In these cases it is important for parents to show the less capable child their approval and acceptance of what he is achieving. Praise for those areas in which he does better than his more successful sibling also helps, as well as involvement in activities where he will not be competing with the sibling.

Through an individual study, the school psychologist can provide valuable information to the school staff and parents regarding the academic potential of the child, including an analysis of his strengths and weaknesses. With the teacher, the psychologist may plan specific prescriptive teaching techniques that can be utilized with the child to help him realize his potential. The psychologist may also help parents to establish expectations for the child that are commensurate with his abilities.

### School and Parent Relations—a Teamwork Approach

A sound working relationship between the parent and the school is essential. Neither the school nor the parent deals with all facets of the child's life. Each adult working with the child views him from a different vantage point and has his own concerns and goals. Through working together as a team, information can be shared and a mutually acceptable approach to the child can be developed. Teamwork is also essential for maintaining consistency of approach.

### *Responsibility of the School Guidance Team*

The purpose of the school guidance team is to present a coordinated approach for helping pupils with learning and/or behavioral difficulties. The principal coordinates the functions of the teacher, counselor, school psychologist, welfare and attendance worker, school nurse, school physician, and other pupil-personnel service workers. Unfortunately, problems of insufficient staffing often make it difficult for these specialists to function as a complete or efficient team. One experienced school counselor commented wryly that he approved of the "team approach" to guidance, but so far he had been unable to find out who else was on his "team!"

Regardless of the availability of the various school personnel to serve on the guidance team, the parent should always be viewed as an important member. Decisions that affect the school program for the pupil should be made whenever possible through consultation with the parent. Decisions that are made by the school without the involvement of the parent are often rejected or not fully accepted. It is understandable that a parent may be reluctant to make a commitment to a plan that he did not help to develop. The parent should be accepted as a partner in the educational planning for his child. His participation on the guidance team can be the most important factor in its successful operation.

### Involvement of the Child in Conferences

In the typical home-school conference, information is shared, the child's problem is defined, and plans are made to ameliorate the situation, without involving the child at any stage of this procedure. If we take the point of view that the child has the prime responsibility for participating in the solution of his own problems, it would seem logical to involve him in conferences. There are, of course, some kinds of information that the school and home should share without the presence of the child. Such instances might occur when the school needs to inform the parent of a child's limited academic potential or when the parent is communicating information about a particularly sensitive home situation.

However, in most conferences it is important to have the child present. This has the advantage of making the child aware of all transactions between his parents and the school and serves to relieve any anxieties he may feel about what goes on behind the closed door. In the information-sharing process, the child can state how he feels about his problems better than anyone else.

In helping the child to develop a sense of responsibility for his own actions, he should be encouraged to utilize a problem-solving approach in formulating plans and making commitments for himself. Commitments developed by a child are more likely to be kept than those made for him by adults. As part of follow-up conferences, the child needs to contribute his observations and feelings regarding the success or failure of his planning and to suggest any modifications that may be necessary.

Having the child present at each conference also minimizes distortions that may occur when all parties do not hear the same thing at the same time. The possibility of the child or parent being able to manipulate the situation through half-truths or more flagrant misrepresentations is thus reduced.

## Responsibility of the Parent and Child

The parent must accept his responsibility for sharing in the school's efforts to help the child solve his problems. In contrast to this viewpoint, many parents have expressed the feeling that schools should work out the solutions to children's school problems without involving the parents—"You take care of him at school, and I'll take care of him at home." This approach is not possible, because a child's problems cannot be neatly labeled "school" or "family." There is a considerable carry-over between the home and school when problems occur. When parents accept this interrelationship between "school" and "home" problems and work constructively with the school, the chances for a resolution of the problem are greatly increased.

The child must also accept his own responsibility, including working toward the solution of his problems. Unless the child is guided into assuming appropriate responsibility for his behavior, it is unlikely that he will develop those coping mechanisms that are essential to functioning as a mature, self-sufficient adult. Where this positive development is lacking, feelings of inadequacy and dependency can result. This, in turn, may produce ego-defensive mechanisms that are characterized by a variety of inappropriate behaviors such as withdrawal or aggression. The school and parents should provide needed encouragement and support, but the basic responsibility for solving a child's problems lies with the child.

## Record Keeping as an Aid to Planning and Evaluation

Plotting the progress of the pupil in relation to the various interventions that the school and home have attempted is an important guidance function. This can be helpful to the guidance team from the standpoint of knowing "what works" with a particular pupil if the same problem is repeated at a future time. It is also desirable to have an accurate record of commitments made by the school, the pupil, and the parents, and to what degree the commitments are kept. These records should not be secret files, which parents would rightfully resent, but should be an available, objective accounting of the transactions that have occurred between the school and the home. In addition to benefiting school personnel, accurate record keeping may assist parents in planning future goals and objectives for the child.

## FORMS OF GUIDANCE INTERVENTIONS

The word "intervention" implies an action or change that must occur in order to improve a child's situation. This section does not attempt a comprehensive coverage of all interventions that may be undertaken. Rather, some basic techniques of guidance are described in which the school and parents may work together to effect change.

### Parent Conferences

Probably the most commonly used school-initiated guidance technique is the parent conference. All parent conferences, however, do not constitute effective interventions. Too often, parent conferences are only discussion sessions that may help in the understanding of a problem situation, but do not effect positive movement toward a solution or improvement. The outcome of a parent-school conference or series of conferences focusing on a child's school problems must be in the form of agreed upon actions that are designed to remedy the child's difficulty. If this objective is realized, the conference has been effective.

The individual parent conference is also the principal vehicle through which parent counseling occurs. Parent counseling is itself a large topic, beyond the scope of this chapter. We will point out, however, that counseling should not consist primarily of giving information or advice, since this would mean one-way transmittal from "expert" to parents, rather than a cooperative effort. Counseling should be regarded as a process in which the parent and guidance worker mutually think through a child's problems, decide upon constructive interventions, and evaluate change.

## Overcoming Barriers of Time and Place

We have discussed the desirability of the parent and school working together as a team for the solution of a child's problems. However, many parents feel that they cannot become involved in school concerns because of other demands on their energy and time. At many PTA meetings the observation is often heard from teachers, "These are not the parents that need to be here!"

Schools need to be concerned about overcoming barriers so that parental involvement can more readily become a part of the school program. One approach might be to expand the school's field of operation beyond the working day and have activities after school and on Saturdays. Another plan that would increase the frequency of parent-teacher contacts is the substitution of parent conferences for report cards. This would have the additional advantage of providing regular contact between the school and home, as contrasted with arranging conferences only when problems occur. In order to provide for working parents, it may be necessary to reimburse teachers for time spent in late afternoon, evening, or Saturday conferences.

When trying to establish contact with parents who are reluctant to come to school, consideration should be given to holding the conference in the home. This would certainly not be advocated for parents who would feel threatened by a school person's visit to their home, nor should it be forced on teachers who might feel insecure in such a situation. However, a home visit would be helpful in many instances when it is difficult for a parent to come to school, or where the parent must overcome some initial shyness or fear of school authority figures.

Along with the general need for increased parental involvement is the specific need for the increased participation of fathers. Too often it is the mother only who responds to the school's request for a conference. This is usually due to the father's working hours, but may also represent mother's wish to keep father out of the picture. Father's absence from a conference is keenly felt when planning requires the cooperation of both parents. The suggestions outlined previously for late afternoon, evening, Saturday, or home conferences might help to increase father participation.

## Environmental Manipulation

The first consideration in planning an intervention is to analyze the environmental circumstances the child is unable to cope with. Parents and the school may then consider how these environmental elements could be manipulated to make it more possible for the child to succeed. If a child is showing withdrawal tendencies, participation in group activities might be arranged. If a child is fighting on the playground during the noon hour, it might be better for him to eat lunch at home for a time. A child who is uninterested in a social studies unit and consequently is disruptive in class might be stimulated by related field trips that the family can take.

An evaluation of environmental pressures may reveal elements that cannot be basically changed. However, even in these instances certain environmental modifications can be made. For example, a school guidance worker may find that a boy's lack of identification with a father figure results from the fact that the father works nights and seldom has time for interaction with his son. Although the father might not be able to change his hours of employment, additional weekend activities together might help improve the father-son relationship.

Another illustration is the child who has great difficulty in sharing materials with other children because family financial limitations require him to share toys, games and bedroom space with his siblings. Although the family cannot afford a separate bedroom for the child, arrangements might be made so that he might have a special, inviolate corner of a room that he can call his own. In a third example, a child's aggressive school behavior might be partially due to sibling rivalry. This rivalry may have some basis in fact in that more attention is being given a younger or handicapped brother or sister. Although the presence of the sibling in the home and the degree of attention paid to him are factors that cannot be altered, some counterbalances might be arranged. The aggressive child could be asked to help mother or father with special shopping trips or interesting projects while his siblings are engaged in other activities as a way of providing him with more parental attention. The child might also be given special privileges such as staying up later at night or a special story time.

## Success-Oriented Experiences

Children who experience serious school problems are frequently victims of a failure syndrome that has gripped them for a long time. These children can be placed on a "no fail" program so that they can experience success on a guaranteed basis. For example, if the parents and school are trying to build a child's ability to accept responsibility, a start might be made in setting goals for the performance of certain household tasks. The initial task selected might be to take the trash container outside each night, with a parental reminder permitted. After the successful performance of this task for a period of time, other tasks can be selected that represent small advances in difficulty. This increase in ability to accept responsibility might be carried over in school with the assignment of minor responsibilities within the classroom. It is essential that a task be chosen that the child can easily complete. It is also important to avoid a task toward which the child has developed negative feelings. After recognition is given the child for the successful performance of a simple task such as opening the classroom windows each morning, small increments can be taken in the progression toward more complex responsibilities.

## Consistency of Approach

There are three major questions involved in maintaining consistency of approach to a child: (a) Is the school internally consistent in its guidelines and requirements for the child? (b) Are the parents consistent in their approach to the child? and (c) Are the methods the school is using consistent with the parent's approach? The answer to the first question regarding the school's consistency lies in the degree of teamwork the school has achieved in its guidance program. If school staff communication is good and if a joint plan has been agreed upon for dealing with a child, it is quite likely that a high degree of consistency will prevail. However, if staff members are using different methods with a child, it is equally likely that confusion will result. The degree of consistency of parents is more difficult to determine. If there is consistency between the mother and father in the handling of the child, either a strict or lenient philosophy of discipline and management seems to work to advantage. When parents are markedly different from each other in their child-management practices, the child frequently becomes confused. He does not know what to expect; his guidelines to behavior are fuzzy. There is also the question of internal consistency of a parent. For example, does mother usually give the same reaction when her child is manifesting unacceptable behavior? Or does she often shrug it off the first three or four times and wait until it becomes unbearably annoying to her before clamping down?

An important point in regard to the home-school relationship is whether parents and school personnel are consistent with each other in their approaches to the child. For example, the school may be encouraging children who are accidentally or deliberately punched to talk things out or seek adult intervention before striking back. The parents may be advising their children to hit back regardless of the situation. The child is caught between these two conflicting sets of instructions and is unsure of how he should respond. He will be blamed by the school if he reacts in the way he has been instructed by his parents. On the other hand, his father may regard him as a sissy if he has followed the school's instructions. If the parents and school personnel can agree on a mutually acceptable response the child should make in a given situation, the child can then be held to that mode of behavior. Another resolution would be for conflicting instructions from parent and school to be clarified for the child on the basis that some behavior is acceptable at home while not acceptable at school. In the example given above, a compromise might be reached with instructions to the child that he might hit back at home, but that he would seek an alternate solution at school.

### Parental Involvement in Tutoring

When a child has problems in his academic work at school, teachers often recommend that he be tutored at home. When the possibility of tutoring is raised, the first question to be explored is whether the child should indeed be tutored. If the answer to this is affirmative, the second question is who should tutor him. The first question is often more complex than it may appear on the surface. A child who is not responding well to a group-learning situation may need more individual help than the teacher can provide. In determining whether tutoring is advisable, however, the need for individualized instruction must be weighed in relation to the child's willingness to accept additional instruction. If the child is saturated with academic learning at school, he may be very resistant to tutoring. Other factors to be considered include whether the child is being expected to produce more than he is capable of and the possibility that the child's struggle with academics is a growth-producing one that may resolve the learning problem without outside intervention.

The question of who is to tutor the child can be equally complicated. Parents often attempt to tutor their own children, with varying results. On the positive side, parent tutoring may demonstrate to the child that the parent is supportive and wants to help him. When successful, the tutoring may create a warm bond between parent and child. On the other hand, parents are limited by lack of training in teaching techniques. In addition, they may be too close to the problem and too emotionally involved to be of real help to the child. If such is the case it will be difficult for the parent to tutor the child with a learning block. Tutoring will likely be counterproductive if it results in parent-child conflict.

When the tutoring situation is carefully thought out and skillfully planned, it can have the added value of reassuring the child that the parent is tuned in to his needs. If the parent and the school feel that remedial help is needed and that the parent should not be the tutor, care should be taken to select a person to whom the child can relate easily. A good tutor can make the experience an enjoyable, productive one for the child. Whoever tutors the child should maintain regular communication with the teacher so that instructional objectives will be consistent.

### Temporary Suspension from School

The suspension of a child from school should be used only as a last resort, since the pupil must be present if school is to teach him positive behavioral concepts. If suspension is used, it should not be regarded as a punitive measure but rather as a conditioning mechanism and a learning device to teach the child that there are certain behaviors that are not acceptable at school. Prior to a suspension, there should be a clearly defined agreement between school, parent, and child regarding the kinds of behavior that are unacceptable and that will result in suspension.

The value of a suspension is based on the assumption that a child likes school and will tend to avoid a specific unacceptable behavior because it comes to be associated with deprivation of his school experiences. A suspension is likely to be ineffective if the child dislikes school and is allowed to engage in enjoyable experiences at home during a suspension. If the parents can be persuaded to deprive the suspended child of all pleasurable activities at home during school hours, the effectiveness of the behavioral conditioning approach will be greater. Suspensions may be more effective if they are of short duration, perhaps for the day of unacceptable behavior only, with the child starting the next day with a clean slate. Suspensions should be accompanied by as little lecturing on the part of school personnel as possible. This policy can make it clearer to the child that his suspension is the result of a violation of a previously agreed-upon commitment on his part and is therefore a natural consequence of his behavior.

Where parents have not made themselves available for discussion or have not been responsive to the school regarding the social or emotional adjustment of a pupil, suspension may be used to reinforce the demand for parental involvement. However, it would be better to gain parental involvement through other means before a suspension becomes necessary.

## Motivational Manipulation

Another consideration in deciding on an intervention is the motivation of a child to behave or misbehave in a given situation. If we are going to encourage a child to be responsible for solving his own problems, we must be sure that he has motivation to do so. A solution to a problem may have a great deal of appeal for the adults involved. If it does not have the same appeal to the child, however, little movement in problem-solving by the child can be anticipated. Rewards help. The concept that a child should experience a reward for an action is looked upon unfavorably by some adults as a bribe for better behavior. These same adults, however, would look with disfavor at any suggestion that they perform their work functions without any hope of receiving a paycheck.

Immediate rewards are far more effective than delayed rewards. Many parents and teachers have set up a reward system that fails because the reward is delayed for days or even weeks. Many children cannot mobilize their resources sufficiently to work for a reward that appears distant. An example of this is the parent or teacher who tells the child, "If you don't get good grades in school, you can't go to college!" This approach might work for the high school senior, but it would hardly have any effect on a sixth grader. When a reward cannot immediately be given, it is often helpful to set up some system of points, cards, tokens, etc. so that the child can see concrete evidence of progress toward the reward.

We must also consider whether the child views an action he is asked to perform as either useful to himself or relevant to his interests. For example, a thirteen-year-old boy reading at a third grade level will respond more readily to a book about automobiles than to a "Dick and Jane" third grade reader.

## Group Counseling with Parents

Group counseling of parents is a technique that has gained increasing use in recent years. It has been noted that the group approach can be more effective than individual counseling in some situations. Most of the problems discussed in a parent group have common application for all children. Parents can learn a great deal from a sharing of experience when guided by a skillful group guidance worker. Insights into problems may be gained more quickly than in individual counseling because parents accept critique and guidance more readily from a parent-peer than from a counseling authority.

The group experience constitutes a learning laboratory where experiences and ideas can be shared and results of different approaches to children's problems can be evaluated. Parent's anxieties are often relieved when they realize that other parents have similar problems in coping with their children. Through the group process a parent can analyze his own attitudes and behaviors that may be contributing to his child's problems.

Group counseling can also provide a vehicle through which the school's educational program can be explained to parents. This procedure should be a two-way interchange, in which the parents can present their views on modifications needed at school. Through small group discussion, the curriculum could become a cooperative venture between parents and educators.

## Referrals to Agencies

When a child's problem is too acute or chronic to expect the school or the parent to resolve it, there is a need to consider other resources. Schools should have comprehensive information regarding community resources that can help with various kinds of problems. This information should be presented to the parents so that they may make a selection from available facilities.

At this point, the internal communication system of the school guidance team may be tested. If communication between school staff members is not effective, a parent may receive conflicting advice regarding referrals. There have been unfortunate instances of parents proceeding with referrals to several agencies at the same time.

School personnel should be certain that the parents feel a definite need for a referral before suggesting this course of action. This is particularly important when referring to a guidance facility. Unless the parents approach the resource with a felt need for help, it is doubtful that there will be positive results.

Schools must be careful to utilize the referral process in such a way that they are not abdicating their own responsibility to the child. All of the school's resources should be exhausted before suggesting referral. However, referrals should not be delayed until problems have reached a crisis stage. In this sense, referrals should be thought of as preventive in nature—preventive of more serious problems developing.

Once a referral to an agency has been made, it is important that a three-way communication be maintained between the school, the parents, and the agency. This is not to suggest that confidentiality between the agency and the parents should be breached, but rather that pertinent information should be shared that will be helpful in the solution of the child's problems. Parental permission should be obtained, when appropriate, for information interchange. In order to facilitate this sharing of information on the part of the school, one school staff member delegated as the liaison between the school and agency should be responsible for all follow-up contacts.

## SOME SPECIFIC GUIDANCE APPROACHES

The preceding sections of this chapter discussed concepts of effective guidance with parents of children who are experiencing learning and behavioral difficulties. No attempt was made to relate the general guidance concepts to any specific approach to counseling and guidance. In this section of the chapter we shall outline four systematic approaches to school guidance that are being implemented in many school districts.

Specific methods of working with parents will be discussed in the context of (a) the "Reality Therapy" of William Glasser, (b) the approach to "Individual Psychology" as developed by Rudolf Dreikurs, (c) the principles of "Teacher Effectiveness Training" and "Parent Effectiveness Training" as outlined by Thomas Gordon, and (e) the basic concepts of "Behavior Modification" as adapted by Frank Hewett, Dwight Goodwin, Madeline Hunter, and others.

### Glasser's Reality Therapy

William Glasser's concept of reality therapy[4] grew out of his work with a group of delinquent girls at the Ventura School for Girls, located in California. He became convinced that delinquency, withdrawal, and other types of irresponsible behavior were the result of repeated experiences of failure. The needs of such individuals to love and be loved and to experience feelings of self-worth were inadequately gratified. The school, as an institution, is viewed by Glasser as the major instigator and perpetuator of feelings of failure and inadequacy in the lives of individuals. His views and conclusions are dramatically presented in his book, *Schools Without Failure.*[5]

Involvement and commitment on the part of a caring, responsible person is seen by Glasser as the only way of helping a person who has failed. The "failure" is viewed as a person who is unhappy and has chosen the pathway of delinquency or withdrawal as a means of coping with an unpleasant reality. Since the delinquent or withdrawn person is unable to help himself across the barrier which separates him from successful, responsible behavior, he needs the committed involvement of a significant, responsible fellow human being to encourage him as he takes that step.

Viewing traditional approaches to psychotherapy as inadequate,

Glasser outlined his own approach to effective psychotherapeutic involvement in which he places stress on the need for the personal involvement of the therapist. The client must feel that the therapist, as a person, cares about his well-being. In contrast to traditional therapy, Glasser emphasizes dealing with the present and working toward the future when relating to the client. The temptation to deal with and focus on the past is avoided. This approach results in minimal attention to past failures.

By insisting that the therapist concern himself with the client's "here and now" behavior and not his feelings about his situation, Glasser again contrasts his approach with traditional therapeutic models. The objective evaluation of the client's current behavior is the primary focus of the therapy session. The client is led to view his actions and their consequence in a more responsible, objective manner without being bogged down in the nebulous area of feelings and emotions. Dealing with the client's behavior in terms of current realities, the therapist helps him make his own value judgments regarding his behavior as a basis for making wiser choices. Unless the client arrives at his own set of value judgments, there can be no real change.

Another essential step in the reality therapy concept is that of helping the client to make a commitment. Based on increased knowledge of the client, his problems and personality dynamics gained through personal involvement, the therapist is able to assist the client in making a commitment to a task or behavioral goal commensurate with his ability to achieve success.

The therapy structure emphasizes the development of self-discipline, as the therapist accepts no excuses and holds the client to his commitments. The client sees that someone cares enough to help him face his problems. This continued personal involvement by the therapist in helping the client to work toward his commitment generates a situation in which the client can evaluate his own behavior in a realistic, systematic manner.

The school guidance worker employing the Glasser model in his contact with a parent would pursue a dual goal. First, he would utilize reality therapy principles in his relationship with the parent. Second, he would explain those principles to the parents so that they in turn could assist the child in dealing with specific problems. Through open discussion in a nonjudgmental atmosphere the guidance worker would help parent and child focus on present behavior and needs. By avoiding preoccupation with the child's inadequate past performance, a more positive and productive conference takes place. A major goal of the conference is to delineate constructive alternatives to the child's current performance and then to obtain from the child a commitment to positive change. The involvement of the child in the reality-therapy guidance sessions is mandatory. The child must participate in evaluating the problem, accept responsibility for participating in the resolution of the difficulty, and make a specific commitment in terms of his own behavior. A case illustration follows:

> Mark was a fourth-grader whose attention-getting, disruptive behavior interfered with his ability to complete classroom assignments and frequently led to interpersonal conflicts with peers. Mark's behavior was not related to any neurological impairment or intellectual deficit. The problem appeared to be that of teaching Mark to respond to both academic and social situations in more responsible ways. Teacher and counselor worked directly with Mark in diagnosing and prescribing for his academic needs. They agreed that the involvement of the parent was necessary. Mark's mother, Mrs. R, was called in for a conference. The counselor made every effort to demonstrate a personal concern for Mark. The first person singular was used to convey this concern to the parent, in such expressions as "I have come to know Mark quite well and am concerned about his apparent dislike of school," "I am worried about Mark's increasing difficulty in getting along with others," and "I have been trying to understand why Mark seems unable to concentrate on his school work."
>
> An attempt was made to draw Mark's mother into a more personal involvement by defining specific roles that she could play in the guidance process. Some approaches which were intended to carry out this objective were suggested by the counselor: "Mrs. R, it is important that we share our observations and views regarding Mark's attitude toward school," "We need to plan ways of helping Mark to experience success and recognition both at school and at home," "What seem to be his main interests at home?" "Our actions, more than our words tell Mark how we feel about him. Let us discuss some things that you might be able to do each day to show Mark that you care for him personally, with no strings attached."
>
> It was necessary to avoid undue emphasis on Mark's past failures during parent conferences. Both the counselor and the parent had to resist this natural tendency. Mrs. R seemed relieved and encouraged by the positive and objective thrust of the conference. When a point

came up about Mark's educational or developmental background, the counselor related it to a basic question, "Knowing this about Mark, how can we best proceed to help him now?"

Keeping the focus on Mark's behavior rather than on feelings was not always easy, as feelings were expressed and could not be ignored. However, when a particular behavior to be eliminated or modified was being considered, zeroing in on the behavior was found to be a more productive approach. There were two essential questions that the counselor sought to keep before the child and the parent in discussing Mark's unacceptable responses in the classroom: What did you do? and How is that helping you?

It was helpful to relate to Mrs. R an example of the teacher's use of the reality-therapy approach. During an arithmetic lesson, Mark, under provocation, left his seat and aggressively shoved another boy. In confronting Mark about his actions, the teacher skillfully avoided an emotionally charged reaction by challenging Mark with the question, What did you do?, instead of Why did you do it? The teacher rejected Mark's efforts to shift the discussion to the reasons why he shoved the other boy. Thus, Mark was not allowed to avoid giving an objective description of his behavior, which he finally stated as "left my seat and shoved another boy." Mark was at a loss to tell just how that particular behavior helped him complete the arithmetic assignment. It was in this systematic approach to a reality situation that Mark was helped to make a value judgment regarding his behavior. With teacher's assistance, Mark decided upon an alternative behavior that he would employ if he were to be provoked. This behavior would be consistent with his responsibility to the reality situation of classwork. He was then led to make a commitment to use the alternative.

The guidance worker used the example above to illustrate the approach Mrs. R could use at home. Mrs. R easily grasped the concept of not accepting excuses from Mark for not keeping his commitment. However, Mrs. R raised the question, "What do I do when Mark fails to keep a commitment?" The counselor pointed out that Mrs. R must show Mark that she really cares that he keeps the commitment. Mother must demonstrate her personal involvement through verbal expression of concern and open discussion regarding the difficulties he is encountering in keeping his commitments. Above all, she must not succumb to the temptation to either give in to Mark's attempts to avoid responsibility or take the "easy" way out of giving up on him. An illustration of the determination needed by the parent was given by Mrs. R in relating to the counselor a situation at home in which Mark had agreed to complete his homework assignment before watching television. Mark sought permission to watch a special program that came on earlier in the evening before his homework was finished. His mother, consistent with the "accept no excuse" approach, denied the request, although she admitted that she felt a bit like a witch. The counselor commended her for having enough love for Mark to hold him to his commitment, although it seemed to hurt at the time. This showed true caring.

## Dreikurs' Individual Psychology

Rudolf Dreikurs has been concerned with helping teachers deal more effectively with children. An advocate of the Adlerian school of psychiatry, Dreikurs views man as a social being whose actions are always purposeful and goal directed. The personality of man is viewed as unique and indivisible. In his book, *Psychology in the Classroom: A Manual for Teachers*,[3] he develops his educational philosophy: to understand children, to influence them, and to correct their deficiencies requires knowledge about the development of their personality. This involves a recognition of the basic needs of children and a systematic approach toward interpreting the child's present goals and motivations. Consequently, an approach to school guidance based on Dreikurs' concepts requires an awareness of the principles of child growth and development as well as of the dynamics of individual and group behavior.

An extensive analysis of Dreikurs' views on the dynamics of personality development and behavorial adjustment is beyond the scope of this chapter. However, certain of his basic concepts will be presented to suggest the rationale for Dreikurs' conception of the behavior of children and the methods for correcting their misbehavior.

### Basic Concepts

As a social being, man can fully function only in a group. A primary need is to feel that one is an accepted, participating group member. Dreikurs asserts that every action of a child has a purpose, the basic aim being to secure a place in the group. Family life provides the atmosphere in which the child first begins to develop attitudes toward social living. The relationship between father and mother to a large extent establishes the family pattern, which has a profound effect on the emotional and social development of the child.

The family constellation, to a large degree, defines the parameters within which the child functions. A kind of "power politics" develops within the family as each member seeks to establish and maintain his identity and status. The child's attitude toward life, indeed his life style, is largely determined at a very early stage by the manner in which he seeks to gratify his group identification needs.

The well-adjusted child is meeting social acceptance through conformity and positive contributions to his social environment. The misbehaving child, however, is generally responding to inferiority feelings created by experiences which have caused him to feel rejected and unsuccessful. Inferiority feelings act to inhibit or restrict the development of adequate social motivation and participation.

Some people may be led to socially acceptable behavioral roles as they compensate for inferiority feelings; for example, one child might seek security in the "bookworm" role; another, as the "family comedian" or "classroom comic." When, however, inferiority feelings have become so generalized as to constitute an inferiority complex, negative or deviant social behavior results.[2] Some examples of this might be children who exhibit characteristic signs of withdrawal, unacceptable aggression or hostility, chronic lying or stealing.

The guidance worker who utilizes Dreikurs' concepts of individual psychology will emphasize the assessment of the life style of the child who has learning and behavorial difficulties. The family background will be evaluated both from its developmental and current impact. The child's adjustment difficulties at school will be viewed and dealt with as a continuing effort by the child to gain and maintain recognition and status with authority figures and peers. The role of the guidance worker becomes that of helping parents and teachers to identify and interpret the behavior of the child as directed toward the goal of his personal acceptance as a valued member of the group, in both family and school.

Dreikurs emphasizes a number of concepts to reinforce his view that in order to guide a child, one must understand him as a unique, striving individual with basic needs. He points out that any actions designed to teach the child must be characterized by mutual respect, and that this respect is shown by one's actions and expectations. Encouragement of the child to learn and behave more appropriately is another key concept. This encouragement must be consistent and sincere and should be reflected in deeds as well as words. The principle of encouragement is so important in Dreikurs' approach that he collaborated in writing a book on the topic.[1] Some of Dreikurs' guideposts to effective child guidance are given below, with illustrative vignettes that involve parent participation.

*Understanding the Goal of the Child's Behavior* is an important concept. Among Dreikurs' contributions to education is the development of a systematic basis for interpreting and responding to the misbehavior of children. The child's misbehavior is considered purposeful and consistent with his interpretation of his place in the family or social group. Dreikurs postulates four goals of misbehavior: (a) *attention*—a desire for attention or service, (b) *power*—a need to be the boss, (c) *revenge*—a desire to hurt another, and (d) *reaction to inadequacy*—a desire to be left alone without pressure or demands.

How others relate to the child and his behavior or misbehavior is of prime importance to effective guidance efforts. One's intuitive reaction to the child's misbehavior often gives a clue as to its purpose. For example, when the child's goal is attention, one is apt to respond by feeling annoyed because of the need to remind and coax him. There is a danger that a response to a child's misbehavior might serve to magnify or reinforce the negative behavior if one does not carefully assess and control his own responses to the situation. For example, the rejection of a child who is exhibiting attention-getting behavior might reinforce the feeling of alienation, thereby causing the child to demonstrate this behavior even more intensively. The child is generally unaware of the goals of his misbehavior, for an awareness of the goal of a particular misbehavior tends to inhibit the exercise of that behavior. A major task of the guidance worker or parent is to identify the goal the child is striving to satisfy.

Mrs. W related to the guidance counselor her concern about her six-year-old daughter Jane's tendency to be "quiet and withdrawn." Jane did not participate in play with her brother or sister or with the neighborhood children. Mrs. W had tried to encourage Jane to be more outgoing, but the girl resisted mother's attempts to get her to socialize. When mother attempted to talk to Jane about this, the girl would cry or run off to be by herself. Mrs. W was worried about the situation and felt that Jane might have serious emotional problems.

The guidance counselor asked Mrs. W to reflect on the purpose of Jane's behavior, to consider what this behavior might be expressing. Mrs. W replied that she sensed that unhappiness or fear was the cause of Jane's avoidance of social contact with peers. Mother wondered if Jane was not sure of herself when she was around other children, since she seemed to be more at ease when she was by herself. The guidance

worker then suggested to Mrs. W the possibility that Jane was reacting to a strong feeling of inadequacy, and that in the face of personal involvement and challenge the girl wanted to escape and be left
alone. Mrs. W concluded that Jane was indeed unsure of herself, that
she was a "loner" rather than "withdrawn," and that enhancing the
girl's self-concept would be the route to making Jane more sociable.
In the light of further discussion about Jane, it appeared that this
explanation was more plausible than a diagnosis of serious emotional
problems. Mother and the guidance worker then worked out a plan
of building Jane's self-esteem through developing some of her innate
talents in music and art at a nearby community center where Jane
could have a more comfortable contact with other children on the
basis of demonstrated strengths rather than self-perceived weaknesses.

*The Principle of Natural Consequences* is constantly operating to
influence behavior. It is rooted in the law of cause and effect and is
a basic concept in learning theories. It indicates the relationship between a given stimulus situation and a natural, predictable response.
The natural consequence of one's specific behavior provides a practical basis on which to evaluate it. Thus, personal experience can be an
effective, though sometimes a harsh teacher. When seeking to modify
the behavior of children, Dreikurs holds that it is often helpful to
allow them to experience the logical consequences of their misbehavior. The child is led to a more realistic assessment of his behavior
because of the heightened level of physical and emotional involvement. Utilization of this principle allows parents and guidance workers to expose a child to corrective pressure with minimum negative
interpersonal feedback.

> Tommy was frequently tardy in arriving at school. Following a
> parent-teacher conference in which Tommy participated, a decision
> was made to apply the principle of natural consequences. Whenever
> Tommy was tardy, he was to be kept after school for half an hour.
> Moreover, an agreement was made with his mother regarding the loss
> of television privileges for the day. Tommy quickly came to recog-
> nize that the natural consequences of his tardiness was a restriction of
> freedom at school and home. With conscientious effort he reduced
> considerably the frequency of his tardiness.

*Never Do for a Child What He Can Do for Himself* is a concept
that is intended to prevent or reduce excessive dependency needs.
This principle can be effectively used by parents. It is easy to under-
estimate the ability of children and consequently have too limited

expectations of them. It is unwise to deprive them of the opportunity for personal growth by unnecessarily performing tasks for them. Parents should resist the tendency to respond for the child or to accept too readily the child's avoidance efforts in a learning situation. Dependency needs are often unintentionally reinforced.

Dreikurs emphasizes that a dependent child is a demanding child. Delayed speech, in some instances, might be a consequence of a child's having no need to speak because all his needs are anticipated and fulfilled without his having to verbalize. Through open or subtle displays of personal inadequacy the child can manipulate parents, siblings, and others into doing things for him. Guidance workers can help parents to recognize the real goals of the child's behavior. Parents may need support in becoming strong enough to establish order and assign responsibilities in the family. By encouragement coupled with firmness, parents are able to make the child more responsible for his own behavior. Parents, thereby, establish their own independence as well.

*Acting Instead of Talking* is a principle that should be followed by more parents. The tendency of many parents is to talk to the misbehaving child and to then let the matter rest. A parent may feel that talking alone is sufficient to affect a change in a misbehaving child. However, unless the child is generally conforming and values pleasing authority figures, merely talking with him will not dissuade the misbehaving child from his disturbing behavior.

Action is much more effective than words in conflict situations. Talking provides an opportunity for arguments in which some children are more adept than their parents. Children also learn early the tactic of "tuning people out." Children, moreover, usually know what is expected of them. It is neither wise nor necessary to explain to a child what he already knows he is expected to do.

Dreikurs also points out that talking should be restricted to friendly conversations and should not be used as a disciplinary means.

Paul is an eight-year-old whose mother was concerned because he would not respond promptly to her request that he come to the dinner table. He would continue to watch the television or play instead of complying. His mother would call to him repeatedly. She had talked to him about this behavior many times. The school counselor was informed of the situation during a conference with Paul's mother. The counselor suggested that Paul's supper be removed from the table and that he go without supper should he fail to come to the table when called. Paul soon learned to come when called, as he learned that the food would be put away if he did not respond promptly. Action was indeed more effective than words.

Dreikurs' concept of guidance provides a model of constructive parent-child interaction, with the goal of involving and supporting the child in a meaningful interpersonal relationship. As the parent is guided in following this model, a closer relationship between parent and child should develop as the child's self-concept is enhanced and his behavior becomes more acceptable.

## Gordon's Parent-Effectiveness Training

Thomas Gordon is a clinical psychologist who believes that society's serious mental health problems cannot be solved by waiting to treat people after they have developed psychological problems. He believes that preventive approaches need to be explored and programs developed. Recognizing that the home and the school are the two most influential factors in the life of a child, Gordon proposed ways of modifying parent-child and student-teacher relationships. His aim was to prevent or reduce the incidence of personal and interpersonal difficulties being experienced by parents, children, and teachers.

Gordon's research and professional experience confirmed that most parents want to do what is best for their children. However, he also found that parents were often confused about how to relate to their children and were making the same basic mistakes and asking therapists the same kinds of questions. Gordon concluded that parents lacked confidence in their relationships with their children and did not have knowledge of proper ways for raising responsible children. Gordon's views on effective parenting and his approach for training parents are presented below.

The authoritarian approach of many parents is often ineffectual or detrimental to the emotional and social adjustment of their children. The permissive approach of other parents can be equally faulty and harmful. It became apparent to Gordon that parents need training to prepare them to be effective in the role. The need for training is both recognized and sought in the preparation for all professional and vocational roles. Training for the complex role of a parent should be no less needed or required than is training to become a teacher or a plumber.

## Parent-Effectiveness Training (P.E.T.)[7]

A program developed by Gordon, stresses the concept of training before trouble occurs, and deals with prevention rather than treatment of parent-child problems. P.E.T. is a program of education rather than therapy. Both professional and lay personnel are trained to serve as resource leaders to school districts and parent groups in presenting Gordon's program.

As a program designed to help a person establish sound, mutually satisfying relationships with another, P.E.T. is not limited to parents. Gordon contends that the program provides the critical requirements for all human relationships. He considers the "no lose" conflict resolution approach as applicable to husband-wife, teacher-student, employer-employee, and other interpersonal relationships.

The course in Parent Effectiveness Training consists of a series of training sessions in which parents are taught skills, methods, and procedures for improving the parent-child relationship and for resolving problems in that relationship. The total of twenty-four hours of classroom instruction includes lectures, demonstrations, tape recordings, classroom participation experiences, role-playing, buzz sessions, and classroom discussions. Gordon's book[7] is used in the sessions, along with a supplementary activity workbook. The program focuses on modifying the parent rather than the child. The premise is that a parent should become a more effective agent for promoting change as his knowledge and skills increase in the areas of personality development, verbal communications, and interpersonal relationships and strategies for influencing the behavior of others. The child will then respond positively as his needs are better met in an atmosphere of mutual respect.

Training in verbal communication skills is an important aspect of P.E.T. Children need the reassurance gained from knowing what their parents are feeling. Parents should be able to discuss their needs and feelings with their children in an open, honest manner. The children of parents who can be open will tend themselves to be more open and honest in communicating their feelings and also more sensitive to the feelings of others. Besides being more respectful of their parents, such children are apt to be more responsive to authority, without fearing it. Effective parenting, therefore, requires skill and practice in the techniques of communication. Communication provides a basis for dealing with feelings of alienation, indifference, distrust, and resentment that often develop between parent and child. Gordon believes that many parents need training both in how to talk to children and how to "listen to their talk."

> Bobby W, a ten-year-old boy, was disruptive in class and insolent to his teacher. He was sullen when disciplined and gave the teacher no clues as to the cause of his behavior. In conferencing with Mrs. W about Bobby's classroom difficulty, the guidance counselor could see that Mrs. W was confused and distraught. Mrs. W felt inadequate and helpless; she could not respond to the counselor's efforts to explore ways that might help Bobby be more respectful of the teacher. Mrs. W stated that she did not understand Bobby and always had trouble with him. Mrs. W was unable to name any of her son's interests or concerns. The counselor saw that there was a communication gap between mother and son, and that Mrs. W needed help in understanding her child. In addition, it was clear that Mrs. W also needed guidance in learning to converse with Bobby.
>
> The counselor explained to Mrs. W the nature of the communication gap and discussed specific ways mother could close it. Each day Mrs. W was to talk to Bobby about specific events at home or in school. She was to be as pleasant and nonjudgmental as possible, and was to listen attentively. At the same time, Mrs. W was encouraged to share her thoughts and feelings with Bobby as spontaneously as she could. Finding out about Bobby's interests and/or worries was to be one of the goals of the verbal interchange.
>
> The counselor told Mrs. W that Bobby's teacher would adopt the same approach and would make a special effort to talk with the boy on the playground or at recess.
>
> A few weeks later, Mrs. W informed the counselor that she was beginning to know her son. The teacher noted some improvement in the classroom. Although the classroom behavior problem was not fully resolved in this short period of time, a start was made in opening up communication with Bobby at home and in the classroom.

The major goal of parent-effectiveness training is to improve the quality of human interaction. Basic to Gordon's concept of a healthy interaction between parent and child is the right, indeed the need, for both parties of the interaction to be authentic, self-actualizing individuals. Problems and conflicts inevitably arise as the parent and the child pursue self-determined needs within a traditionally highly structured role relationship. An overriding theme in Gordon's approach to parent-child guidance is that neither the parent nor the child should suffer damage to his self-concept as a result of their relationship. The principle that neither should be a "loser" is reflected in the title of Gordon's book: *Parent Effectiveness Training—The "No-Lose" Program for Raising Responsible Children.*

The "no lose" approach contrasts with the two most prevalent modes of child-rearing, the authoritarian and the permissive. The authority emphasis results in a parent-wins-and-child-loses situation. Conversely, the child wins and the parent loses in the permissive approach to parenting. Either approach results in interactions which cannot be mutually satisfying to the parent and child. Moreover, neither works toward the constructive development of the child's social attitudes and behavior. In the no-lose method, discussion is held until a problem resolution is worked out that satisfies both parties.

Gordon's program of parent training emphasizes an eclectic approach in recognizing and overcoming the roadblocks to communication. He postulates that there are a dozen types of verbal communications which tend to create barriers between individuals. These communications emphasize what the parent wants the child to do, without sufficient regard for the child's feelings or needs. Included in this category are communications which direct, command, admonish, threaten, advise, criticize, analyze, tease, and probe. Gordon would have parents become more adept in actively listening to the needs and feelings of the other, relying less on authoritarian communication. It is in the search for solutions to situations that are acceptable to both child and parent that sound relationships can be established.

## Behavior Modification

A number of psychologists have applied the principles of operant conditioning and reinforcement theory to the educational process. Prominent among these are Dwight Goodwin,[6] Frank Hewett,[8] and Madeline Hunter.[9] Although there are variations in the approaches used by each advocate of reinforcement theory, the underlying principles and their application to parent guidance are fundamentally the same.

### Reinforcement Theory

A positive reinforcer is defined as anything that is needed or desired by the learner. Money or food can be used as reinforcers. However, the most powerful reinforcers for a child are social in nature, such as the love, interest, and attention of his family and friends.

If positive reinforcement follows a behavior, that behavior will tend to occur more frequently in the future. For example, if a child who is sitting quietly in his seat and working is rewarded with a smile, a word of approval, or a pat on the back, he will be more likely to work quietly at his seat in subsequent time periods. It should be noted that what is a positive reinforcer for one child may not be for another. Some children may relish praise from a teacher, while others may shrink from it. Experimentation is often necessary to determine what sort of reinforcement is most effective with a particular child.

It is important to realize how we may be accidentally reinforcing a child's behavior. If, for example, a child who is seeking attention is scolded by the teacher every time he leaves his seat, the harsh words of the teacher may constitute positive reinforcement. Consequently, the behavior of leaving his seat is being strengthened by the scolding.

Negative reinforcement is anything that is unpleasant or not desired by the learner. In keeping with this definition, negative reinforcement is synonymous with punishment. Logically, one might assume that if negative reinforcement follows some behavior, that behavior will tend to occur less frequently in the future. In fact, however, behavior that brings on a negative reinforcer is only suppressed. When the negative reinforcer is removed the behavior will tend to recur. As an example, the child who is spanked for hitting another child may suppress his aggressive behavior in fear of the physical punishment imposed; however, when the immediate threat of spanking is removed or made less likely, the child may again resort to hitting.

We should also realize that whatever behavior takes away the negative reinforcer is also being strengthened. The child in the example above might resort to lying, in order to place the blame for the hitting incident on the other child. If this subterfuge is successful in removing the threatened spanking, the untruthful behavior is being strengthened and will be more likely to recur.

Behavior is extinguished by withholding any kind of reinforcement. This is often demonstrated by the child who engages in many minor, irritating actions in the classroom to get the attention of his teacher and peers. If he receives no attention as a result of his actions, those particular actions will tend to disappear. It is possible, however, that the child may switch to other, more disrupting actions to obtain the attention he seeks.

## *Procedure*

Behavior modification should be utilized as a learning device that will *teach* desirable or acceptable behavior in children. The first step in the procedure is to identify the behavior that we wish to change. Some authors refer to this as the "target behavior." Next, we should identify the new behavior that we want to occur in place of the undesired conduct. This new behavior must either already be in the repertoire of the child, or be made part of his repertoire by the shaping process. "Shaping" is the procedure by which existing actions are reinforced that are increasingly closer to the desired behavior. For example, if we wish to reinforce silent reading with the child who always vocalizes when he reads, we would reinforce progressively lower levels of vocalization as they occur until silent reading is obtained. As another illustration, the parent may wish to reinforce a child for doing his homework, but states that the child never accomplishes this task. The parent might start by reinforcing him for bringing a textbook home. A next step might be to reinforce him when the child picks up the textbook during the evening to glance through it. The child's actions in getting paper and pencil ready may represent another behavior that is selected for reinforcement. The child's behavior is "shaped" by this procedure until he is actually doing his homework, which would then be reinforced further.

We have shown above how a parent might employ behavior modification techniques. School guidance workers may serve as consultants to parents as well as to teachers in explaining how these procedures can be utilized both at home and in school. This home-school approach is most helpful when a child is evidencing the same kind of undesirable conduct at home as he is in school. Both parent and teacher can utilize the same techniques to modify a child's behavior. For example, the parent and teacher both report that a child does not pay attention to them when they speak to him, but instead turns away or daydreams. This in turn causes further problems because the child does not respond to requests or directions, either at school or at home. In this instance, daydreaming or looking away constitutes the undesired action. Looking directly at the adult who is talking to him is the behavior we wish to have substituted.

Following this defining of "undesirable" and "desirable" behavior, we would then decide on the type of reinforcement to be utilized. In this case, the teacher and parent may simply smile at the child every time he looks directly at them when they are speaking. In the beginning it will be necessary to be consistent in applying this reinforcement every time the child pays attention. Such a regular schedule of reinforcement results in rapid learning of the new behavior. While this procedure is being instituted, it may be necessary to suppress the unwanted conduct with negative reinforcement if it is strongly established. The parent or teacher may need to interrupt the child's daydreaming with reminders to pay attention. This may serve to temporarily suppress the daydreaming and provide increased opportunities for the child to be reinforced for looking at adults when they speak to him.

After a new behavior has been well established, a switch should be made to an intermittent schedule of reinforcement. In our example the parent and teacher would not smile at the child every time he looked at them while speaking, but would smile with decreasing frequency, making the intervals increasingly long. Intermittent reinforcement tends to result in making the new behavior resistant to forgetting. At this point, any negative reinforcement should be removed, so that the undesirable behavior, in this case looking away or daydreaming, can occur with no reinforcement and thus be extinguished.

The school guidance person can work out behavior modification techniques that parents can use in a variety of situations. It is important that the parent clearly understand the principles involved and follow a methodical and consistent approach with the child.

## RECOMMENDATIONS

The thrust of this chapter has been the principles and methods of working with parents whose children are experiencing school problems. We believe that parents have much to contribute; they should be an integral part of guidance work with children who have school difficulties. Thus, an emphasis has been placed on the importance of having school guidance personnel listen more objectively and with keener perception to what parents tell them. Direct involvement of the child as well as the parent in the parent conference has been suggested. It is essential that extensive staff development programs be developed that can enable school personnel to work more effectively with parents. To implement these recommendations, however, it is clear that a fuller commitment to parent guidance must be made in terms of larger budgets and increased staffing.

The underlying premise of this chapter is that work with parents and families is essential to an effective guidance program for all children. Communication between home and school should be maintained on a regular basis rather than being initiated only when problems arise. More open and relevant communication with parents and community could result in an ongoing dialogue with the goal of basic agreement on the objectives of the curriculum.

If schools are able to communicate with and actively involve all parents, a preventive guidance program could be a reality. Such a program would concentrate its efforts on not allowing children to fail rather than on attempting to rescue them from failure syndromes. We could then look forward to seeing more children realize their full potential as happy, productive people.

## REFERENCES

1. Dinkmeyer, D., and Dreikurs, R.: *Encouraging Children to Learn: The Encouragement Process.* Englewood, New Jersey, Prentice-Hall, 1963.
2. Dreikurs, R., and Stoltz, V.: *Children: The Challenge,* New York, Duell, Sloan & Pearce, 1964.
3. Dreikurs, R.: *Psychology in the Classroom. A Manual for Teachers,* 2nd ed. New York, Harper & Row, 1968.
4. Glasser, W.: *Realty Therapy: A New Approach to Psychiatry.* New York, Harper & Row, 1965.
5. Glasser, W.: *Schools Without Failure.* New York, Harper & Row, 1969.
6. Goodwin, D.: Joint venture; one view: innovation and behavior change through collaboration with a school staff. *J School Psychol, 8,* 1970.
7. Gordon T.: *Parent Effectiveness Training; The No-Lose Program for Raising Responsible Children.* New York, Peter H. Wyden, 1970.

8. Hewett, F.M.: *The Emotionally Disturbed Child in the Classroom; A Developmental Strategy for Educating Children with Maladaptive Behavior.* Boston, Allyn & Bacon, 1968.
9. Hunter, M.: *Reinforcement Theory for Teachers; A Programmed Book.* El Segundo, California, TIP Publications, 1967.

*Chapter XII*

# SOME SPECIAL PROBLEMS AND GUIDANCE NEEDS OF FAMILIES WITH HANDICAPPED CHILDREN

Evis J. Coda and Gerald I. Lubin

In our experience with school programs for the handicapped, we have been impressed by the influence of the family on the child's school adjustment. Guidance of parents of handicapped children is essential, therefore, if the handicapped are to reach their educational potential. School guidance personnel have an especially challenging role in this endeavor. The purpose of this chapter is to review some of the special problems and guidance needs of families with handicapped children. The term "handicapped child," as used here, refers to the child with a significant impairment in intellectual, physical, emotional, or social functioning, requiring special care and assistance. In the first section of the chapter we shall present an overview of family attitudes and responses to the handicapped child with special attention to the implications for school learning and behavior disorders. In the second section we shall discuss the need to take parental feelings and family stress into account during the evaluation of and planning for the handicapped child.

## ATTITUDES TOWARD AND RESPONSES TO THE HANDICAPPED CHILD

The impact of a handicap on a given family can be related to a wide variety of factors. One of the significant influences is the understanding, acceptance and attitudes of family members, including that of the involved child toward himself and his handicap. The very young child has considerably more awareness of what is going on about him than is generally suspected. From the earliest months of life, he is continually reacting and being reacted to. The attitude of parents upon whom he depends for physical and emotional comfort

321

and gratification will greatly influence his attitude toward himself. The otherwise normal, healthy infant meets with much spontaneous show of affection and pleasure. The handicapped infant, especially the one with various degrees of associated physical abnormalities, meets with a complexity of feelings and attitudes, some of which are detailed below.

## Initial Responses

In addition to the normal response of love and concern, there is the initial response to the handicap itself. Concern and anxiety as to the child's future level of development and achievement, considerable sorrow, disappointment, anguish, and at times, rejection is not uncommon. This is not to imply that such parents do not love their children; these responses are normal. They are considered as initial reactions to the defect rather than to the child himself. Under such stressful circumstances, many parents are unable to differentiate and separate out conflicting responses; love and acceptance on one hand, rejection and disappointment on the other. To these parents the child and his disability are one. The child is also unable to make such a differentiation. He senses the parental reaction as being toward him directly and not toward his disability. Feelings of insecurity, anxiety, and rejection can result. In most instances, parents adequately resolve these conflictual feelings with relatively little adverse effect upon their child's behavior and learning patterns. However, where such feelings are unresolved and persist into later childhood and the adolescent years, there can be profound effects upon the handicapped child's concept of self, subsequent behavior, and school adjustment.

## Compensatory Responses and Their Consequences

Parents of a handicapped child experience some feelings toward their child from time to time that are unacceptable to them. These feelings, such as anger or disappointment, are compensated for by certain mental attitudes or responses. In the compensatory response the individual attempts to make up for actual, or at times, fantasied deficiences. Among the more common compensatory responses of parents to the handicapped child are denial and overacceptance. Compensation responses may occur singly or in varying combinations. In overemphasizing the disability, there is an accompanying sympathy, pity, and an overprotective desire to do more for the handicapped child than is actually needed or required; for example, dressing, feeding, help with personal hygiene. This, in turn, can inhibit or limit the child's potential development. Not being encouraged to work out his own problems can lead to overdependency and a demanding attitude on the part of the child. In school, for example, overdependency may result in the child's unwillingness to learn academics unless he receives an inordinate amount of individual attention from the teacher. Feelings of sorrow and pity may inhibit the parents from setting reasonable limits and taking disciplinary measures that are essential for the child if he is to recognize and respect the differences between what is his and what is anothers, and what he is free to do or not to do. Much confusion around personal identity, authority, dependency and independency may develop, and classroom behavior difficulties may follow. In the reverse situation of denial, there is deemphasis of the disability to the point of minimizing or even denying its existence. An unrealistically high expectation is a frequent resultant as the parent attempts to bring the child to the expected level of the nonhandicapped child. The child's best efforts may meet with the parental expectancy to "do even better next time," and thus he does not gain the sense of the true approval and acceptance necessary for his growth.

In other situations, there is a surface overacceptance or too ready an acceptance of a disability, accompanied by an air of casualness and seeming indifference—"That's the way he is, there is little we can do about it." This response may conceal an attitude of hopeless resignation which is manifested in the parents' subtly avoiding involvement with the child and his problems. Such a response frequently contains an underlying note of rejection. Some teachers may have similar responses in which they rationalize this attitude by emphasizing what may be a realistic limitation in the amount of individual attention they can give the child. Attitudes of overprotection, overexpectation, denial, indifference, and hopelessness are but some of the many complex responses and reactions to a handicapped child. These reactions may prevent parents from recognizing their own capabilities as parents and may inhibit teachers from using their talents to help the handicapped child. In both cases, the child's potential abilities may be underestimated and therefore not developed. School difficulties are apt to follow. A case illustration follows:

The compensatory response of denial can be seen in the case of L.K. L.K. is a fifteen-year-old, mildly retarded boy who had an associated physical handicap of congenital heart disease and congenital foot deformity. His father had become overly involved with his son since early childhood. He had considerable difficulty adjusting to his son's physical handicaps and spent many hours in exercise and play with him in an attempt to compensate for this handicap. L responded with a similar determination and as a result of much practice, he was able to participate adequately with his own age group in sports and other physical activities.

Academic difficulties were noted soon after starting school. Psychological testing showed him to be mildly retarded, with an IQ in the mid 60's. Father seemed unable to accept or adjust to the fact of his son's retardation and questioned the findings of psychological tests. He had his son retested on several occasions and despite similar findings, persisted in his denial of the retardation. He pressured the school into maintaining L in a regular class instead of a special class for the retarded by stressing L's physical accomplishments that were achieved despite the handicap, and speculating that with sufficient effort L might be able to keep up with his classmates academically. L continued to fall further behind his peers in schoolwork but was able to learn at a level commensurate with his measured intelligence. Special class placement was again considered by the school, but at father's insistence the school continued him in regular class on a "social promotion" basis, based on age and physical size rather than academic achievement. The school's rationale for going along with father was that association with nonretarded students of his own age group could be of more benefit to him than placement at his academic achievement level with either much smaller and younger normal children or placement in a class with mentally retarded children at approximately his own age level. It was speculated that either of the latter two placements would result in a sense of inadequacy and lowered self-esteem.

During his adolescent years, L's poor social judgment and limited capabilities became increasingly apparent and stood in marked contrast to his nonhandicapped classmates. He was progressively excluded by his peers from the school social events, dances, and parties. Father reported that L frequently questioned why he was not invited to parties and why he couldn't have a girlfriend. Father became very tearful and embittered when describing such events. L vehemently and steadfastly refused to participate in any community, social, or educational programs for the mildly retarded adolescents, insisting that he was not retarded. L's distortion and denial of his handicap was apparently reinforced by a similar earlier pattern of denial by father.

Marital difficulties resulted in L's parents becoming separated. Mr. K attributed much of this difficulty to his own marked overinvolvement with his son. L became increasingly moody, and school performance and behavior gradually declined. He began to absent himself from school, finally refusing to go at all. Following a divorce by his parents, he was eventually placed in a private residential school for retarded adolescents.*

In this situation, it was felt that L's distortion and denial of his handicap was reinforced by his father. This denial in turn was a major obstacle to both L's and his father's ability to participate in the educational and special programs for the retarded and their families that were offered to them and from which they might have been able to receive considerable benefit.

## The Type of Handicap as a Factor

The nature of the handicap, including its type and severity, may have significance in the response it brings from the family and community as well as within the child himself. There may be both a real awareness of limitations imposed by a specific handicap that exists and also imagined limitations that do not exist. The child must be helped to realistically assess his ability and neither overvalue or undervalue himself in the light of the handicap. This tendency to overvalue or undervalue certain abilities because of inner needs and attitudes can also occur with people who may have feelings of insecurity about their own abilities. If a parent is obsessed with avoiding or denying any weakness in himself, he may be unable to accept his child's limitations. These feelings may lead parents and educators to push the handicapped child too hard and too fast. The motivation for this pressure comes from within themselves rather than from a genuine wish to help the child. A case example follows:

ML was born with complete paralysis of one side of the body. Her parents were physical culture enthusiasts. ML had a great deal of difficulty in winning acceptance by the family. Father in particular was concerned with his own physique and lifted weights, exercised vigorously, etc. He could not tolerate his child's limitations. He had a need to struggle against any weakness in himself and pushed his

---

*L's educational placement with normal children, rather than in a special class for children of similar handicaps appeared to have an adverse effect both educationally and socially. It is to be noted, however, that a number of handicapped children appear to do quite well when placed in regular rather than special classes; particularly where both child and parents have a realistic acceptance of the handicap, and opportunities for social interaction are provided.

daughter much to hard to correct the weaknesses he saw in her. The school personnel were very pleased with the child's academic and social progress and they tried to get father to reduce excessive pressure on her, particularly in the area of motor behavior and speech. The school was concerned that the constant pressure would lead to the child's refusing to try or just giving up, thereby jeopardizing the academic gains she had already acquired. This father had such a strong attitude about weakness in himself that he could not believe his daughter was unable to use her paralyzed limbs.

The tenacity of this belief was astonishing to the school personnel. In spite of several conferences in which father was confronted with clear and conclusive evidence of the extensive brain damage, he continued to believe that the destroyed brain tissue could regenerate or that other parts of the brain could take over for ML's complete hemiplegia. In this case we have the unfortunate situation in which the type of handicap, which limited physical activity, interfered with the parents' preoccupation with physical culture and represented a threat to their need to be physically completely functional. Father's last words in the final conference were, "When will my little girl walk?"

## Severity of Handicap

If the handicap is a severe one, it may significantly damage the child's self-concept. The child responds to his inner awareness of what his body is like and how it functions. We call this his body image. This image is affected by what he perceives he is like, and what he can and cannot do. His ability to perceive accurately can be limited by a handicap involving the sense organs or the central nervous system. Perception can also be distorted by emotional factors or diminished by mental retardation. It is significantly influenced by the attitudes of parents, siblings, peers, teachers, and other professionals. Even if the disability is correctly perceived, however, it may be so extensive that the child is clearly different from others, with the result that self-esteem is low.

When a handicap is severe enough to block communication between parent and child, internal attitudes may build up in the child and the parent that can lead to the child's gradual exclusion from the family and placement in a residential facility. In families where some verbal and/or nonverbal channels of communications are kept open, an opposite development often takes place. The entire family structure seems to be strengthened by the common purpose of caring for the child, and all the family members seem to be drawn to this goal. In special schools designed to handle a severely handicapped child the same attitudes are seen at times. The staff usually draws together in these schools and works toward actively including a problem child in the treatment program. When communication between child and school personnel (as well as between various school personnel) breaks down, the group may move toward excluding the problem child from the school. If there is an opportunity for channels of communication to be reopened, either through consultation around the child or an informal discussion session for personnel, the problem child may be given another chance. When the total staff resolve in caring for the child is strengthened, the individual staff members directly involved with the child may then be willing to see a difficult situation through.

## Responsiveness and Temperament

Parents look forward to a pleasurable interchange with their infant. The quality of the emotional bond that develops between the child and his parents, especially his mother, will depend in part on the infant or young child's emotional responsiveness. The handicapped child's emotional responsiveness reflects, as with all children, his inborn ability to give of himself and receive from others, as well as the nature of the stimulation he receives. If there is impairment of the infant's ability to smile spontaneously, to readily accept attention from others, and to manifest other signs of responsiveness, then mother's spontaneous, stimulating response to the child may be minimal. Even intense stimulation, however, is limited in its effect by the child's constitutional makeup. On the other hand, if the ability to react is intact, there must still be interaction with mother in order for the child to develop. If mother rejects the handicapped infant, it is not likely that there will be the meshing between mother and child that is so vital for emotional, social, and intellectual development. It should be noted that the handicapped child may be rejected by the mother either with or without awareness of the rejection on her part. In either case, the child will have an interruption, either partial or complete, in the necessary developmental stimulus mother provides. When the child's handicap is such that interactive ability is seriously impaired, or if the parent behaves as if the child could not respond, the child may remain at an infantile level.

Rejection is not the only response of a parent that may result in understimulation of a handicapped child. Overprotection, anxious overconcern, misinformation, and lack of information can be determining factors. The following case illustration points up the need to inform and guide the parents of a handicapped child.

> Lisa J, an eight-year-old girl, had never been in a nursery or school program because of severe mental retardation. Lisa had no speech, was a nonambulatory spastic child with cerebral palsy. She was unable to feed herself or take care of her basic needs. Mother felt overburdened to the point of near exhaustion. Lisa was a heavy child and mother felt she had to carry her frequently from place to place. Mother was of the opinion that her child's multiple handicaps were of such severity that there was no purpose in trying to get her admitted to any type of day care program.
>
> The child was admitted to a special school for an extended diagnostic workup. In observing mother's relationship, it was felt that she was overprotective and anticipated the child's needs, and presented the child with no stimulation or challenging experiences. The physical therapist outlined an activity program which was carried out by the teacher and aide. After four months of this special stimulation, Lisa was able to spontaneously pull herself up to a standing position and walk with minimal assistance and also take a number of steps on her own without assistance. She became self-feeding and more communicative, and although she did not have actual speech, she could vocalize, and was able to indicate wants and feelings at times through sounds. There was a definite change from a vacuous facial expression to one that could communicate both positive and negative feelings.

The above example is illustrative of how an overprotective mother could deprive a child of stimulating experiences, which resulted in a significantly lower level of intellectual and social achievement than was possible with this child. Mother was a warm, oversolicitous, well-meaning, but uninformed parent regarding severe handicaps. When appropriate guidance was given, mother changed her attitude toward Lisa. She readily supported and cooperated with the supplemental home training program.

Another factor that enters into the parent-child interaction is temperament. Thomas, Birch, and Chess[2] consider temperament to be a critical element in a child's behavior. They suggest further that differences in temperament between parent and child may lead to difficulties in their relationships. A child's handicap may exaggerate the effect of temperament differences. For example, the placid parents of a hyperactive child with minimal brain dysfunction may find the high activity level very upsetting to them. This is due not only to the child's hyperactivity, which is frequently associated with learning or behavioral difficulties at home or in school, but also to the parents' own quiescent nature and their preference for placidity in their children. However, in an active, energetic, competitive family that is continually on the go, this child may be viewed as having only a mild handicap until the parents are faced with complaints by school.

## Family Patterns of Interaction

The entry of a handicapped child into a family often results in considerable stress. The family's cohesiveness and coping mechanisms may be put to a severe test. The family in which there is warmth, mutual support, and constructive interdependence linked to acceptance and respect for individual differences can work together as a family unit and sustain itself. In a family that lacks these traits, the handicapped child may be experienced as a disruptive burden. Pre-existing patterns of family interaction largely structure the impact of the family on the handicapped child, and conversely the effect of the child on the family. Thus, if the family's interactive style reflects significant role distortion, the adjustment of the handicapped child in the family, school, and society will be adversely affected.

One pattern of role distortion that negatively affects the handicapped child is that of an excessively strong mother-child tie, with father partially or totally excluded. This may tend toward the development of mother-child separation anxiety, with the child manifesting excessive crying, tantrums, headaches, abdominal pain, or vomiting when attempts are made to have the child go to school or otherwise physically separate from mother. The fact of the child's handicap may change what would have been a mild-to-moderate overprotective mother-child relationship into one which produces severe separation anxiety. In such instances, the mother may not be able to allow her child to attend a special school, especially if it is a boarding school.

A second type of family-role difficulty occurs when a husband and wife are unable or unwilling to expand their marital roles to that of mother and father to meet the needs of their newly arrived child.[1] The child is viewed as an interference. Without a close sense of belonging, the child tends to be isolated and withdrawn, or if he does relate, it is at a superficial level. These children appear very needy of emotional support and acceptance. Their limited ability to relate and their general inattentiveness make them high risks for learning disabilities. The handicapped child in this situation is considered unusually burdensome to the parents, and out of home placement may be sought, even when special educational programs are available in the community.

Another pattern of distorted family development is seen when there is an excessively strong family tie, a form of overprotectiveness and overtogetherness. Individuality and independence are limited. Community and social life are deemphasized unless the family participates as a group. The child goes everywhere with the parent and vice versa. Dependency is fostered in this situation; individuality is devalued. While these parents may be active in parent-teacher associations or other school activities, any threat to the excessive family closeness, such as day camps (particularly overnight camps), may be unacceptable to the family. Creative teaching techniques that stress individuality are viewed with suspicion. Learning is hampered by the lack of independent motivation. The handicapped child, in a sense, becomes doubly disadvantaged.

The opposite of the "smothering" pattern described above is the family style in which there is excessive emphasis on individuality, with relative isolation, poor communication and a lack of mutual support among family members. A handicapped child reared in this style may be left to his own resources sooner than he should be and may therefore have difficulty in requesting needed assistance in the classroom and elsewhere. Even when assistance is offered, he frequently rejects it, viewing help as a threat to his independence and individuality. This exaggerated independence leads to difficulties in his conforming to classroom routines and rules.

## Comment

Earlier we have reviewed various factors and determinants of some of the problems of handicapped children and their families. The attitudes and responses of the handicapped child, his parents, teachers, and peers, the handicapping condition itself, and the child's personality and temperament were discussed. To illustrate the interaction of all these factors in the etiology of a handicapped child's problem, the case of K.W. is presented below.

KW was a seven-year-old, hyperactive male with learning disability associated with a wide scatter of intellectual abilities ranging from borderline retarded to bright normal. Mother described K as having been an extremely active infant, "always into everything," and "constantly on the go." In personality, he was considered as stubborn, nonconforming, disobedient, and belligerent. He had frequent temper tantrums both at home and in public and was difficult to discipline.

K's parents stated they tried all means known to them to get him to obey. They had tried being permissive, restrictive, punitive, and combinations of these methods. They also felt they tried both consistent approaches and flexible ones, all to little avail. By mutual agreement, mother had recently assumed the disciplinarian role as both she and father felt that K's behavior had stirred up too many angry feelings in father and that he would be too punitive.

At the time of request for counseling help, mother felt she was at the point of exhaustion. She stated that when they were out in public K would invariably have a tantrum when he was minimally frustrated by not getting what he wanted, causing mother tremendous embarrassment. She stated, "When he's having one of these tantrums in public and people look at me, I just wish I had a sign on me saying 'I have really tried.' "

K had already been excluded from one school for his disruptive classroom behavior and was again being considered for exclusion from his current school. His teacher gave the following description of his school behavior and performance:

"K rarely, if ever, obeys anything I tell him. He is tense and destructive, he moves, walks, or wiggles constantly. He seems unable to play with other children, he races around the playground; if anyone gets in his way, be it child or teacher, he simply runs into them or over them, and keeps on going. He enjoys throwing sand on girls. I have corrected him many times, but he is right back doing the same thing. I have never seen him play nicely with any child. In the classroom, he wrinkles or crumples every paper he has. He picks up other children's number cards and throws them around the classroom. He seems bright and intelligent enough. I find him a great disturbance in the class."

K's psychological and pediatric neurological examinations had revealed clinical manifestations of a definite perceptual disorder with signs and symptoms of minimal brain dysfunction.* Medications for

---

*It is not always evident that in the condition of minimal brain dysfunction the term "minimal," refers to the difficulty in demonstrating any structural or physiological evidence of gross brain pathology. Frequently, the behavioral correlates of this syndrome are not minimal, but severe.

hyperactivity were prescribed, with minimal improvement noted. K was asked not to return to school at midterm and was transferred to public school, where he was placed in a social adjustment class for one year and later transferred to a class for the perceptually handicapped. After three years of placement in this class, his hyperactive, aggressive, destructive behavior subsided to a point where he was given a trial in a regular junior high school.

This section of the chapter has concentrated on some of the unique factors that school guidance for the handicapped child and his parents must take into account, factors that may underlie a school learning or behavior difficulty. Constructive intervention, based on an understanding of these factors, can enhance the value of the school experience. Intervention may be provided by the school guidance worker in the form of individual or group parent counseling. When the problems are deep-seated and long-standing, referral to a community mental health facility may be necessary.

School guidance personnel who work with the handicapped often function as key members of diagnostic and planning teams. These teams may function separately from or as part of the school program. The next section of the chapter highlights some special problems that arise during these phases of programming for the handicapped.

## EVALUATION, PLANNING, AND THE FAMILY

### Diagnosis, Evaluation, and Planning

A child with a handicap usually has difficulty in multiple areas of functioning. The interdisciplinary team fulfills the need for comprehensive evaluation and planning. Team members may include the child psychiatrist, school psychologist, dentist, nurse, nutritionist, occupational therapist, orthopedic surgeon, pediatrician, physical educator, physical therapist, educational or clinical psychologist, social worker, special educator, speech and hearing therapist, and urologist or other medical or paramedical specialist. The interdisciplinary team, with experts in these various fields, can focus on the specific areas involved with the handicap and bring together total expertise in arriving at a diagnosis as a basis for an overall plan. The selection of an appropriate school placement and the setting of realistic educational goals is an essential part of a treatment program.

The parents should also be considered as part of the team. They should not be passive members, but integral participants. Parents

have their own expertise in the sense of best knowing their own resources—emotional, social, and financial—that must be considered if
planning is to be effective. Parents should be given a clear, sensitive,
supportive, and detailed interpretation of findings. If the team fails
to communicate to parents and school personnel the pertinent facts
of the evaluation or uses language that the parents do not understand, problems may arise. For example, if the parents feel that decisions are made that do not take into account their concerns and
feelings about their child's needs they may be dissatisfied and tend
to search elsewhere for help. It is also difficult for school personnel
to support a treatment program if an overview of the problem has
not been shared with them. A case illustration follows:

> TN, a seven-year-old boy, developed purpura fulminans, a severe
> but self-limiting sensitivity type reaction that led to gangrene in both
> legs and required amputation above the knees. He also had severe
> damage to his genitourinary system. He recovered quite rapidly how-
> ever, and was placed in a special school for the handicapped. The par-
> ents had great difficulty pulling together the various specialty reports
> and reporting these findings to the school. Reports from the school
> suggested increased difficulties with behavior even though the physical
> state of the patient continued to improve. In their frustration the par-
> ents discussed going to another hospital for assistance and even made
> some inquiries, but because of the complicated nature of the case were
> advised to return to the facility where T had been first treated. The
> psychiatrist was appealed to by the parents and took on the role of case
> coordinator, meeting with the various specialists and pulling the case
> together. A three-way conference between the child psychiatrist, par-
> ents, and school disclosed the underlying problem. The patient's teach-
> er believed T's condition to be rapidly approaching the terminal
> phase, and was overreacting with excessive concern and anxiety to
> T's bladder spasm which occurred when he felt upset and frustrated.
> She had assigned an aide to work with him individually, and tended to
> isolate him from the group. When the teacher was included in the
> collation of the reports and the planning conference, her attitude
> changed and T's problems in school subsided in response to a stance
> of kind firmness that her changed attitude made possible.

The importance of including teachers and other professionals who
have worked with the child over the years cannot be emphasized
too strongly. Their information on the child's progress or regression
furnishes a point of reference for the interdisciplinary team. The
variety of their experience with the child enriches the data on which
decisions must be based.

After the team evolves a plan of therapy, there should be co-ordination among those who will carry it out. The parents also need ongoing guidance, and the child should be reevaluated at regular intervals. The first plan is only a point of departure which then must undergo revision as the child's response to the therapy is observed. The readiness and capability of the child and the parents to cooperate with a treatment regimen must always be considered.

The parents' initial reaction to the diagnosis needs to be carefully appraised. Parental responses that have been observed in this situation include apprehension, anxiety, anguish, despondency, denial, shock, anger, and even overt hostility. After the initial evaluative phase some of these reactions are to be expected in view of the stress that handicapping conditions may impose on a family. If these reactions persist, however, further discussion is necessary. The need for reinterpretive interviews is illustrated by the case of T, a three-year-old girl who had been examined by the pediatrician because of suspected mental retardation. On a subsequent occasion, T's mother told the pediatrician, "After you mentioned the words 'mental retardation,' I was in such a state of shock I didn't hear another word you said."

It should be noted that there may be pitfalls in planning interviews that relate to learning and behavior problems in school. If the interviewer paints too grim a picture, parents may give up. Conversely, if too rosy a picture is painted, parents may not work hard enough at helping. The effect of parent reactions and attitudes on the child's school adjustment can be considerable.

### Family Needs and Community Resources

The needs of handicapped children and their families are complex and varied. For one family, the major need may be for information, for another it may be assistance in sorting out the conflicting information and recommendations given by a number of specialists. Parents may require ongoing counseling help with their feelings of guilt, frustration, anger, or rejection. Some families may be going through a period of emotional crisis around a decision regarding placement of their child in a residential setting. For other families, the lack of financial means to carry out treatment recommendations may precipitate a crisis.

The care and treatment of the handicapped child, particularly in those cases of greater severity and chronicity, are frequently beyond the physical, emotional, and financial resources of an individual family. To assist in the provision of care, numerous organizations of parent groups and concerned citizens have been formed at national, state, and local levels. The National Association for Retarded Children, with its state and local chapters, the Crippled Children's Society, the California Association for Neurologically Handicapped Children, and the National Association for Mental Health are examples of such groups. There has been a group organized for virtually every category of handicapping condition. Parents and relatives of handicapped children have constructively utilized their personal experiences and frustrations in meeting the needs of their handicapped children by becoming the catalysts and major force in developing and promoting these organizations and their programs. They have also been the major stimulus in securing legislation at Federal and state levels which have helped bring these services physically closer and more attuned to family and community needs.

Parent groups have also supported the current trend to keep the more severely handicapped children in the community rather than dispersed to large residential facilities that are often at a considerable distance from the children's homes. In the past, residential placement was favored because of the lack of placement alternatives at the local level. It has been increasingly recognized, however, that a better adjustment to the handicap and a fuller and healthier personality development occur when the child can be cared for in his home. This is particularly the case with very young children, who need the closer personal attention, love, and support that is difficult, if not impossible, to obtain in the large, typically understaffed institutions. There are times, however, when unusual stress within the family makes an out-of-home placement necessary. To assist families at such periods, a variety of community programs are required, ranging from respite-care program for brief periods of time to longer placements in special-care homes, group or foster homes. Brief periods of hospitalization may be indicated for those children who are multiply handicapped and who present complicated diagnostic and management problems that may not respond to ordinary outpatient or day care. Examples of such situations are those hyperactive, retarded, or brain-injured children with seizures that are not controlled by medication, and the visually or aurally handicapped child who is manifesting signs of physical or emotional regression for undetermined reasons. During periods of crises, partial hospitalization or day-treatment programs where the child may return home during evenings or weekends may be necessary. For children with lesser degrees of handicap than those requiring out-of-home care, special educational, rehabilitation, social, and recreational programs are essential for their optimum care. Helping parents understand and accept the need for the special interventions delineated above is an important guidance function.

The dispersion and lack of coordination of resources for the handicapped have been major problems. Can a single, conveniently located resource be developed that is readily available to meet the varied needs of families with handicapped children? One attempt to provide such a program is the State of California's Lanterman Mental Retardation Services Act. Excerpts from the act and program description[3] given below clearly highlight the importance of parent and family in planning services for the handicapped:

> In the past, available services lacked a continuity necessary for the mentally retarded individual to reach his fullest potential. The Lanterman Act seeks to join fragmented services, eliminate duplicated services, and provide services where none exist so that a parent may find help for a child at the earliest possible moment after mental retardation is suspected.
>
> In order to provide fixed points of referral in the community for the mentally retarded and their families; establish ongoing points of contact with the mentally retarded and their families so that they may have a place of entry for services and return as the need may appear; provide a link between the mentally retarded and services in the community, including state-operated services, to the end that the mentally retarded and their families may have access to the facilities best suited to them throughout the life of the retarded person; offer alternatives to state hospital placement; and encourage the placement of persons from the state hospital, it is the intent that a network of regional diagnostic, counseling, and service centers for mentally retarded persons and their families, easily accessible to every family, be established throughout the state. There are nine centers now in operation.
>
> The family is usually invited to come to the Center for an interview and for additional diagnostic tests and evaluations. These are performed by the center staff, often with assistance from local specialists and laboratories. When this has been completed, the Center staff team

meets, reviews its findings, and prepares a comprehensive diagnosis and evaluation, and, with the participation of the family, plans for the care and treatment of the child. The team and the family together work out plans for care, treatment, and for the many services that may be needed. Plans are also made to reexamine and reevaluate the mentally retarded child as often and as extensively as needed. A counselor is assigned to work with the family and arranges for special medical care, family counseling, summer camping, day care, and any other services that are needed.

Since the care and service needs of an individual change as he grows, develops, and as his physical condition changes, the Center provides continuing, systematic contact with the family so that necessary reevaluations and changes in the plans for care and supervision can be made. These plans and services are made with the full participation and approval of the family.

As the parents get older, many families become more concerned about the future of their retarded child or relative. The Regional Centers provide counseling about future care.

Diagnostic and counseling services of the Regional Centers are, by law, provided without charge to individuals or families.

It is currently planned that the scope of the Lanterman Act will be expanded to cover all developmental disabilities. This legislation represents a significant step forward in the response to some of the special problems of families with handicapped children.

Another approach to expanding services for the handicapped child and his family is the University Affiliated Training Programs (U.A.P.). There are twenty-six such programs affiliated with universities throughout the United States, supported wholly or in part by federal funds.* Training in the interdisciplinary team concept is the major emphasis of the U.A.P. School guidance personnel are an integral part of the program, whose goal is to train personnel to provide comprehensive services for the handicapped child in his adaptation to home, school, and the community.

*Dr. Lubin's work at the University Affiliated Training Program is supported by a grant (MCH Project No. 914) from the Maternal and Child Health Services, Department of Health, Education, and Welfare.

## REFERENCES

1. Allen, F.H.: *Positive Aspects of Child Psychiatry.* New York, N. W. Norton, 1963.
2. Thomas, A.; Chess, S., and Birch, H.G.: *Temperament and Behavior Disorders of Children.* New York, NYU Press, 1968.
3. Lanterman Mental Retardation Services Act. State of California. Human Relations Agency, Sacramento, 1971.

# AUTHOR INDEX

339

# SUBJECT INDEX